THE STORY OF WIPRO

A journey from 1945

BUSINESS

Published by Westland Business, an imprint of Westland Publications Private Limited, in 2021

1st Floor, A Block, East Wing, Plot No. 40, SP Infocity, Dr MGR Salai, Perungudi, Kandanchavadi, Chennai 600096

Westland, the Westland logo, Westland Business and the Westland Business logo are the trademarks of Westland Publications Private Limited, or its affiliates.

ISBN: 9788194879084

Printed and bound at Thomson Press

THE STORY OF WIPRO

A journey from 1945

TEXT
Anindita Mitra

VISUALS
Dileep Prakash

DESIGN
Wari Watai

wipro | BUSINESS

Amalner, where the
Wipro story began.

Contents

NOTE: For reasons of clarity, The Story of Wipro *retains the names of cities as they were for much of the seventy-five years of Wipro's history. Bombay changed to Mumbai in 1995 while Madras switched to Chennai a year later, in 1996. Calcutta became Kolkata in 2001 and Bangalore adopted Bengaluru in 2014, Mysore became Mysuru, and Burma and Rangoon changed to Myanmar and Yangon respectively in 1989.*

Foreword

The unremarkable mid-sized oval wooden table that used to occupy the center of the room was gone. That was the first thing I noticed walking into the room I had occupied for many years at the Wipro Corporate Office. This was in early 2016. With increasing alarm, I checked for its whereabouts. No one seemed to know. The best guess seemed to be that it had been disposed of as scrap, so must have been cut up for reuse.

The table was unremarkable only in form. It was a bearer of Wipro's history and legacy. It was the table used for all Wipro board meetings, as far back as anyone could remember, while the company was headquartered in Bombay. It had been moved to Bangalore when the headquarters shifted.

The horror at the fate of this unique artefact from Wipro's past did not last long. Raghu, a man for many a crisis, called me with the news that they had located the table, it had not been chopped, and was being reclaimed. The table now adorns a special place at the Foundation, befitting its past.

The episode was a stark reminder of the near zero attention that we had paid to the history of this company, which is now seventy-five years old. Unsurprising, given the don't-pay-attention-to-yourself culture that all of us at Wipro have grown up with, combined perhaps with the Indian penchant for oral histories with its many possibilities, rather than any formal historical record.

At about the same time as when the table went missing, Rishad participated in a lovely, warm, Wipro alumni meet. One day soon after that, he, Saurabh and I got talking. It seemed impossibly irresponsible that we had anecdotes galore but no history of this company. We decided to do something about it. But to do something we needed someone who could do that something.

Mitu and I had known each other for years. We met in a coffee shop in late 2016, and I made her an offer, literally on a paper napkin, to build this project, both in its imagination and execution. As far as Rishad, Saurabh and I were concerned, there were no boundaries; we had the basic idea but not its contours and implications. We wanted everything possible collected, archived and converted into various forms of communication, so that we had the histories of Wipro in as much detail and nuance as possible. I use the word 'histories', because we were conscious that the life of an institution such as this, over a period of seventy-five years, cannot be reduced to one simple narrative. Mitu took on the responsibility for this idea.

The story of the birth of the Wipro Story Project (as we named it) is incomplete, without sharing AHP's reaction to it. It won't surprise anyone who knows AHP to learn that he dismissed the idea summarily, saying, 'you guys seem to have no work, so you want to create some, and waste the time of others.' After all, he is the fountainhead of this don't-pay-attention-to-yourself culture. The three of us did not listen to him. Which is also equally our culture — you can disagree with AHP totally and act based on your conviction in the interest of the organization — and this too has equally been fostered by him.

Over the next year, as Mitu and the Wipro Story team discovered wondrous artefacts from our past, recorded poignant accounts from Wipro alumni and the project came to life, his stance changed from outright dismissal to irritated tolerance, and finally to genuine endorsement. The inescapable depth of feeling and sincerity with which hundreds of people started contributing spontaneously is what changed his mind, I think.

So here we are, the first output of what has become over the past four years, a super-exciting, and often moving endeavour. Moving, because underneath our get-on-with-it exteriors, Wiproites, past and present, have deep emotional bonds to this institution. Wipro has made us, infinitely more than we have made Wipro.

Wipro has made me, for sure. Going right back to when I was in college.

Wipro had an enigmatic reputation in my engineering college days of the 1980s. Few companies even had a reputation. First, it was a techie's paradise. If you fancied your chops as an engineer, Wipro was the company you wanted to join after graduation. Second, bribing was not allowed at Wipro. Stories were told and retold of the company losing a Rs 5 million contract after refusing the demand of a fifty-paisa bribe. None of this was the company's sales spiel; we knew this with certainty. Because it was our friends who had joined Wipro that narrated anecdote after anecdote from their own lives. In the India of mid- and late 1980s, a company that would simply refuse to bribe, under any circumstances, was unheard of.

At some point after my MBA, I had four job offers. All in the same week. All from then well-known companies. My decision did not take a heartbeat. I joined Wipro. Its reputation as a tech leader did not matter to me, the reluctant engineer that I was. By then, it had also come to be known for its superb professional management, which was good to know, but did not matter much. The knowledge that, in this company, I would not be expected to bribe ever was the all-important consideration.

In the nearly three decades since then, I have traveled a dream-like journey. From being a rookie frontline executive to moving into the top management of the company. And now being responsible for the Foundation that serves some of the most vulnerable and disadvantaged people in the world, striving for justice, equity and humaneness. With Wipro's success directly enabling this mission, as 67 per cent of the economic ownership of Wipro rests with the Foundation. The reason I joined Wipro has held true every moment, from the very first day. If I could relive my life, I would make the same decision, with even more conviction.

During these decades, tumultuous for the whole world, Wipro too has transformed. I have been an inside witness to these many unfolding histories of Wipro, and sometimes an actor. What are these many histories?

One of them is a real-life enactment of a classic journey recognised in all cultures across the world — how a young man saved a family business and then led it to global heights, finally rediscovering a greater higher moral purpose from his past. How an institution can be built that is more than the sum of the individuals who have built it. How one company has been shaped by and has also shaped India's economy. How the global tech industry has evolved and Wipro with it. How so many entrepreneurs have emerged from this one company. There is also the standard story format of a business with its many shifts and turns, successes and failures, and of resilience. The many stories of the personal struggles, sacrifices and triumphs of the pioneers that led the way. The even more everyday stories of the average unsung Wiproite — whom few remember — but without whom Wipro would not have been.

The Story of Wipro is all this and more. But even as one journeys and straddles these many histories, stories and experiences, there is an unchanging essence of Wipro. It is that essence that has really built Wipro and thus made us. Unflinching commitment to values, with integrity, honesty and fairness at the core, is that unmistakable essence. This, the first book of the Wipro Story Project, gives you some slices of these many histories, along with that unchanging essence. Let's wait for more.

Anurag Behar
CEO, Azim Premji Foundation

Postscript: The contribution of many to Wipro, and their understanding of this remarkable institution, is manifold more than mine. Thus, the privilege of writing this opening piece for this book is thoroughly undeserved. It's just one of those things arising from being at a certain place at a certain time.

2005–2010	2002–2004	1996–2001

1996

Wipro-Acer, joint venture set up.

Registered office of Wipro moves to Bangalore from Mumbai.

1996–99

Takes up quality initiatives, wins top certificates under SEI-CMM and Six Sigma.

1998

Becomes India's largest publicly held software company.

Launches new brand identity with the rainbow flower.

2000

Lists on the New York Stock Exchange on October 19.

2000–01

Turnover grows to ~$635 million from ~$176 million in 1990-91.

Wipro Applying Thought in Schools program launched in Bangalore in May 2001.

Azim Premji Foundation set up in March 2001.

First company globally to be assessed at PCMM level 5 in December 2001.

Employee headcount touches 14,000; 11,500 in IT business.

2002

Acquires Spectramind.

2003–04

Wipro Consumer buys Glucovita, its first acquisition.

Wipro acquires NerveWire.

Crosses billion-dollar mark in IT business and at Corporation level.

2005–06

Combined IT business revenue crosses $2 billion.

Wipro Ltd employee headcount touches 55,000; operations in 16 countries.

2007

Rishad Premji joins the BFSI vertical.

Wipro Consumer acquires Unza for $246 million.

2008

WIN launches Eco-Energy green business.

2009–10

WCCLG revenues cross $500 million; acquires Yardley in December.

2009–10

Premji transfers 9% of Wipro Ltd shares to a Trust supporting his philanthropic entities at Azim Premji Foundation.

2019

Total value of philanthropic endowment corpus is $21 billion (including 67% of economic ownership of Wipro Ltd).

2019

Azim Premji retires as Chairman and Managing Director of Wipro Ltd.

Rishad Premji appointed Executive Chairman of Wipro Ltd.

2020

Azim Premji Foundation, Wipro Limited and Wipro Enterprises commit ~$150 million in April to tackle the health and humanitarian crises of the Covid-19 pandemic.

2014–15

Wipro Ventures launches $100 million fund for early and mid-stage start-ups.

Wipro Ltd acquires Designit, the world's second-largest strategic design firm.

Wipro Ltd develops AI platform Wipro Holmes.

2015

In April, Premji transfers additional economic benefits of 18% of shareholding in Wipro Ltd to the Trust, which now holds a total of 39% of shares of Wipro Ltd.

2017–18

WCCLG crosses $1 billion in revenue.

Santoor becomes number two brand in value in personal wash category in India.

Wipro recasts logo, values to mark new brand identity.

2011

Wipro, a $7 billion enterprise, crosses $5 billion in revenues in IT services business.

2012

Sells Sunflower brand.

2013

Wipro Ltd demerges to focus on IT services. Consumer, Infrastructure Engineering, Healthcare businesses grouped under privately held Wipro Enterprises Ltd.

Wipro Ltd employee headcount touches 140,000, serving 950 clients.

Premji transfers an additional 12% Wipro Ltd shares to the Trust.

The Wipro Timeline

Azim Premji Foundation
Wipro Ltd
Wipro Enterprises Ltd
Wipro Consumer Care and Lighting
Wipro Infrastructure Engineering
Initial Years

1990–1995

1990

Wipro-GE joint venture set up to manufacture healthcare equipment. Factory comes up in Bangalore.

Wipro Systems bags first big IT services account with GE.

1991

Wipro Fluid Power ties up with Eaton Corp, USA.

Launches Wipro Lighting.

Wipro Infotech's R&D begins 'lab on hire' operations.

1992

Diversifies into financial services business with Wipro Finance.

1993

Wipro Infotech and Wipro Systems come together as Wipro Infotech Group.

1994–95

Ranks among top 50 publicly held corporations in India.

Wipro-BT, joint venture with British Telecom, set up.

1981–1989

1981

Wipro Consumer starts using flexipacks for vanaspati, an industry first.

Wipro Infotech rolls out prototype of Series 86.

1982

Wipro Products renamed Wipro Ltd.

1983

Dr Gulbanoo Premji relinquishes chairmanship to Azim Premji.

Wipro Systems incorporated on July 14.

1984

Wipro Consumer Products Division sets up toilet soap production, with annual capacity of 4,000 tonnes.

1984–85

Wipro Infotech launches computer peripherals with Epson, Japan.

1986

Wipro Consumer Products Division launches Santoor sandal-turmeric bath soap.

1987

Wipro Infotech launches Wipro Series 386.

Wipro Systems rolls out InstaPlan in US.

1971–1980

1971

Wipro Beliefs articulated.

1976

First diversification, a fluid power business called Wintrol,commences production in Peenya, Bangalore.

HQ moves to Bakhtawar building, Nariman Point.

1977

WIVP changes name to Wipro Products Ltd.

1979

Diversifies into Information Technology.

1980

Sets up IT Division in Bangalore with manufacturing facilities in Mysore.

Wipro PAT is $1.16 million.

1945–1970

1945

Western India Vegetable Products incorporated on 29 December.

1946

Vanaspati factory comes up in Amalner.

1947

Lists on Bombay Stock Exchange on 13 June.

1966

Mohamedhusain Hasham Premji dies on 11 August.

Dr Gulbanoo Premji appointed Chairman.

Azim Premji returns from Stanford University.

1968

Azim Premji appointed Managing Director.

wipro

Be passionate about clients' success

Treat each person with respect

Be global and responsible

Unyielding integrity in everything we do

*The Spirit of Wipro is the core of Wipro. These are our Values. It is about who we are. It is our character.

WIPRO
Wipro GE
Medical Systems Ltd
YARDLEY
SANTOOR
Max. Price
Rs. 3.00
ocal Taxes
Extra

Chapter | **1** | 2020

A Fresh Approach

Older than independent India, Wipro took its first breath in the aftermath of World War II in 1945. These early years were suffused with the euphoria of India's independence and the human tragedy of the Partition. As it turns seventy-five, Wipro remains contemporary, having kept pace as the world changed around it and, in some instances, helping the world change. It diversified and reinvented itself several times over while nurturing an exceptional value system, fostering innovation, and committing to the creation of a just, equitable, humane and sustainable world.

Like its contemporaries (about seventy pre-Independence Indian businesses listed on the Bombay Stock Exchange survive today), Wipro is privileged to be both maker and keeper of India's history. From a traditional, family-run business, it grew into a professional, diversified, global corporation respected the world over for its integrity and purpose. In its avatar as an information technology (IT) company, Wipro has had an indelible impact on the country's economy and changed the way the world thinks of technology.

Wipro's story is inseparable from the story of Azim Premji. As the heart and mind that guided Wipro for fifty-three of its seventy-five years, he took an unexceptional manufacturing business in a small town in central India and grew it into a global IT giant. With decades of accumulated success and wealth, and much more to come, Premji turned over the ownership of the company to a philanthropic foundation, the Azim Premji Foundation (Foundation), to serve and support some of the most disadvantaged populations in the world.

This is the story of that exceptional entrepreneurial journey.

This tale began when Mohamedhusain Hasham Premji, a Bombay-based trader and trade activist, bought a ghee manufacturing unit from Larsen & Toubro for Rs 25,750 on 6 November 1945. A few days later, it set sail from a port in Great Britain to India, along with a Greaves Cotton and Co steam boiler, two diesel oil engines and an air compressor. Mohamedhusain set up Western India Vegetable Products Ltd (WIVP) on 29 December of that year to manufacture a kind of vegetable shortening known as vanaspati. The factory in Amalner was an eight-hour drive from Bombay.

Today, Wipro no longer makes vanaspati. The consumer business, the starting point of the Wipro story, and the technology giant that is Wipro Ltd are today demerged. The older business is now part of Wipro Enterprises Private Limited (WEL), a privately held company that includes Wipro Consumer Care and Lighting (WCCLG) and Wipro Infrastructure Engineering (WIN), as well as two joint ventures, Wipro GE Healthcare Private Limited and Wipro Kawasaki Precision Machinery Private Limited. WEL is a rapidly growing business with revenues of more than $2 billion, united with Wipro Ltd in the belief of creating an inclusive, sustainable future and the ability to do good.

Wipro Ltd (New York Stock Exchange [NYSE]: WIT; National Stock Exchange of India [NSE]: WIPRO; BSE: 507685) is today the more globally prominent part of the Wipro conglomerate, a leading global IT, consulting and business process services company. With over 180,000 employees, Wipro is recognized for its comprehensive portfolio of services, strong commitment to sustainability and good corporate citizenship.

Even as it changes constantly, leading and responding to technology shifts and addressing market needs, the core of Wipro is unchanging, anchored in its foundational value system. These intangibles have always played a critical, if often unarticulated, role in Wipro's success. Right from navigating the first offshoring wave in the 1990s, Wipro's values continue to be a draw for global clients, many of whom have witnessed first-hand the company's meteoric rise from its unassuming beginnings. These relationships are a testament as much to the trust invested in a little-known company in a faraway country as the ability of that company to recognize and respond to new opportunities in shifting global realities.

❖❖❖

Rarely in history has this agility—and also Wipro's resilience in the face of adversity—been as crucial as it was in 2020, with the world negotiating the COVID-19 pandemic. It helped that Wipro had envisioned a digital-first future much ahead of its peers and was able to help many of its clients complete the digital transition even as countries and economies locked down and work shifted to the domestic space.

Unknown to its clients, in a matter of weeks, Wipro also enabled a significant section of its employees to work from home for an extended period. Many of them were stranded in remote parts of the country and overcame impossible odds to keep working. A member of the Data Domain team, for instance, found himself hitching a 150-km ride each morning in a milk truck to access a secure internet connection.

Chances are that, with time, his story will become part of the Wipro legend. It would find company in the story of the factory manager who stood up to a bureaucrat and refused to pay a bribe for grid electricity, and then ran an entire factory on diesel generators for eighteen months. Or the company official who confronted a powerful union leader for claiming first-class fares for second-class travel, and then sacked him. Unprompted, undirected, owning it from within, people of Wipro have always lived by the values explicitly articulated by the company in 1971.

The Spirit of Wipro, as they are now known, is the core of the company. These values define the character of Wipro and are touchstones for all that it does. While deeply rooted in the unchanging essence of the company, the Spirit of Wipro also embraces its identified aspirations. As the indivisible synthesis of four values, this value system is a beacon, giving direction and a clear sense of purpose, energizing Wipro.

While transitions pose a challenge, when moored in unshakeable values, they make for a purposeful journey. Through three generations of leaders, in Wipro, this has indeed been the case.

This is where Wipro stands apart, in creating an inclusive, sustainable future for all stakeholders and in profit finding purpose. By 2019, 67 per cent of the economic ownership of Wipro Ltd came to rest with the Azim Premji Foundation, which works to help improve India's public education system, supports other not-for-profits that help people with deep vulnerabilities and runs the Azim Premji University.

Set up in 2001, the Foundation has been the beneficiary of multiple tranches of Premji's personal shareholding in Wipro Ltd, making it the largest stakeholder in the technology business. It has also received much of Premji's wealth in other assets, including ownership of Wipro Enterprises Ltd. Significant direct benefits of any value creation by

1945

1977

1998

2017

ABOVE
Wipro's logos over the years, which have evolved in response to shifts in markets and technologies.

Wipro, in terms of profits or share price increases, goes to philanthropy. This has set Wipro on a new trajectory.

Today, there's a new leadership in place to build upon Wipro's legacy of deep knowledge of technology and uncompromising values. Rishad Premji became the Executive Chairman of Wipro Ltd in July 2019. He was joined by Thierry Delaporte, who assumed office in July 2020 as chief executive officer and managing director.

Delaporte, formerly the chief operating officer at Capgemini, had known Wipro as an industry insider and a competitor for almost twenty-five years. He was considering going on a sabbatical after his time at Capgemini, when the offer from Wipro came. On his visit to India, Delaporte asked to spend some time at the Foundation, a cause which resonates deeply with this co-founder and president of a non-profit, Life Project 4 Youth. 'I knew about what Azim Premji had done and his legacy. I learned more about it, and I was incredibly touched,' says Delaporte.

He comes in at a crucial juncture of Wipro's history, committed to restoring Wipro to its position of leadership in the global IT services industry. It does not promise to be an easy transformation, but, as Delaporte takes on the challenge, he is confident of at least one element: the values of this 'emotionally intense company', where the heart leads the head. As he points out, 'These are incredible values, different from anyone else's in the industry. And I know this industry well.'

As Rishad Premji stepped into the Chairman's office, these were the very values he promised to protect. 'The legacy of Wipro is now my responsibility,' he said in his first letter to the company as chairperson. ◆

Rishad Premji, Bangalore, 2020.

The legacy of Wipro is now my responsibility

In conversation with Rishad Premji

Rishad Premji worked at Wipro for more than twelve years before taking over as Chairman. The erstwhile chief strategy officer of Wipro was also the Chairman of the National Association of Software and Service Companies (Nasscom), a trade body that furthers the cause of India's $170 billion software industry. Since stepping into his new role, he has focused on creating habits that manifest the Wipro culture, ones that address not only business but also society. Each Wiproite is committed to five habits: being respectful, being responsive, being communicative, demonstrating stewardship and building trust.

As a serving board member of the Azim Premji Foundation, Wipro's Chairman represents the largest stakeholder in Wipro Ltd as well. While Rishad Premji has lived his life with the values that Wipro embodies, he is now also their custodian.

Did you always know you were going to work for Wipro?
I have been asked this question before, and the answer is, absolutely not. Wipro was a job my father did. He was very focused on creating a professional set-up. My grandmother, Dr Gulbanoo Premji—a profound influence on my life—was the chairperson till the early 1980s, but we never discussed Wipro. I don't know how involved she was with it.

In Bombay, I went to a Jesuit all-boys', very diverse school called St Mary's, where one could meet kids from all walks of life. My life centered around my neighborhood friends, many of whom

After graduation, I started with GE's flagship Financial Management Program and went on to join the bond-insurance business. I was based in New York City. But I realized I wasn't enjoying it very much. So I decided to go to business school. Harvard was one of the best experiences of my life. You meet people from every walk of life, as diverse a group as possible. It's an amazing bubble while it lasts.

ABOVE
Harvard Business School,
Boston, Massachusetts.

also went to St Mary's. I remember going to Amalner every January, cycling inside the factory, enjoying the food. I also remember a lot of Wipro's senior leaders, who were based elsewhere, staying with us when they came to Bombay. I distinctly remember Mr Soota [who led Wipro's IT business in the 1980s and 1990s] staying with us on many occasions, Mr Prasanna [the first head of Wipro-GE] and Mr Narasimhan [the founding CEO of Wipro Infotech] as well.

In many other structured family businesses in India, the children work part-time or full-time in their family's offices, but it was never part of Wipro's culture. There was never any sense of entitlement or unique belonging or, frankly, even affection in my formative years for Wipro.

Did you know what you'd do after college?
You know, I don't over-plan. This is something that has helped me tremendously. If you overthink situations, you can ruin them.

I went to college in the US. I did liberal arts with a major in economics. And I loved it. It really stimulates the way you think, more broadly, how you approach and address problems. I had very little money, so I worked at a pizza place on campus. I did a year abroad at the London School of Economics, and over the summer of 1998, I worked at Barclays Bank. I needed some suits [to wear to work], but I didn't have the money. So I had to write to my father saying, this is how much it'll cost, this is how much you'll need to send me. I had friends from home who were well-to-do, whose pocket money was more generous than mine, and they could spend more easily, but I couldn't because of my very constrained budget, which my father thought was fair.

My grandmother, on the other hand, was very generous. I remember she sent me $200 asking me to buy myself something nice. It was a huge amount of money in those days. It still is.

A year before graduation, I started thinking about what I should do. My father recommended GE. I joined GE's flagship Financial Management Program with GE Capital. This was the late 1990s, the Jack Welch era. And I really enjoyed it, learning a lot, living across the US. After graduating from the program, I joined a bond-insurance business, Financial Guaranty Insurance Company, which GE subsequently sold. One of the reasons was that it was based in New York City—I wanted to be in a big city.

After a year and a half, I realized I wasn't enjoying it very much. I decided I wanted to do something different and so, I went to business school, and that was one of the best experiences of my life. It was a phenomenal two years at Harvard Business School. You meet people from every walk of life. It's a bubble, but an amazing bubble while it lasts.

Mr Premji talks about his mother being a big influence in his life. So do you. What do you remember of your grandmother?
We were a unit of five, and my mother and my grandmother were very close. She [my grandmother] was a very principled person, very non-judgmental. A great listener, great conversationalist, very generous. There are two people in our family who are unconditionally generous—my grandmother and my brother.

She was very, very involved in our formative years, and I was very close to her. Tariq and I used to visit her at the Children's Orthopaedic Hospital, and she'd take us out for lunch. We had an independent relationship with her that was very warm and very close. She used to play cards at the Orient Club in Bombay. I remember, at eighteen [years of age], driving her there on Sundays. She would proudly show off her grandson to her friends, not that there was much to show off! When I went to college, I would talk to her on the phone. I enjoyed coming home and spending time with her in the summers. Later, when I was applying to Harvard Business School, I remember coming home for Christmas and reading my essays to her. I went back to the US and she died a few days later.

Coming back home for holidays, did you get to know Wipro? Did you know much about your dad's work life?
Very little. Clearly, I knew Wipro was successful. I started my first rotation at GE's Financial Management Program in 1999. I remember *The Wall Street Journal* carried a front-page article on Narayana Murthy and Azim Premji. My boss called me to his office and asked, 'This guy, are you related to him?' I said, 'No!' I actually denied knowing my father because I didn't want to be treated differently. It was very important to me from the beginning that people respect me for what I am myself and [what I am] capable of—or not. There was no infatuation with the wealth or with leveraging that relationship for my betterment.

After Harvard, I was thinking of going into consulting and had a chat with Vivek Paul, who was then with Wipro [CEO, 1999–2005]. He recommended Bain & Company, I applied, and it worked out. I worked at Bain for a few years in London. Then, in 2007, when I was thirty, I remember

ABOVE

Rishad Premji at the Sarjapur campus in 2010, three years after joining Wipro.

Professionally,
I found Wipro to be as
good as the companies I
had worked for abroad.
It was very structured,
I had good bosses.
I went through
performance appraisal
cycles with conversations
about salary hikes, all
of those things that
people go through.
But I'd be unfair if
I didn't acknowledge that
I was different.
I was as mainstream
as I could be
with the uniqueness
of my situation.

thinking—and there was no pressure—that if I want to come back to India and live here, this was the right time. I'd lived away for twelve years, I was doing well at Bain, enjoying my life as an independent working professional. But I remember thinking, if I don't come back now, I never will.

Why were you thinking of coming back?

I always wanted to give myself a chance to return and live in India. And then I figured if in India, I should seriously look at Wipro as an option. But it wasn't like my father was saying, 'Come back and work for Wipro. This is the job you must do.'

A lot of people externally assumed that I was always on a very structured path from 2007 to 2019, and it was meticulously managed. Actually, it was not clear to me at all at that time. If you'd asked me when I joined Wipro, if I'd still be here, I'd have said, 'I have no clue.'

Did you have a choice?

Yeah, absolutely. Nobody pushed me to come back when I was twenty-one or twenty-two. You know, Kumar Mangalam Birla made a very interesting comment. He said that he gave his children the choice to pursue what they wanted, a choice he didn't have. I think I had the choices. Today, I feel a responsibility. Twenty years ago, I did not feel that pressure to have to be part of Wipro. But coming back to India for another corporate job didn't make much sense.

What were you thinking, coming in?

It was a big change for us. One, I was joining Wipro, which had its own unique culture, with the added complexity that my father was the Chairman. Aditi and I were expecting a baby. I'd never lived in Bangalore before and didn't know a soul here. But I think we handled it pretty well. AHP [Azim Premji] had me meet some board members. He had also told some of his direct reports about me. I'd met Girish Paranjpe [joint CEO of Wipro, 2008–2011] in London. He recommended a couple of things that I could do, and I joined Banking and Financial Services [BFSI], where I helped set up the mortgage business.

Did you have any advice from anyone on how to handle that?

I can't remember, to be honest. But I remember telling myself to take it one day at a time and not to overthink it. I also remember telling myself, 'Look, it's not going to be easy. People will judge you, arguably more harshly than they'd judge someone else.' I don't think that happened.

What helped was that I was inducted into the company at a level commensurate with my experience. I was not coming in to a big job. We were evaluating Business Process as a Service [BPaaS] in the mortgage business, and we put together a small team.

What was the job like for you?

Professionally, I found Wipro to be as good as the companies I had worked for abroad. It was more Indian-dominated, culturally, than what I'd been used to, but the professionalism wasn't very different. It was very structured, I had good bosses. My first boss was Soumitro Ghosh, head of Banking and Financial Services. Later, I suggested I report to Sriram Srinivasan, the head of the banking business, who I was working with more closely in practice.

How long was it before the others got over you? The value of the Premji name, the awkwardness?

Quickly. Because I was able to relate to and connect to people easily, I think they found me disarming. And that's perhaps a difference between AHP and me—I'd argue perhaps a strength. People are intimidated by him, there's an aura of formality and stature around him.

Was Wipro fair in treating you? In terms of performance reviews, promotions?

Yes, I would say 90 per cent of the time. I went through performance appraisal cycles, with conversations about salary hikes—all of those things that people go through. But I'd be unfair if I didn't acknowledge that I was different. I was as mainstream as I could be with the uniqueness of my situation.

How did your career move? Did it move the way you wanted it to, the organization wanted it to, AHP wanted it to?

There was no specific plan in 2007, none whatsoever. A lot of my moves within Wipro happened organically as opportunities presented themselves.

At Banking and Financial Services, I went into this special project building the mortgage business. We bought a 100-people company as part of that, Gallagher Financial Systems, which settled well into the business. After a point, I felt I was getting a bit siloed and thought I should figure out what to do next. Maybe I discussed it with AHP. And I don't know whether I came up with the idea or someone suggested it, but there was an opening in Investor Relations [IR]. And I thought it'd be interesting to engage with investors—it'd give me a more holistic view of the company.

People ask me what I've learned from AHP. The remarkable thing about AHP is that he is unaffected by success. I have learned from him to not let things go to your head. The second thing is hard work, there's no substitute for it. The third is attention to detail. And the fourth is learning from people at all levels.

ABOVE
Azim Premji, Founder Chairman of Wipro, with son Rishad at the Azim Premji Foundation Office, Sarjapur, Bangalore, 2020.

Rajendra Shreemal was then treasurer of Wipro, he also ran IR. I remember Soumitro tried to convince me not to go. In hindsight, I think that reflects well—everyone in Wipro fights to keep back a person they have regard for.

How long were you in the IR function for?

I worked there for six quarters, till about September 2010. As part of this role, I started connecting with the top thirty to forty leaders for two weeks every quarter before the results—it gives you a real view of what's happening inside the company. During that job, they put up my name for general manager. I didn't care too much about titles or hierarchy. But I did care about becoming a vice president because then you could travel business class overseas. That had to wait till 2011. Till that time, I had always traveled economy.

In 2010, Lan [K.R. Lakshminarayana, now the chief endowment officer at the Azim Premji Foundation] wanted to leave Wipro. So his job—head of Strategy—opened up. Initially, I was apprehensive [of stepping into his shoes]. It was a big job, and I would have to report to Suresh [Vaswani, joint CEO of Wipro, 2008–2011] and Girish. In September 2010, I moved to the strategy job to overlap with Lan, and a few months later, I took up the mergers and acquisitions [M&A] role as well.

It's your longest portfolio, right?

The job evolved. But it was not a mainstream function, except maybe for the M&A part. Lan described this to me very well. He said, 'The strategy function focuses on how you can optimally allocate the resources of the company so that they can have the best returns for the company.' What are the resources for the company? People and dollars. So, how can you optimally allocate these resources for impact? M&A is one mechanism of executing on strategy. He said, 'Strategy is like salt in food. You can't see it, but if it isn't there, the food doesn't taste so good.' I thought it was a fabulous description.

The new piece we added in 2015 was Wipro Ventures, our $100 million fund, which I feel proud of having helped start from scratch. We've now gotten to a place where we have more than twenty investments—our typical check size is $3–$10 million—and we are doing more than 100 deals with our customers, the value of that portfolio has increased. That really became exciting. So, I started spending a lot more time on that.

We don't take a technology risk at Wipro Ventures. We want to be comfortable with the technology that a company has built, [ensure] that it is reasonably validated. But we're very happy to take a market adoption risk. We bring three things to these companies: We work with the top 100 of the Fortune 500 large enterprises, so we provide market access and help with market adoption. Two, we understand technology so we can add value on the product management part. And three, we have access to people so we can value-add there. But our predominant value is the first. And it has played out quite well, actually. What I'm most

LEFT
The Premji family with the Wipro Consumer Products team at Amalner in the mid-1980s.

CLOCKWISE FROM TOP
Designit employees from around the world in Rotterdam, The Netherlands, for their annual innovation meet in 2017.

An image from a Microsoft store, where Rational Interaction—part of Wipro Digital—helped Microsoft transform its stores into an experiential hub for its products, services and partners.

Rishad Premji at the launch of Wipro's Silicon Valley Innovation Center in Mountain View, California.

An aerial view of Wipro Ltd's campus in Mountain View, California, September 2020.

proud of with Wipro Ventures is that we've done this with the right sensibility. Unlike many corporate funds, the team we found and the nature and the sensibility with which Wipro Ventures was created are very strongly aligned to Wipro.

I also spent a lot of time on M&A, meeting the team on the other side, the promoters and the CEOs. Even today, in my new job, I would spend three hours in a management presentation to understand a company and its people. I am still involved in the investment committee of Ventures because I feel very passionate about what we do here.

From your first job up until you became the Chairman, you've had three or four bosses. How has that been for you?

I was able to experience different leaders with their different styles and ways of working. I learned a lot from the way they conducted conversations. I got a much better sense of the company, the mindset, the ways of thinking. I remember something TK [Kurien, Wipro CEO, 2011–2016] told me: If somebody's a high performer and never experiences failure then they're in their comfort zone. I tell my teams this a lot: Sometimes you have to fail to get better at what you do.

People also ask me what I've learned from AHP. And I say three or four things. The remarkable thing about AHP is that he has not changed in fifty years. He is unaffected by success. I have learned from him to not let things go to your head. The second thing is hard work, there's no substitute for it. But I caveat that—you have to find the right balance between working hard and working smart. The third thing is attention to detail. And the fourth is learning from people at all levels. Not being afraid to say, I don't know. Not being afraid to ask questions. Not being afraid to be learning from people across the hierarchy. His discipline at his job is remarkable.

Didn't you ever want to move into a business vertical or a business function role?

Not really. Ownership and management are very different. And as an owner, you want the best manager in the job. My strength is in relationships, in people, in customers and employees. My strength is understanding prioritization of investments and assets, in things like Ventures and M&A. That's why I'm more involved, more hands-on on those two components.

But I am also clear as Chairman that the CEO runs the company. They are accountable for delivering the plan. My job is to enable them. My value-add is also in things in India—connecting with the government, meeting customers in India—because the CEO is based overseas.

But I am involved in the business. I show up at work every day. And I have an advantage in that I have been in the company since 2007. I know the people, I know the stakeholders. I know the system. I know what works and what doesn't. I have been raised in the system without being seen as a threat for more than a dozen years, which is a long time.

Performance-wise, the last ten years haven't been the best for Wipro. Between 2000 and 2010, the IT business grew from $400 million to $5 billion, a once-in-a-lifetime thing. Between 2010 and now, it has grown to $8.5 billion. How do you equate the two decades? Does this bother you personally that you're not top of the heap anymore?

Of course. Wipro's lackluster performance has been very disillusioning and disappointing. And that bothers everybody who's associated with Wipro. If you have a unique connect with Wipro—which a lot of our leaders do—it hurts. The challenge is that there's no 'Aha! This is the problem, and this is the solution'. If there was, it'd have been an easy fix. The situation is more nuanced than that.

You know, we did a poor job of mining our accounts. We leaked accounts as opposed to our competition. One thing Abid [Ali Neemuchwala, Wipro CEO, 2016–2020] cleaned up tremendously is customer-satisfaction issues, which challenge your right to play. Certainly, it has been a time of dramatic change in the industry—nobody is growing at the same pace as before because you're becoming bigger and bigger. Between 2000 and 2008, the industry grew at about 36 per cent to 37 per cent. Between 2008 and 2016, it grew by 12 per cent. And between 2016 and 2019, it grew sub 10 per cent. So, things are slowing down also because of the base effect.

What is your vision for Wipro?

In the last four or five years, we have moved to a world that is highly mobile first, very data rich, very cloud-centric. It is changing how large enterprises engage with their end customers. Consequently, their expectations from partners like us are changing profoundly. I feel very strongly that a lot of the successes that have brought IT services companies where they are today is not necessarily going to be what takes them to success tomorrow.

In the last few years, Wipro has made an effort to invest in new technology. I think there's tremendous potential in technology services for helping customers think through

ABOVE
Rishad Premji with wife Aditi (left), daughter Rhea and son Rohaan in Bangalore, 2020.

It has been an interesting first year as Chairman of Wipro, to say the least. In the middle of an unparalleled global pandemic, we were also going through a CEO change. We made some very fundamental calls upfront. Employee safety and enablement were first. Personally, I realized how blessed I am ... it has been a year of great learning.

the power of being digital first, of the cloud and of the data. Many enterprises are still struggling in the very, very early days of: 'How do we intelligently understand our customers better, take them much more pointed solutions, cross-sell, up-sell them better, use our data much more smartly?'

At Wipro, we also deeply believe that we exist to serve beyond just our customers and employees. We are part of communities where we have to play a very involved and responsible role. Yet we are, as we should be, strongly focused on the returns for our shareholders as well.

What did the pandemic mean for Wipro? How did it affect the plans you had before taking over as Chairman?

It's been an interesting first year as Chairman of Wipro, to say the least. We've had an unparalleled situation in the world. We went through a CEO change right in the middle of all of this. I joke with people and say, 'It's been a challenging first year. But things get better from here on.'

In the technology industry, one feels quite blessed because this is actually the space where people are going to spend. The new way of engaging with customers is going to be a different medium, a digital medium. This is the reality. This journey had already begun, but it's only gotten that much more accelerated in this new world.

If you'd asked us a few months ago if 100 per cent or nearly 100 per cent of our people could work from home and work from home impactfully, one would have just laughed and said, 'Not possible.' The reality is that it's happening. The Indian government has even approved some form of work from home permanently, so it's [a] totally changed world.

We did a few things smartly right from the beginning. Just before the lockdown, we had anticipated that the situation could be more precarious than it was at that point in time. So, we had already started to enable people to work from home. It got accelerated as we went deeper into the lockdown. And, fortunately, IT was declared an essential service. So, I think we were quite well prepared.

I think we made some very fundamental calls upfront. The first call we made was for the safety of our people. [It] was paramount. That was a call we made very, very, quickly and we set up four task forces. One focused on employee enablement and employee safety, spearheaded by our COO. Once we realized the enormity of what we were facing, we very quickly set up a group addressing cost, headed by our Chief Human Resource Officer (CHRO). A third task force looked at opportunities around COVID-19. And the fourth looked at long-term implications of change, how we think industries will change eighteen or twenty-four months down the road, and how we start anticipating, preparing and planning for them.

I think they've worked quite impactfully. And I think things are looking a lot better today than they were in the first quarter of 2020.

How has your life changed personally? Like all of us, did you experience some moments of panic, anxiety, a low as well?

No. I mean, I realized how blessed I am. I have the luxury of space, I have the luxury of a home office, which many people don't have. My family has been well. My children, I think, are made for lockdown; they've been quite comfortable being at home. So, it's been okay for us. I realize that it has been much harder for many people who've been out of work, who are living in confined spaces, in multigenerational families.

But I've also learned very strongly not to judge people on how they are coping because people are coping with it differently. There are moments of hoping that this will end, moments of being able to be mobile and commute and travel, which I used to do a lot prior to this. But I realize it's not been as okay for many other people, and so one is just trying to be sensitive to friends, to family, to work colleagues, and trying to just over-communicate and encourage people to just make sure that everybody is doing okay.

You finished a year in the middle of all of this. What's that first year been like as Chairman of Wipro? What were the things you assumed coming in that didn't play out? Things you learned along the way?

It's been a year of great learning and moments of great demand. Mr Premji has been very graceful. For the founder, who has been at the helm of things and really been the soul of the company for fifty-three years, to take a step back and truly let me play the role that I should be playing, that's incredible. He's been incredibly supportive—always available but never visible, in his own way, which has been terrific.

I began playing a much more involved role after Abid announced he was leaving. I was spending much more time meeting customers, both customers I knew and new ones as well. And building relationships in a virtual format because we went into lockdown and the world pretty much slowed down from early March. I realized that you can connect and build equations with people even in this medium and form. It's been very interesting to learn that you can actually construct opportunities, close deals and transition in this virtual format. So, that's been a big learning.

I believe the smell of an organization is as important as your competency and capability. Those two, coming together impactfully, make a huge difference. I'm a huge believer in the power of culture to unlock the potential of the organization. In terms of our customer mix, our people, our capabilities, we are positioned very well.

ABOVE
Wipro Ltd's Board members, Bangalore, 2019. From left: Chairman Rishad Premji; independent directors Narayanan Vaghul, Ashok Ganguly and Ireena Vittal; Founder Chairman Azim Premji; CEO Abidali Neemuchwala; and independent directors William Owens, Patrick Ennis, Mahendra Sharma and Patrick Dupuis.

It's also been a big learning as to how much you can do virtually and that there are certain things about in-person meetings that cannot be replaced, like seeing a person face-to-face and judging their body language or catching up for a coffee or a drink after the formalities. So, those things you miss. You also realize how many things you perhaps don't have to travel for.

And then, it's been a learning experience to bring in a new leader for the company in this virtual format. I had the chance to meet Thierry in person. But he's still not had the chance to meet many of his direct reports in person. But again, I feel I've learned so much by the fact that you can bring in such a profound change into the company and make it work. And I can tell you I'm very, very excited about where we sit at the moment. Thierry has settled in really well and gotten to know people, gotten under the skin of the company, all without having met most reports or visiting a single Wipro office, except for the office in Paris, where he is currently based.

So, doing the Chairman's role for a year, do you feel closer to Mr Premji than you did before? This is the first time you are performing a role he did. Do you talk about it with him?
I don't talk about the role so much. But I certainly reach out to him for advice. I keep him updated on certain things [that] I think are important for him to know. I will bounce off ideas as and when required. So, as I said, it's been a remarkable partnership that I really appreciate, where he has given me the freedom to discover my own way of doing things and my own style. And that has been the help that I needed. Sometimes the help can be letting go.

Were there any moments where you hesitated in implementing anything you thought of in early 2020? Over the first few months when the world didn't know what was going to happen, did you feel like putting the brakes on any initiative you thought of for Wipro, including announcing the new CEO? Or were you always clear that you'll go ahead, no matter what?
Of course, there were moments of anxiety. That's just the natural environment. But we were able to think long term and stay strong with the view that we were not trying to make decisions only for the next six months, but for the long term. And so, I look at this also as an opportunity because moments of crisis can also be an opportunity to address things, to double down, to drive right when everybody is focused on going left, to move against the tide. And I think that's an opportunity that we should take and we must take and we've tried to take. The fact that we have stable ownership in the company allows us to think longer term and take decisions longer term. If anything, we wanted to accelerate our decisions on our new CEO coming in, given the change that we were going through.

How do you feel about 2021 as you go into it?
I feel great. I'm quite a pragmatic person; I'm not an eternal optimist. But I feel more energized about where we are at Wipro Ltd than I've felt in a long time. I think Thierry brings in a great style of leadership, a great set of fresh ideas. We're thinking through some fundamental things for the company. We work well together, we work closely together, and I think this is the time for us to be building a bolder future for the company and that's the journey that we are on.

While this new medium of work is interesting and exciting, I think it'll be very important for people to come back to work. So, one of the things we are very focused on, at least at Wipro Ltd, we want all of our people to come back some of the time. And all of our people to be able to work from home some of the time as well. Because we believe that coming together physically is incredibly important for two things. One is to nurture and build culture, because culture is incredibly, incredibly powerful and often grows informally, in conversations around the water cooler or the coffee machine. That's one. The second is for innovation and ideation. Innovation and ideation often don't happen with structured Zoom calls but often happen in downtime, when you are sitting frustrated in a conference room and suddenly something strikes. So, I'm a big believer that while things have changed, it's important for us to come together.

The other thing that I've spent a lot of time on in the past twelve months is this most important thing—the culture of the company, specifically the ways of working with each other, what we are calling the 'five habits'. I've personally done sixty-two sessions, each of them between two and a half and three hours long. I was reaching more than 15,000 Wipro employees, starting with the senior most, going down to key managers in the company, talking about my observations, the importance of change, the importance of how we work and how we come together for impactful results. Because I really believe the smell of an organization, the smell of a place is as important as your competency and capability. And those two coming together impactfully will make a huge difference. I'm a huge believer in the power of culture to unlock the potential of the organization. I genuinely feel that in terms of our customer mix, in terms of our people, in terms of our capabilities, we are positioned very well.

We have a very strong sense of purpose. People really resonate with and care about working with organizations that believe in the larger community and giving back. Wipro is built on a bedrock of integrity, on a bedrock of doing right, on a bedrock of doing clean business. These things are unparalleled. They matter to employees; they matter to customers.

ABOVE
A glimpse of communities across India, where Wipro Foundation works to create a sustainable future.

How do you know that with certainty?
I benchmark. I look at our customer base. I look at the breadth and depth and quality of the customer names we have. I cannot blame portfolio imbalance. When I talk to stakeholders, when we benchmark our top people, and I meet our competition stakeholders and benchmark one on one, we're as good, if not better. I don't think the strategic priorities we are driving are the wrong ones. We can always have an argument about whether we're investing enough, investing fast enough. Those are healthy conversations for a company. But our leadership position—as per the industry analysts—is moving and growing tremendously. It gives me validation that what we are investing in is being recognized by the market. These are the right things.

We have a very strong sense of purpose. People really resonate and care about working with organizations that believe in the larger community and giving back. This company is built on a bedrock of integrity, on a bedrock of doing right, on a bedrock of doing clean business. Those are things that are unparalleled. They matter to employees; they matter to customers.

We need to focus on our habits. They can really, really make all the difference in what an organization can become. We're calling it the growth mindset. We've not performed as a company for ten years. So, we have to try different things. But our habits, the way people work, need to change. Habits are what you inculcate by doing [things] yourself and, as a consequence, build the way the organization works. This is critical.

You also represent continuity in the Azim Premji Foundation, in the private enterprise and in Wipro Ltd. How do you see your role vis-à-vis the other two entities? The Foundation owns 67 per cent of Wipro Ltd today. How do you see that? And what role have you had in the making of that?
The Indian family context is unique because, you know, a lot of people have not created the wealth, they've inherited the wealth in large traditional family businesses. So, it's not theirs to give away.

I find the philosophy of first-generation entrepreneurs very different. My father was very clear that there was so much [wealth] and there was no way he was going to leave it to his next of kin for personal use. We discussed it, but it was, as it should be, his decision.

Two, frankly, it was never a wrestle in my mind to disagree with that because of what we were taught. Our lives haven't changed much from the time I was born. We were very comfortable even then. How much can you actually consume? Money becomes notional beyond a certain point. And even if you leave a very small proportion of this to your children, it's still a lot to live on very comfortably anywhere in the world. So, there was no disagreement in terms of thinking on this.

I feel a deeper responsibility in the fact that Wipro's largest shareholder is a foundation, and what value Wipro creates, a large chunk of that goes to a great cause.

Is it more responsibility for you?
It certainly puts more expectation. But it would hurt just as much to lose even otherwise. I find it energizing that the benefits of Wipro's success ultimately go to a worthy cause. That it's not only just pure, raw capitalistic ego and the satisfaction of winning alone. I find this purpose matters to employees, to people joining the company and also to customers.

The Azim Premji Foundation also has played a significant role in helping communities go through the pandemic, especially in India. What has that been like? Have you been involved in some activities there?
Yeah, that's something that we take great pride in. I remember having these conversations in mid-March in 2020 with Anurag [Behar of the Azim Premji Foundation] and [PS] Narayan of the Wipro Foundation. And we said, these are the moments that count, we really need to step up and do something on a substantive scale. And let us combine this with all the different parts of Wipro, be it Wipro Enterprises Ltd, Wipro Ltd [or] the Azim Premji Foundation. And we committed Rs11,250 million, about $150 million, to the cause. In the first three to four months, we were all on a daily call. Now we're on a fortnightly call. If you cannot be there and help in these times of need, then when does it really matter? We're proud of the work we've done across the Wipro family.

The other thing that I feel incredibly proud of is, how we used the Wipro Ltd infrastructure smartly. We have these large campuses, so we decided to use our industrial kitchens in Pune, Calcutta and predominantly in Bangalore to produce hot meals. So, for the first seventy-five days [of the lockdown], we were able to produce almost 3 million meals, 60,000 meals a day at our peak. We've been working with the government of Karnataka, which has been incredibly supportive, and the other state governments on this since the early months.

We also converted our campus in Pune, which was lying

ABOVE
Wipro's newest campus
at Kodathi, Bangalore.

idle, into a 450-bed COVID-19 hospital and handed it over to the government of Maharashtra in a record time of five to six weeks. It has come to good use and served as a tertiary care hospital—1,700 to 1,800 patients have been through its doors so far. Being able to do these kinds of things, being able to help and support the community has been very important.

We've also said categorically that we won't let a single employee go on account of COVID-19. And we've done our best to stay with that.

ABOVE
Thierry Delaporte took charge as chief executive officer and managing director of Wipro Ltd in July 2020.

What's the one habit that you have picked up, one change you've made during the lockdown and this general slowing down?

I don't know if I made a fundamental change. I just learned—or at least I've tried and not succeeded fully—to be more patient with people because people deal with this situation very differently. So, you're just trying to be more understanding about people's contexts and trying to be more empathetic and patient, which is something that I should continuously work on.

But I've also doubled down on things that I feel are important for me personally, for my own sanity. I've tried to be very disciplined with exercise and with sleeping. I'm a big believer in both those components for just a balanced, stable life. I've tried to maintain both those components, and I've been quite successful at it.

You take responsibility for upholding the legacy of Wipro. What is this legacy?

The minute you think of Wipro, you think of the highest standards of governance and integrity—unyielding integrity. We command a deep respect across stakeholders as a formidable competitor, a fair and responsible employer, a partner that delivers value, and a kind and compassionate company. This is the kind of company we are. We have stayed true to our values, the Spirit of Wipro. We have been able to stay current and relevant and move with the times in the fast-changing space of the technology industry. We have created value for all our stakeholders and, in the bargain, created value for our largest shareholder, the Azim Premji Foundation.

Wipro is celebrating its seventy-fifth anniversary in 2021. What is your feeling about it?

A feeling of great pride. You have to reflect on what an incredible achievement it has been to have built a company over these last seventy-five years in various different industries. Not only in the IT industry but also in the consumer care industry as well as in the infrastructure engineering space, in the healthcare space, and with partnerships and joint ventures with GE. To have built a company on the bedrock of integrity, strong governance and uncompromised values ... it's just quite remarkable. To have created a kind of loyalty, to have built the kind of leaders who have also gone out and done fabulous things on their own, and to have helped put the technology industry and India on the global map, to have built a part of that respect that has become a celebrated part of India today and the potential that we have, I think that's remarkable.

Then there is a huge element of gratitude. Because luck plays a huge component in this. You know, there are lots of people that are incredibly bright, incredibly hardworking, do all the things right, and do not achieve this kind of success. You have to marvel at the good fortune that has allowed us to get here as a company. ◆

Interviewed by Mitu Jayashankar, 2020

*Recreated from a plaster relief-work found on the wall of the Amalner factory.

1945–1966

The real property that a parent can transmit to all equally
is his or her character and educational facilities.

Mohandas Karamchand Gandhi

Mohamedhusain Hasham Premji was only twenty-one when he took over his late father's grain trade. Its footprint stretched from Burma to Africa. But the young man was aware that the world order was about to change. In 1945, he branched into manufacturing. His first project was an oil mill in the Indian heartland. Western India Vegetable Products, which would grow into Wipro, sold its first tins of vanaspati in 1947, the year India won independence.

Chapter | **2** | 1945-1966

A Very Small Company

ABOVE
Mohamedhusain Hasham Premji as a young man.

LEFT
Mohamedhusain Premji with his parents Sakina and Khan Bahadur Hasham Mohamed Premji, circa 1929.

The seed of Wipro's growth, now spread over fifty countries, can be traced to events that occurred more than a century ago.

Economic historians and social theorists point out how India had participated in globalization right from the nineteenth century, with trade and migration, and a 'readiness to resettle, relocate and change one's circumstances by joining cross-cultural transactions.'[1] In case of the Premjis, it started with Hasham Premji. He traveled from his village in Kutch, a district in the modern Indian state of Gujarat, to settle down in Bombay, a mercantile center and a city of promise for enterprising people, in the late nineteenth century.

It is not clear what Hasham Premji did when he first arrived in Bombay, but over time, he joined the rice trade. Rangoon, Calcutta and Bombay were the nerve centers of the trade, and Hasham Premji quickly learned that, to make a mark, he would have to import the grain directly from Burma, the largest hub of wholesale rice. He set up an office in Rangoon and soon earned the sobriquet of 'Rice King'. The office continued to be operational till the 1960s, when it was nationalized by the Burmese government.

Hasham Premji's son, Mohamedhusain Hasham Premji, arrived late in his father's life. A bright young man, he graduated from Fergusson College in Poona (now Pune) and joined his father's business as a partner, quickly picking up the ropes. He was only twenty-one when his father died in 1936, leaving him to handle the business alone. But before his demise, Hasham Premji saw his son engaged to Dr Gulbanoo Patel.

LEFT
Mohamedhusain and Dr Gulbanoo Premji visited Rangoon, a stronghold of the family's grain business, shortly after their wedding in 1936.

ABOVE
Newlyweds Dr Gulbanoo and Mohamedhusain Premji.

Mohamedhusain Premji married Gulbanoo Patel in 1936. They were both twenty-one. He was a suave businessman, she a qualified doctor. They made for a remarkable couple. He was committed to his honorary roles in various trade bodies and boards. She raised their children and championed large healthcare causes. And together, they shared a common altruistic ethos.

Mohamedhusain was very much the progressive, Westernized young man about town, organizing balls for the governor and his lady and hosting dinners at the Willingdon Club in Bombay. But he quickly established himself as a leader in the grain trade and became known as an advocate of trade interests, filling his father's shoes.

Burma, part of the British Indian territory till 1937, was the biggest bastion of Mohamedhusain's grain business until World War II. As the Japanese moved in during the war, thousands of Indians journeyed back to their motherland.

Anticipating economic, political and social changes, Mohamedhusain looked to move away from trade and into manufacturing. The ambitious businessman already had a formidable reputation in Bombay and was unanimously elected the president of the Indian Merchants' Chamber (IMC) in 1945 at the age of just thirty—the youngest ever to hold this post. A nonprofit set up in 1907 to represent Indian businesses, the IMC was as powerful as it was respected. Its members played a crucial role in the Swadeshi movement, supporting the boycott of foreign-made goods and encouraging domestic manufacture. The IMC counted no less a personage than Mahatma Gandhi as an honorary member. The list of IMC's presidents is an absolute education in Indian business history.[2] Among the most notable are Sir Purshottamdas Thakurdas—one of the leading industrialist-nationalists who shaped the Bombay Plan (see: The Bombay Plan) before Independence—and post-Independence stalwarts like Naval H Tata and SP Godrej.

Right after he was elected IMC president, Mohamedhusain founded Western India Vegetable Products Limited on 29 December 1945. Its first unit was an oil mill in Amalner, deep in the groundnut-growing region of Khandesh, part of the erstwhile princely state of Sachin (in present-day Gujarat). Mohamedhusain's long-time deputy, Natwarlal Vansia, belonged to the ruling family of Sachin. With Vansia in charge, most of Mohamedhusain's workforce moved from his Burma outfit to Amalner.

Western India Vegetable Products looked to manufacture vanaspati and refined oil out of groundnut, alongside laundry soap—786 that was later renamed 787—as a byproduct of the oil-refining process.

❖❖❖

These were an unsettled times. While independence from 200 years of British rule was in sight, there was no clarity on who would take the reins of the newly birthed country. Multinational firms expectedly hedged their bets while Indian family-owned businesses—many had prospered during World War II—threw their weight behind Indian leaders.

Amid the uncertainty, Pranlal Devkaran Nanjee (see: The First directors of Western India Vegetable Products), a former president of IMC, founder of Dena Bank and one of Western India Vegetable Products' founder-directors, hosted the new company's first meeting. Their primary mandate was to get the factory running. Despite the late delivery of machinery, Western India Vegetable Products' first products rolled out in 1947—they had registered the brand names Sunflower, Kisan and Camel—making it among

LEFT
Mohamedhusain Premji (fourth from left at the table) at a reception in Burma.

Mohamedhusain Premji worked closely with industry bodies, drafting appeals and urging change. He was a critic of the ever-expanding role of the State in the private sector. As vanaspati manufacturing became mired in punishing controls, he emerged as a spokesman for the industry.

ABOVE
A view of the Amalner vanaspati factory. A railway siding, from where this photo was taken, ran adjacent to the factory, making it convenient to transport raw materials and finished products.

BELOW, RIGHT
Ganesh festival celebrations in the town of Amalner.

BELOW, LEFT
Mohamedhusain Premji (in dark jacket) with Morarji Desai (fourth from left), then chief minister of Bombay State and future prime minister of India, at the inauguration of a plant in Amalner.

ABOVE
Mohamedhusain Premji (seated on chair, fourth from right) with the workforce at the Western India Vegetable Products Ltd factory in Amalner, 1964.

the first new vanaspati factories to start manufacturing post Independence.

❖❖❖

On 3 June 1947, the British government announced the Mountbatten Plan, confirming the proposed partition of India. The British parliament passed the Indian Independence Act the next month and, on 15 August 1947, the sovereign States of India and Pakistan came into existence.

Against this cataclysmic backdrop, Western India Vegetable Products went public. The initial ordinary shares were priced at Rs 100—the cost of 33 gm of gold in those days—each.[3] The company raised Rs 1.7 million in its first year through its public listing and other sources. It would next raise funds from the public only fifty-three years later in 2000, when Wipro listed on the New York Stock Exchange.

Vanaspati was an industry with a future (see: What is Vanaspati?). For most Indians, dairy-derived cooking fats such as ghee and butter were expensive. A vegetable-based alternative, vanaspati was perfect for deep frying, both at home and for commercial sweet-makers. Proving Mohamedhusain's bet right, vanaspati would go on to become the largest industry of its kind in Asia and the fifth largest in the world by 1955.

Shortly after its listing, Western India Vegetable Products sold its first batch of refined oil. It found a ready market around Amalner—in Bombay, Poona, Gujarat—and further afield, in Calcutta and Agra. The laundry soap also found takers across northern India. Western India Vegetable Products predicted 'tremendous demand' for its products. This optimism grew as India gained independence. To mark the occasion, Western India Vegetable Products employees received a month's salary as Independence Day bonus.

While Amalner was the heart of Western India Vegetable Products, the registered headquarters was located in Bombay, at Hasham Premji House on Ghoga Street, Fort. Despite State controls on price in Bombay,

The First Directors of Western India Vegetable Products Limited

On the first board of directors for Western India Vegetable Products Ltd were several known names from Bombay's trading and business circle. Several of them had a Kutchi Gujarati background, and almost all shared the zeal to serve the nation and its people, colloquially known as Bombay philanthropy.

Banker, businessman and philanthropist Pranlal Devkaran Nanjee, the founder of Dena Bank, was one. Sir Rahimtoola M Chinoy, who had served as president, Federation of Indian Chambers of Commerce and Industry in 1937, was another. Both men resigned from the WIVP Board by 1949 due to ill health. While Sir Rahimtoola was replaced by his son Mahommed Husain R. Chinoy, Abdultyeb E Maskati was co-opted in place of Nanjee. Maskati is credited with expanding his grandfather's textile business that spread from Siam to Singapore, Cambodia, and Burma further up to Japan. The firm still exists in India and Thailand.

Ratilal Mulji Gandhi served on WIVP's Board till 1975. He was a leading trader of grain, wheat and oilseeds and was an expert on oilseed-crushing, which saw him installed as a member of several expert committees. A trustee of the Port of Bombay, Gandhi was later elected to Assembly from Bombay City.

Sir Behram N Karanjia, a fourth member of the first Board, had served as mayor of Bombay during 1939–40. Not much is known about Rao Bahadur Devji Tokarsee Muljee who passed away in 1951, Gangaram Vallabhji who resigned in 1961, and Ratansey Karsondas Vissanji.

ABOVE
Mohamedhusain Premji addresses a meeting, flanked by Maulana Abul Kalam Azad (to his right) and Jawaharlal Nehru and Sardar Vallabhbhai Patel (to his left), 1946.

We Stand by the Fight for Freedom ...

Revered Maulana Saheb and Panditji,

I consider this as quite a unique and glorious event in the history of this Chamber. It is, indeed, a rare privilege to have both the retiring and the incoming Presidents of the Indian National Congress in our midst, and we are very grateful to you, Sirs, for having kindly spared time to come over here this evening, in the midst of your crowded programme, to give us your message of hope and encouragement.

The Nation is greatly indebted to you, Maulana Saheb, for the steadfast manner in which you steered the ship of' the national struggle, particularly during the last six years of tempest and storm. With devotion and steadfastness, and with a faith that continued undimmed amidst the severest discouragements, you inspired the country to hold aloft the banner of freedom. The country is on the threshold of a new era, taking us one step nearer our goal. You have thus the added satisfaction that you are giving over charge with a clearer and a more precise vision of the future.

The mantle of leadership has naturally fallen on Pandit Jawaharlal Nehru who is considered the young old man of India. Panditji combines the wisdom of age with the impetuousness and enthusiasm of youth. He has never faltered. He embodies in his person all that is high and noble in our land.

It is rested with him he would: "With fate conspire to grasp this sorry scheme of things entire" and then "shatter it to bits ... Remould it nearer to the heart's desire."

The country is today passing through a critical phase. It is a matter for great satisfaction that you, Panditji, will be at the helm of the most important political party at this juncture. We offer you our sincere felicitations and wish you Godspeed and success in your task ahead.

The world has changed and people are inspired with a new vision. It is now futile to think that we shall go back to the old hum-drum days. In the words of Robert Bartlett, the refrain seems to be:

"Don't send us back to a life that is flat again, Haven't you something that is more in our line, We specialise in the impossible, Doing things nobody could ever do!"

From what we know of you, you will be undertaking your new duties and responsibilities with that determination and in that spirit and we cherish the hope that side by side with Indian freedom, it will fall to your privileged lot to achieve Indian unity also in your regime as President.

I have no desire to utilise this occasion for initiating a discussion on any of the aspects connected with the current political developments. In fact, you have been so engrossed with those aspects for the last few days that I feel that I would not be justified in requesting you to go over the ground again here. Our silence should not, however, be taken to mean that we are not alive to the intricate and serious nature of the problems awaiting solution. The Indian Merchants' Chamber and the Indian commercial community generally have always stood by those who were in the vanguard of the country's right for freedom. You have immediately before you the important task of harnessing the resources and organisational strength of the Congress in the work of the Constituent Assembly.

There is no one better qualified than you, Panditji, to fill this important role. The country is already pulsating with a subdued feeling of hope that it is on the threshold of its cherished goal of freedom and independence. We fervently hope and pray that the coping stone of India's edifice of freedom shall be shaped and placed in its position by you during your regime as President of the Congress.

I again thank you, Maulana Saheb and Panditji, for having honoured us by your presence here today.

Mohamedhusain Hasham Premji, President, Indian Merchants' Chamber, at the Reception in honour of Maulana Abul Kalam Azad and Pandit Jawaharlal Nehru on 9 July 1946 at 5.30 p.m.

Mohamedhusain Premji pushed back against the State's attempt to nationalize the grain trade in the 1960s. He wrote *Food Problem in India*, a monograph highlighting the institutional neglect of agriculture. He believed India's State policies would lead to totalitarianism. As an activist and chief of the Federation of All India Food Grain Dealers' Associations, he courted arrest in 1964.

ABOVE
Mohamedhusain Premji at a political meeting addressed by C Rajagopalachari, who was home minister under Nehru and, later, launched his own private enterprise-friendly political party.

TOP, LEFT
Mohamedhusain Premji with Lal Bahadur Shastri, prime minister of India between 1964 and 1966.

The Bombay Plan

Published in 1944, the Bombay Plan was an outline for economic development and self-reliant industrialization in independent India. It was created by leading Bombay industrialists and technocrats: Jamshedji Ratanji Dadabhoy Tata, Ghanshyam Das Birla, Ardeshir Dalal, Sri Ram, Kasturbhai Lalbhai, Ardeshir Darabshaw Shroff, Sir Purshottamdas Thakurdas and John Mathai. They sought an investment of $100 billion over fifteen years. The aim was to double agricultural output and five-fold growth of industry.

The Plan envisaged State intervention to be crucial. The assumption was that Indian industries would not be able to compete in a free market and needed government protection against foreign competition. Although Jawaharlal Nehru, India's first prime minister, never officially accepted the Plan, its influence certainly left a mark in the Nehruvian era.

One of the Plan's recommendations was for Indian businessmen to start manufacturing consumer goods required by the growing middle class in India. Refined oil and vanaspati were industries earmarked under this category. The birth of Western India Vegetable Products Ltd was partly in response to this.

Historically, the Plan has received its fair share of brickbats. Some dubbed it too socialistic and some blame it for the regime of licenses that later controlled that India's private sector. This restrictive environment played a significant role in charting Western India Vegetable Products Ltd's future course.

What is Vanaspati?

Vanaspati is the Indian term for vegetable shortening. It's the vegan equivalent of lard, made by hydrogenating edible oil.

It was first introduced in the US in 1911, by Procter and Gamble. The first commercial brand of vegetable shortening was called Crisco. The term was shorthand for crystallized cottonseed oil. It still continues to be on sale, though the brand is now owned by JM Smucker Co.

In India, vegetable shortening was popularized in the 1930s by way of imports from the Netherlands. After World War I, single-seed edible oils were in short supply. India being a milk-deficient nation, butter and dairy fat like ghee were expensive. The term vanaspati, coined from vanas (plant) and pati (lord), served to emphasize its vegan origin.

Hindustan Vanaspati Manufacturing Company, set up by the Lever Brothers (Unilever today and Hindustan Unilever in India,) was one of the first manufacturers. Incidentally, their most popular brand, introduced in 1937—Dalda—had Dutch origins.

Western India Vegetable Products Ltd started production of vanaspati with groundnut oil in 1947. Subsequently, cottonseed oil became a prime ingredient. The first brand from Western India Vegetable Products Ltd stables was Sunflower. In December 2012, Wipro Ltd sold the brand to food multinational Cargill.

Vanaspati was an economical alternative for dairy fats such as butter and ghee. But the industry had to push hard for the product to be accepted in the market.

The Vanaspati Manufacturers' Association ran media campaigns for years to familiarize people with brands and companies.

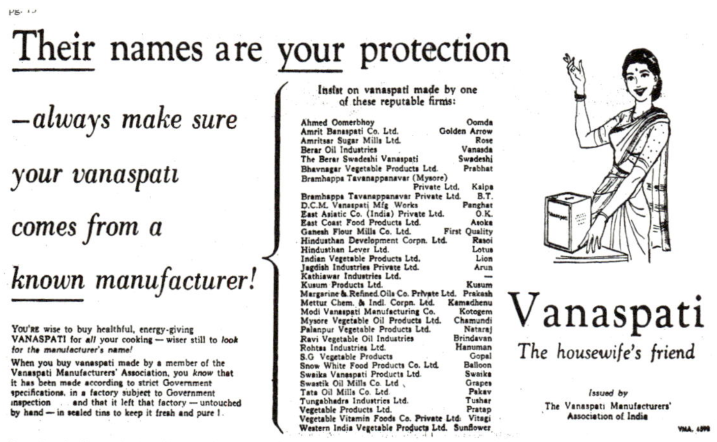

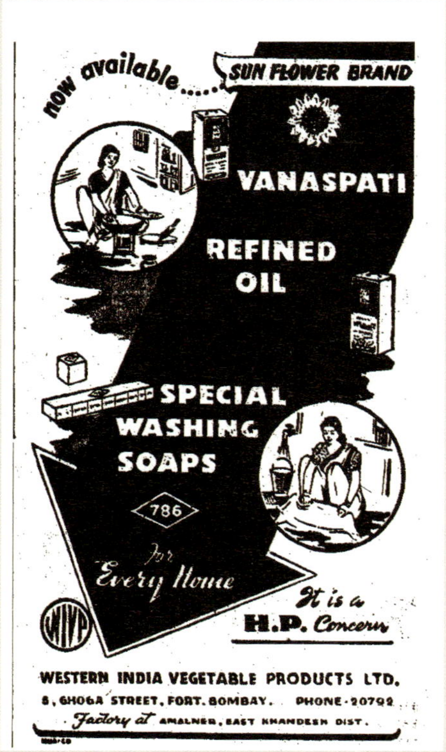

Mohamedhusain insisted on selling some of his products in the metropolis: he believed it would build up goodwill. He also aligned with the Vanaspati Manufacturers' Association of India.

Mohamedhusain found support for his new venture from leading entrepreneurs of the day, a fact borne out by his board of directors—renowned businessmen and traders committed to enterprise and philanthropy alike. Like Mohamedhusain, they too believed they had a role to play in building independent India.

❖❖❖

As the vanaspati industry grew, the economic environment in which it operated changed. To extend its control over the private sector, the government kept tinkering with its policies (see: State Control on the Private Sector). The Vegetable Oil Products (Control) Order, 1947, which regulated the manufacture, distribution and sale of vegetable oil products, including vanaspati, became more stringent.

During 1948–49, even as groundnut prices shot up, the government imposed a price ceiling on vanaspati to keep the product affordable. The year after, regulations barred Western India Vegetable Products from procuring oilseeds from Saurashtra, a major source. To make matters worse, crops failed for three consecutive years till 1952, and Western India Vegetable Products ran into losses.

The euphoria of the early post-Independence years was ebbing away. The private sector, across industries, felt let down. To his credit, Mohamedhusain weathered this storm. As managing agent and Chairman, he ably steered Western India Vegetable Products, balancing its demands with those of the grain trade.

As a business leader who had stepped up to serve the public sector, Mohamedhusain had other things on his plate too. At thirty-nine years of age, he was appointed the first honorary Chairman of the Electricity Board for the State of Bombay. He streamlined the Board to function on sound business principles. He was also part of the first board of directors of the Life Insurance Corporation (LIC). Founded in 1954, LIC was India's only State-owned insurance and investment company. Described by his contemporaries as a man of unimpeachable integrity, Mohamedhusain brought complete commitment to these roles.

However, as the government proposed to nationalize the grain trade and impose new controls on the vanaspati industry, his conviction about the drawbacks of State involvement and interference in the private sector strengthened.[4] 'Some of our public men have not yet appreciated the fact that the progress of the vanaspati industry in India is part of the compelling world trend of a growing hydrogenated oil industry to meet the ever-increasing demand for semi-solid dietary fats,' he rued in a public speech in 1961.[5]

Using convoluted logic, the

ABOVE

Mohamedhusain and Dr Gulbanoo Premji, circa 1960s.

State Control on the Private Sector

The Industrial Policy Resolution of 1948 is a good example of how India's new government started to exercise control on industry. Under this, certain basic industries were open only to government enterprise. These were mostly the heavy industries and infrastructure—industries that required large investment. From 1951, the Planning Commission created five-year plans. The premise of a mixed economy—a public and private sector working working in parallel—informed these plans. The plans, in turn, set up targets for the economy to achieve in each industry and each sector.

The next step was the system of industrial licensing. The Industries (Development and Regulation) Act of 1951 outlined new rules. Established firms had to register. New ones had to apply for licenses. And all needed permits to procure goods and equipment. The State had power to regulate price and distribution of the produced goods.

With foreign exchange becoming scarcer, imports were restricted in the coming years. This was a marked departure from the way of doing business before 1947. Initially, this afforded protection to the new industries. But with time, this devolved into a restrictive, inefficient system. In India, this came to be known as license and permit raj.

LEFT
Gulbanoo Patel, later Dr Gulbanoo Premji (seated right), with her siblings in Bombay in the late 1920s.

BELOW
The Society for the Rehabilitation of Crippled Children (SRCC) in May 1950. Dr Gulbanoo Premji had helped set up the hospital two years previously, the beginning of a long association with the SRCC.

Dr Gulbanoo Premji did not shy away from challenges. Aware of gaps in medical service, she worked to set up the Children's Orthopaedic Hospital in Bombay. Later, she helped set up a cerebral palsy unit. She was an able administrator, inspiring her team to give their best under trying conditions.

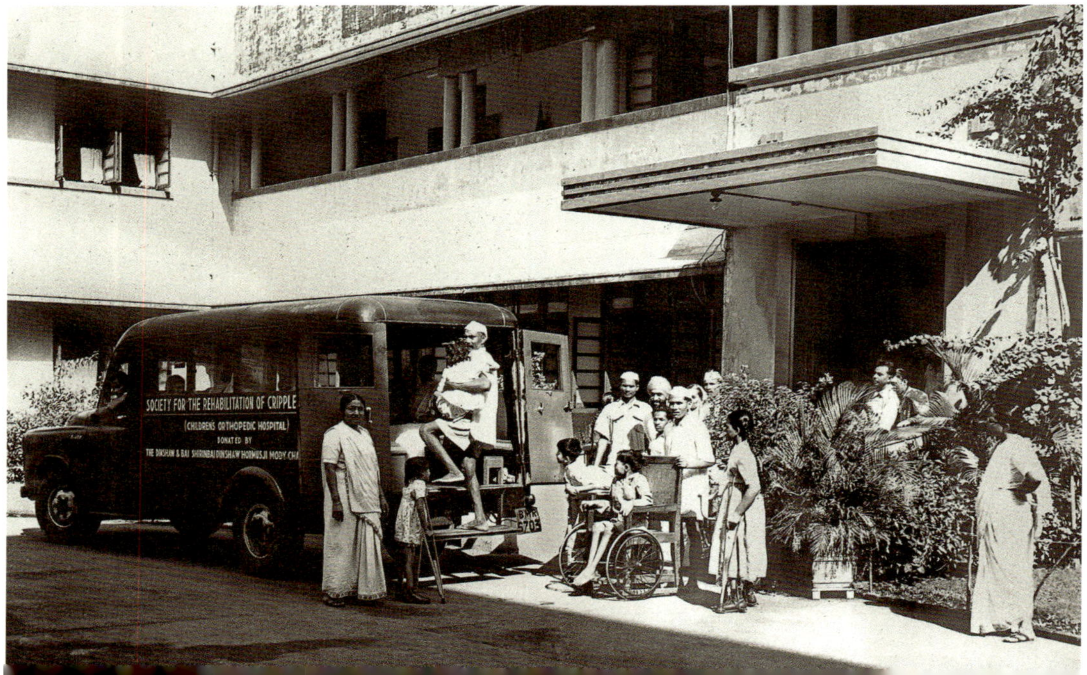

OPPOSITE PAGE

LEFT
A young patient at the Children's Orthopaedic Hospital run by the Society for the Rehabilitation of Crippled Children, 1950.

RIGHT
Prime Minister Jawaharlal Nehru at the Children's Orthopaedic Hospital.

government made it mandatory for manufacturers to add color to vanaspati as an anti-adulteration measure in 1961. The ceiling on production, raw material and prices continued to be in place. The constantly changing constraints made Mohamedhusain consider his options, even though Western India Vegetable Products was by now competitive and profitable. With Western India Vegetable Products, he had moved from trade to industry. And now, he was ready to move beyond consumer goods. By 1965, he wanted to direct Western India Vegetable Products into the ceramics and electrodes industries. On his radar were manufacture, import and export, and dealerships in steel strips, alloys and other metal products.

As he explained to his shareholders in 1965, the business had to expand. But this would require high capital expenditure, and there would be no wishing away the relentless, often arbitrary, State controls. Consequently, Western India Vegetable Products began to explore contracts and order equipment for a stainless steel project. Preparations were on in full swing when Mohamedhusain succumbed to a heart attack on 11 August 1966 at the age of fifty-one.

The board met a mere twelve days after Mohamedhusain's untimely demise. 'But for his intelligence, integrity and honesty of character, the company would not have attained the position it enjoys today. The loss occasioned as a result of his death is irreparable,' the chair, Ratilal Gandhi, read. The vanaspati industry had lost a pioneer, he said, while business and trade had lost an advocate of its interests.

❖❖❖

On 23 August 1966, just twelve days after the demise of her husband, Dr Gulbanoo Premji joined the Western India Vegetable Products board of directors.[6] For the first few months—till her son Azim was able to return from Stanford University to pick up the reins—she held the fort. Those who knew this remarkable woman were not surprised.

Dr Premji had been running the Children's Orthopaedic Hospital for years. The co-founder, Mrs Fatima Ismail, was Dr Premji's inspiration. Mrs Ismail's three-year-old daughter had suffered from polio in the 1940s, and she was determined to provide appropriate care and rehabilitation for similarly afflicted children. Dr Premji was among those who helped make this dream a reality. They established the Society for the Rehabilitation of Crippled Children in 1948.[7] The Indian Council of Medical Research established the Polio Research Unit, the first institute of its kind in India, the next year.[8]

Seventy-odd years later, it is difficult to imagine the harrowing future the disease spelled in India in those days. Many of those who lived with the disease faced isolation and social stigma. There were few options for therapy, making the physical burden of the disease even heavier. Though the first polio vaccine came in 1955, India attained polio-free status, a milestone in global public health, only in 2014.

With Mrs Ismail, Dr Premji put together the first panel of doctors and registered children for therapy. They started with a small clinic in the suburbs before moving to a military hutment near Nariman Point. They went on to build a fifty-bed hospital near the racecourse in Bombay, which was inaugurated in 1950 by India's first prime minister, Jawaharlal Nehru.

People, many from disadvantaged sections of society, flocked to the hospital from far and wide. From administration to fund-raising, Dr Premji juggled many roles. She also wrote on the need for physical therapy for polio-afflicted children in the *Indian Journal of Surgery*.[9]

Alongside, she was a steady, enduring presence in her children's lives. Her generosity and compassion had a lifelong influence on them, inspiring her son Azim to establish the Foundation later in his life.

In 1961, as the superintendent of the hospital, Dr Premji started a cerebral palsy unit. 'We had realized even at that time that care for a disabled child would have to include appropriate education, training and rehabilitation,' she said in an interview to *The Times*

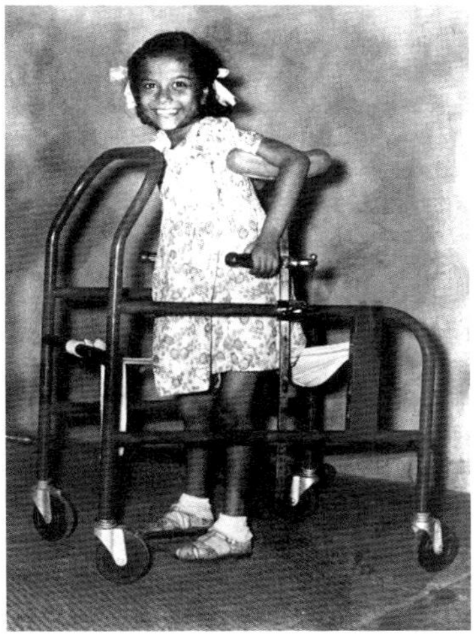

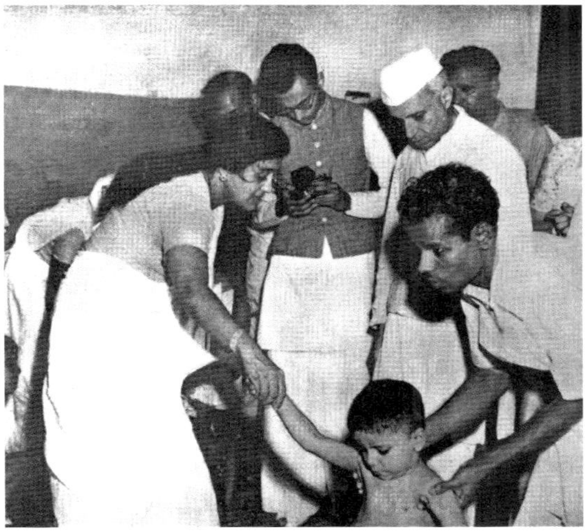

Mohamedhusain Premji's sudden demise at the age of fifty-one thrust Dr Gulbanoo Premji into his seat at WIVP. She had not been involved in the business. But she assumed charge of it with dignity and composure. She thanked shareholders who had kept the faith and took critics head-on. She was never less than optimistic about the future of the family business.

TOP
Dr Gulbanoo Premji (seated extreme right) with members of the first executive committee of the Children's Orthopaedic Hospital.

ABOVE
Dr Gulbanoo Premji (left) with Indira Gandhi, who became India's prime minister in 1966, Vijaya Lakshmi Pandit, first woman president of the United Nations General Assembly, and Shobha Magdolna Friedmann Nehru, wife of Indian diplomat BK Nehru.

of India. Despite the paucity of funds and the lack of a skilled workforce, the unit became a success because of the staff's dedication.

Dr Premji took challenges in her stride. She was a good judge of people's character and had a strong sense of purpose. All these qualities stood her in good stead when she briefly assumed her late husband's role at Western India Vegetable Products in 1966.

❖❖❖

In September 1966, Dr Premji, as the chairperson, faced the Western India Vegetable Products shareholders at her first annual general meeting (AGM). She assured them that the company would continue to make progress, but her confidence was not shared by all.

Moments after a tribute had been read out for Mohamedhusain, a serial dissenter, Feroze S. Wadia, took the floor. A regular at the AGMs since 1962, Wadia was notorious for his pointed questions at various meetings. In fact, in 1965, when Mohamedhusain had been re-elected managing director of Western India Vegetable Products, he had been the lone objector. Now, he held forth to the chair, newly widowed and still unfamiliar with the business, on Western India Vegetable Products' prospects and performance.

The future of the vanaspati industry, Wadia offered, was as dismal as the future of Western India Vegetable Products in the hands of a Chairman who understood little of business, and a young man—referring to Azim—with no experience. 'The time is ripe for this company, when it is earning profits, to amalgamate with a bigger unit,' he said.

Without batting an eyelid, Dr Premji underscored that the company, despite difficult times with crop failures and State controls, had done fairly well. She told the dissenter, 'You are a pessimistic man. But I am sure with the support and goodwill of the members and the cooperation of the directors, Western India Vegetable Products will make good progress and grow from strength to strength.'

By her side was her son, Azim. He had just turned twenty-one.

❖❖❖

After two years at St Xavier's College in Bombay, Azim Premji went to Stanford in 1963. Always a quiet child with a serious bent of mind, he took time getting used to California. In a new, unfamiliar environment, he fell ill. Dr Premji came to help him settle in, and he soon got into the swing of campus life. He played tennis and joined a Stanford Eating Club—a hub of social activities.

In 1963, India had strict limits on the foreign exchange that could be sent abroad. To supplement the money he received from home, Premji worked, for the first time in his life, as a cleaner at the university cafeteria and as a telephone operator, working the graveyard shift.

Though American colleges were throbbing with life in the 1960s, Premji was focused on finishing his degree as soon as possible. In three and a half years, not being able to afford to travel, he came home only once. "We were not an international company then," he says. And then, one fateful phone call from Bombay changed things forever. ◆

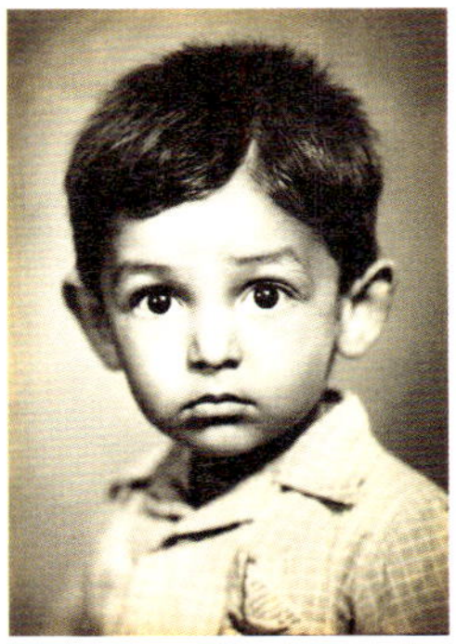

FROM LEFT
Azim Premji, Bombay, June 1947.

Azim Premji as a student at St. Mary's School, Bombay.

Azim Premji, circa 1963.

WIVP

1966–1979

Everything comes to us that belongs to us
if we create the capacity to receive it.

Rabindranath Tagore

The business had to be run. There was not enough professional management to run it. There was no alternative but for me to come back ... [A shareholder predicted I'd run it to the ground.] For me, that statement was a challenge. I made up my mind to prove him wrong and, with each passing day, my resolve strengthened.

Chapter | **3** | 1966–1979

Dreams Come First

'It was not easy. I was dealing with a personal loss and also taking on a role for which I had no training, no experience, no preparation and no demonstrated strengths,' Azim Premji would reminisce years later. 'The business had to be run. There was not enough professional management to run it. There was no alternative but for me to come back.'

Neither his engineering major nor his liberal arts electives had prepared Premji for the struggle of running a business straddling a small factory town and a sophisticated big city. Shareholders breathed contempt; one [Feroze Wadia] predicted Premji would run Western India Vegetable Products to the ground. 'But for me at that point, that statement was a challenge. I made up my mind to prove him wrong, and with each passing day, my resolve strengthened,' Premji would say later of those tumultuous months.[1]

In the seventy-five-year span of Wipro's history, the suddenness of Premji's initiation into the company obscures—frequently and unpardonably—its far-reaching impact. But it is hard to overstate the grit and determination that drove a grief-stricken twenty-one-year-old with a half-finished degree to immerse himself in an unfamiliar reality. Selling the business would have been easier. But Premji decided against it.

Amalner, deep in the Indian heartland, was a world apart from the California campus he had left behind. Summer temperatures in the small town stabilized upwards of 105 degree Fahrenheit. The torpor of the still afternoons seemed to seep into the work culture, upheld by long-established practices. But rather than

ABOVE
Azim Premji (seated, center) with the WIVP team in Amalner, 1973.

FIRST ROW, FROM LEFT:
NI Sheik, RV Sheikh, MZ Syed, NP Vansia, Premji, KN Basrur, KN Vansia, PR Bhagawat, JY Sheik.

SECOND ROW, FROM LEFT:
YB Badgujar, SR Pathan, RB Shedey, BU Syed, TS Syed, MH Syed, NS Syed, DS Sonwane.

LAST ROW, FROM LEFT:
YJ Pathan, RT Sarode, SS Choudhary, TS Choudhary, P Babiskar, YS Syed (of Adarsh Photo Studio).

LEFT
Azim Premji in Amalner, in the mid-1970s.

set these aside, Premji used them to navigate the ecosystem, of which his oil company was a tiny part. 'I read a great deal to understand various business subjects. And then we did a complete re-engineering of our cost-accounting system,' he says.

❖❖❖

The workforce Premji had inherited gave him the obligatory respect due to the owner's son, but did not offer much support on the ground. 'Most of them were very loyal, very committed, but many were completely ineffective in their jobs,' he says.

This impacted every part of the factory. In the summers, for example, production would halt abruptly on account of heatwaves, or erratic power or material supply. Overhead costs would multiply, adversely affecting the bottom line. In a departure from the previous administration, Premji stationed himself in Amalner through the season to dispel the myth that it was too hot to work.

Vanaspati, he learned, was subject to manufacturing controls and the occasional price control, although the prices of its raw materials were market-driven. Each licensed factory had a State-imposed cap on daily production. The only way to enhance profits, Premji realized, was to cut down costs and optimize production.

Besides streamlining the procurement of groundnut, the primary raw material, at optimum prices, Premji introduced an efficient manufacturing process. He mandated maintenance of daily records of profit and loss, production, sales and margins—a practice popular among the Marwari business community in India, but unknown to the vanaspati industry—to maximize oversight.

'We started a practice of weekly calls. We tracked how much vanaspati we sold in each region and the average price, and could then determine the margins against the raw material cost. We even set up a competition among different regions over sales realizations,' Premji recalls. The figures would be logged in a thirteen-column sheet, and every Monday, Premji would pore over the figures. The thirteen-column sheet is still part of the consumer business today.

Alongside cleaning up house, Premji looked out for theoretical and practical guidance. He asked the faculty at the Jamnalal Bajaj Institute of Management Studies in Bombay to recommend books. He approached industry veterans for advice. As the youngest member of every association—the Vanaspati Manufacturers' Association and the Solvent Extractors' Association—he had no compunctions asking questions. 'I was very young. People felt sorry for me and shared a lot of information with me,' he says, laughing, remembering how he would run to the restroom to jot down all that he had learned.

It took the Western India Vegetable Products board two years to acknowledge that the Premji scion had proved his mettle. 'Being of the opinion that the said Mr Azim Hasham Premji is now fully capable of looking after the company's affairs as Managing Director, [the Board of Directors] passed a resolution in their Board meeting dated 3-5-1968 appointing him as Managing Director with effect from 1 September 1968 subject to the Central Government's approval,' reads the Western India Vegetable Products annual report for 1967–68.

Simultaneously, Premji was working to articulate his own goals and mapping a course to achieve them. With his back to the wall, he identified his primary task — induct the right people and set down efficient processes to ensure the institution stayed true to its principles. Each of them would take an enormous amount of time and rigor.

❖❖❖

Premji's vision for Western India Vegetable Products contrasted sharply with the path followed by many family-run businesses in India in the late 1960s. Many were autocratic organizations with centralized decision-making, managed mostly by the owners and their kin.[2] Premji's benchmark instead was Hindustan Lever Limited (HLL, now Hindustan Unilever Limited), the largest

ABOVE
The label on Sunflower tins after 1977. WIVP started production of vanaspati with groundnut oil in 1947. With subsequent controls, cottonseed oil became a prime ingredient. The first brand from WIVP stables was Sunflower. In December 2012, Wipro Ltd sold the brand to food multinational Cargill.

ABOVE
Indian Institute of
Management, Ahmedabad.

When it came to campus recruits, Premji aimed right at the top. His company was largely unknown, his sales turnover insignificant. But, in 1973, Premji went to IIM Ahmedabad to meet the graduating class. They were India's most coveted employees, with their pick of profiles and postings. Premji made offers to three young men. All three said yes.

multinational (MNC) operating in India at the time. 'One compared the way they ran their business versus the way we ran ours. So, one got triggered,' he says.

Perhaps it is the prerogative of the very young to claim impossible dreams and work to actualize them. 'That's the period when we decided to become a brand-oriented company, leaving behind our legacy as a commodity-based vegetable oil-maker,' Premji would say later. 'It was also at this time that we started hiring highly talented people from the best institutions in the country.'

By the early 1970s, HLL had a ubiquitous presence in India, thanks as much to brands like Lux and Liril (soaps) and Anik (ghee) as its expansive distribution network. Premji knew he needed one to build the other, but the first step was the augmentation of his primary product, Sunflower vanaspati. Consequently, Premji's first two hires as managing director in 1969 were purchase officer NR Parikh, a chemical engineer from the Indian Institute of Technology (IIT), Bombay, and consultant PR Bhagwat, then thirty-nine years old, who had a degree from, and had worked in, the UK. For the next few years, they would be in charge of all expansions and engineering needs at Amalner.

'As Premji began building a professional management cadre (see: Early Professionals), along with competence, integrity was the defining quality he looked for. Integrity was a value Premji had inherited and wanted to perpetuate consciously. '[My father] was in various public positions of very major power,' he would say in an interview to the BBC years later. 'He never compromised on integrity ... which really stood out, as that was not the culture at that point of time.'

As Western India Vegetable Products stepped into its twenty-fifth year in 1970, Premji knew he wanted to grow beyond Sunflower. He needed professionals who could create brands and further expansions. The only problem was that at Rs 70 million—the company's annual sales turnover in 1969–70—it simply was not big enough to aim for these objectives.

Or so it seemed on paper.

❖❖❖

Premji understood it was crucial for Western India Vegetable Products to find managers who were the right fit by way of character, qualities and culture. He had neither the deep pockets of the MNCs nor the heft of top business families. But no one could have accused him of lacking ambition. And so, Premji aimed right at the top, targeting graduates of the Indian Institutes of Management (IIMs) in Calcutta and Ahmedabad. The alumni of these premier business schools, set up in 1961, were India's most coveted employees.

Ironically, Premji's first IIM Ahmedabad recruit came to Western India Vegetable Products after working in a major family-run firm. Pradeep Desai, twenty-three, joined the company as export officer in July 1970, impressed, in part, by Premji's team-building approach and the day-long interview. Premji had made the final selection after screening 300 applications and conducting 65 interviews. 'I thought, if this guy is taking so much interest in hiring people, this company has to grow. And if the company grows, I will also grow,' Desai says.

'I remember how I had to spend hours and hours, over multiple days, to attract and interview a single person. It was just relentless,' Premji recalls. For Western India Vegetable Products' first managerial position in finance, the search began in 1969, but it was only in 1972 that MS Sekhar received his letter of appointment—after Premji had screened 145 applications and interviewed 60 candidates (see: The Right Fit).

Premji demanded a similar dedication from all his recruits. When KN Basrur, a lawyer who had handled commodities for M/s Hasham Premji for twenty-five years, moved to Amalner as deputy general manager in 1970, he was put through an intensive work schedule. Besides attending two residential management-development programs at IIM Ahmedabad, he spent months in the field, studying oils, oilseeds and vanaspati markets in Uttar Pradesh, Punjab, Haryana, Delhi, West Bengal, Madhya Pradesh, Maharashtra and Rajasthan. In Amalner, Basrur's first assignment sent him away to the markets in Andhra Pradesh and Gujarat, with pit stops in Mysore and Madras.

As vital as it was for Basrur and his colleagues to keep an ear to the ground, the most formidable factor in the vanaspati business was State policy. Within months of Basrur's joining, license regulations were complicated by the India–Pakistan war of 1971. By then, the factory was producing poly-jars of vanaspati, alongside the 16.5 kg tinned mainstay. It was also making a large profit by exporting de-oiled cakes as cattle feed. But the red tape that governed the vanaspati industry led to the widespread perception that the industry was corrupt, and few outside Western India Vegetable Products knew of Premji's zero-tolerance attitude towards graft (see: License-permit Raj).

Aware that the concern of being tainted by association could discourage

Early Professionals

At the cusp of the 1970s, the little-known Western India Vegetable Products Ltd set about creating a management cadre that matched its ambition rather than its stature. It was possible only because of Premji's rare ability to win over the best of trained professionals with similar values, drive and intensity.

CLOCKWISE FROM TOP LEFT

NR PARIKH
Joined in 1969 as purchase manager in Bombay. He was also the stop-gap deputy factory manager in Amalner till 1979.

NAGJIBHAI SHAH
Joined in 1970 as manager of M/s Hasham Premji in Calcutta. In 1975, he became WIVP's procurement manager, overseeing millions of rupees' worth of inventory and running a complex operation with native wisdom and his legendary black book of oil-price records.

PRADEEP DESAI
Joined in 1970 as WIVP's first export officer. The first IIM Ahmedabad graduate in the company, he contributed significantly to instituting professional ways of working, including processes and reviews.

MS SEKHAR
Joined in 1972 as the finance manager and later went on to be the company secretary. He was the first finance professional—a chartered accountant with a master's in business administration—hired by Premji. His appointment came after Premji had screened 145 applicants and interviewed 60.

RAVI LAJMI
Joined in 1973. He was one of the first three campus recruits from IIM Ahmedabad. WIVP's first marketing professional, he worked on WIVP's branding and subsequent transition to brand Wipro.

MS RAO
Joined in 1974 to spearhead Wintrol, a hydraulics unit and WIVP's first diversification away from vanaspati and edible oils. Desai's classmate from IIM Ahmedabad, Rao was responsible for extending the company's footprint to Bangalore.

DILEEP RANJEKAR
Joined in 1976, straight out of the Tata Institute of Social Sciences, as WIVP's factory personnel supervisor in Amalner. Ranjekar later moved to Bombay and subsequently to Bangalore and played a significant role in building and nourishing Wipro's leadership bench.

RAM AGARWAL
Joined in 1977 as area sales manager in Maharashtra. Recruited from Glaxo, Agarwal had a meteoric rise in Wipro. Later, he switched over to the IT business and handled the international operations division before heading Wipro's peripherals business, which he eventually bought out.

The Right Fit

It was December 1971. I was a chartered accountant in the second year of my MBA at IIM Calcutta. Nagjibhai Shah, who was based in Calcutta for M/s Hasham Premji, reached out to me through the institute and said that I'd been selected for an interview. At that time, the IIMs would place their graduates with the Tata Administrative Service, Hindustan Lever, DCM and the like. Nagjibhai's call, however, came a few weeks before the campus interviews, and he said they would fly me to Bombay for the interview.

My parents lived in Bombay, so this was an opportunity for me to see them. Plus, I'd never traveled by air. So, I said yes to the interview and, one day later that month, found myself on Ghoga Street at 9 a.m., staring at a rickety building with a narrow staircase. I climbed up to the mezzanine, where there were two rooms: a large one for AHP and a small one for visitors.

Western India Vegetable Products Ltd turned twenty-five in 1970. Premji knew he had to grow beyond vanaspati. And for that, he needed trained managers who could further expansion and create brands. But they had to be the right fit by way of character, qualities and culture.

This being my first job interview, I had no idea what to expect. I was handed some case studies, each touching on a different aspect of the business, and informed that I had ninety minutes to analyze them. In those days, profits of new industrial undertakings were exempt from income tax. The vanaspati factory at Amalner had just been expanded, so one problem I had to examine was whether the profits from the expansion could be tax-free. The second case related to costing, deciding how to price a product. I was surprised but not entirely taken aback by the problems; I'd studied them for my CA. But after two years at IIM, I was a bit rusty on taxation laws! At the interview, it was AHP and me. I was arguing for my solutions, with AHP questioning me. Rather than my knowledge of specific provisions, he seemed interested in learning how I would handle certain situations. Three cases in, the clock struck seven and there was a blackout—this was the time India was at war with Pakistan—so I was told to come back at 8 a.m. the next day.

In the morning, we grappled with the cases till 10 a.m., when the oil markets opened and AHP was called away. I was told to come back again at 2 p.m. When I returned, AHP started on the personal interview. He had forty-odd questions written down for me! We spoke about philosophy. I told him I was passionate about playing the mridangam. I was young and ambitious; I said that I wanted to grow fast, become a managing director or CEO. I wasn't great academically, but I was both a CA and an MBA, a rare combination. So that was there.

We had a lot of disagreements:
I would state this is right, he would counter it. I'd say, I'm not convinced, he'd say likewise. We were at it till 6 p.m. or 7 p.m. It was unusual. I had never heard of interviews that went down this way, but I liked the deep conversation. It was evident that AHP was very serious about it.

I also appreciated the fact that the owner was conducting the interview himself, instead of delegating it. That showed his involvement, his dedication. I gathered he was extremely sharp—he was always a little ahead of me—and recognized his tenacity. Also, he was very cordial, talking to me on equal terms. He didn't act like the owner, which could have been intimidating.

After the interview, I stayed back with my parents. In those days, IIM allowed graduating students only two offers and, if you accepted one, you couldn't appear for more interviews. I knew all the big companies would come calling in January, so I needed to know the outcome of this interview. A couple of days later, I called his home. Dr Gulbanoo Premji answered, saying AHP was away but would certainly get back to me. Within a day or two, they sent me the offer letter.

My salary was set at Rs 1,200, plus Rs 200 for housing. I negotiated with AHP and got Rs 100 more. The figure was higher than what Hindustan Lever and others gave their campus recruits at the time, but AHP agreed to it. Then they said they wanted me to start work in April. But I was getting married and said I wanted to spend a month with my wife. They agreed to that too.

I was mocked on campus for accepting the offer; a faculty member even asked me to reconsider. Besides the fact that I wouldn't dream of going back on my word, I knew AHP was a person I wanted to associate with. The size of the company was immaterial. So, finally, on 7 May, I joined Western India Vegetable Products Ltd. I think I was the first qualified finance professional AHP hired.

As told by MS Sekhar
Sekhar joined WIVP as finance manager in 1972. In 1974, he was designated company secretary. In 1978, he left the company, then known as Wipro Products. He is now the managing director of Three D Management that structures and executes corporate governance in organizations.

BELOW, LEFT
Premier institutes like the Indian Institute of Science gave Bangalore a ready pool of intellect. Combined with its overall business-friendliness, the city would alter Wipro's future.

BELOW, RIGHT
MS Rao (right), then chief executive, Wintrol (now Wipro Infrastructure Engineering), in Peenya, Bangalore, circa 1976, the year they produced their first pneumatic cylinders.

Premji planned a diversification into a 'high-growth, high-tech' sector for years. But the first move away from vanaspati was more accidental than strategic. MS Rao came to Premji with a proposal for a hydraulic cylinder business. The investments were not large and the opportunities seemed interesting, so Premji hired him. Wintrol, led by Rao, was Premji's first business in Bangalore.

License-permit Raj

The term was coined in 1961 to describe a period of fierce regulation of the private sector. The most severe of the laws was the Monopolies and Restrictive Trade Practices Act, 1969, which formally curbed the expansion and modernization of industries. Procuring a single license became so time-consuming—it could take up to 400 days—that businesses began installing offices in Delhi with the sole remit of navigating the bureaucracy.

The term, license-permit raj, found greater resonance in the following decade, when political instability, nationalization of the coal and banking industries and a cap on foreign investment created a sharply unfavorable climate for private industry. The 'Raj' climaxed with the twenty-month-long national Emergency imposed by the Indira Gandhi government between 1977 and 1979, suppressing civil rights and liberties in the nation. Between 1970 and 1984, the government also set up over a hundred public sector enterprises.

It was under such hostile conditions that Wipro decided to take its first steps towards diversification into hydraulics and information technology.

prospective employees, Premji, Desai and Sekhar went to the IIMs for the first round of campus recruitments in 1973 with ammunition: application forms that opened with a statement by the American management consultant Peter Drucker. It said, 'Integrity may be difficult to define, but what constitutes lack of integrity of such seriousness as to disqualify a man from a managerial position is not.' The panel made offers to three students. It was a hard sell—Western India Vegetable Products was by no means a known name—but all three said yes.

Confirming Premji's belief that avowed integrity could be an employee magnet, Western India Vegetable Products' first brush with campus recruitment was an eye-opener. The company's first marketing professional, Ravi Lajmi, and his classmates were India's graduating elite. They had their pick of employers, profiles, postings, and little idea of what Western India Vegetable Products actually did Yet, even in their inexperience, they gauged that the intensive interviews and questions about values were extraordinary in an India where business was synonymous with corruption.

Finally, it was Premji's idealism—and his ambition—that drew them in. On joining, all the recruits got, along with tomes like the Income Tax Act of 1962 and Bailey's Industrial Oil and Fat Products, two sets of annual reports. One was Western India Vegetable Products'. The other was HLL's.

❖❖❖

In retrospect, one could say that, with the new generation of managers, Western India Vegetable Products ushered in an era of cultural re-engineering, establishing an ethos of competence and equality.[3] However, it required as much engagement with the world outside as within Western India Vegetable Products.

In the Bombay office, hitherto dominated by long-time employees of the grain trade, the twenty-something-year-olds of Western India Vegetable Products tried to carve their own niche. While Desai shared the first floor with Premji, the management trainees jostled for space outside Parikh's cabin on the floor above. Whether by strategy or design, they were always a chair short; the subliminal message was they should not be sitting around in the office anyway—they learned on the job.

The 'kindergarten years', as they now call it, involved imbibing the steadfast Premji values, including that of hard work. There was much good-natured ribbing about benchmarking against HLL: Western India Vegetable Products replicated processes, right down to the crop surveys that HLL conducted.

By the early 1970s, Premji had won a grudging respect from HLL. His company may not have been among the top businesses of the time, but the quiet yet fiercely driven Premji stood out in the industry. 'We could engage with Lever because we developed a relationship with them,' recalls Desai. If the MNC respected Premji for his professionalism, traditional businesses mocked him for the same reason. 'I recall the head of a very large Indian vanaspati company becoming furious with Premji when he mentioned their black money intake in a business meeting,' says Desai.

Shared values and a common agenda inculcated a rare camaraderie among the young Western India Vegetable Products recruits and their boss. It was an egalitarian culture, Sekhar emphasizes. 'Conversation with Premji was mostly work-related, but on entirely equal terms. Nobody felt intimidated—if you thought you were in the right, you dug in your heels and fought.' Frequently, the conversations would spill over into the Premjis' Bandra home. The larger purpose of business was much debated, while cinema and politics were taboo. 'Initially, it was just us. Then people started getting married, and the wives would also join in. Then the shop talk dropped off, especially if Dr Premji was present,' reminisces Lajmi. 'Those were very pleasant evenings.'

Of course, it wasn't all fun and philosophy. The draconian rules governing the vanaspati industry made business difficult in 1973. Monsoons failed that year, which led to a shortage of oilseed crops. The price of the little edible oil that was available almost doubled. The price of vanaspati, made by hydrogenating these oils, however, remained under a price ceiling. Black markets thrived. The whole industry suffered. For the first time in its history in India, HLL suffered losses through the first half of 1974.[4]

Notwithstanding the market trends, Premji saw no reason to change his practices. The company issued strict advisories to its distributors and retailers to sell the Western India Vegetable Products brand at the designated price. While the bottom line took a hit, Sunflower quickly registered in the consumer consciousness as the only fairly priced brand of vanaspati. Western India Vegetable Products' exports of de-oiled cakes provided a buffer—from Rs 3.4 million in 1969–70, it grew to Rs 39.7 million in 1973–74—but the writing on the wall was getting clearer.[5] Diversification was the need of the day.

❖❖❖

Premji had been on the lookout for a 'high-growth, hi-tech' industry for

Until late into the 1970s, Premji led the vanaspati business from the front. He cranked up the distribution network, built an ace sales team and reinvented Sunflower as a consumer brand. For the first-ever ad campaign, he enlisted Hindustan Thompson Associates, the leading agency of the time. The account was tiny, but Premji's conviction and charm won them over. The first Sunflower ad rolled out in 1977.

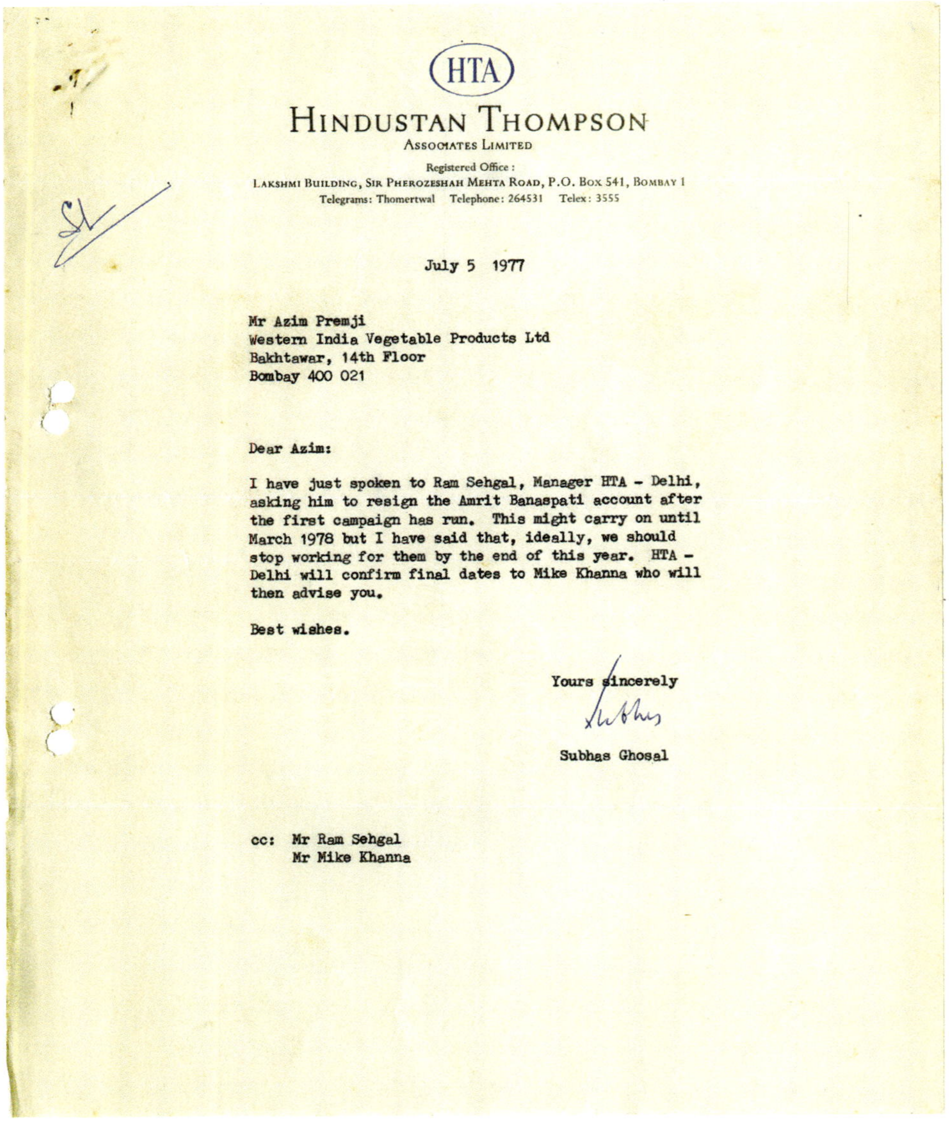

HTA

HINDUSTAN THOMPSON
ASSOCIATES LIMITED
Registered Office :
LAKSHMI BUILDING, SIR PHEROZESHAH MEHTA ROAD, P.O. BOX 541, BOMBAY 1
Telegrams: Thomertwal Telephone: 264531 Telex: 3555

July 5 1977

Mr Azim Premji
Western India Vegetable Products Ltd
Bakhtawar, 14th Floor
Bombay 400 021

Dear Azim:

I have just spoken to Ram Sehgal, Manager HTA - Delhi, asking him to resign the Amrit Banaspati account after the first campaign has run. This might carry on until March 1978 but I have said that, ideally, we should stop working for them by the end of this year. HTA - Delhi will confirm final dates to Mike Khanna who will then advise you.

Best wishes.

Yours sincerely

Subhas Ghosal

cc: Mr Ram Sehgal
Mr Mike Khanna

a long time. In fact, he freely shared his plan to move out of the vanaspati business even as he recruited people for it, and Lajmi was put to work on a plan for just such a business the day he joined. But, the first concrete step towards a business unrelated to vanaspati came about when Desai met MS Rao, a classmate from IIM.

A mechanical engineer, Rao mentioned a project he believed, had huge potential. Desai asked him for a note, which he passed on to Premji, leading to an intensive interview. 'Rao showed me the idea of a fluid power business to make hydraulic and pneumatic cylinders,' recalls Premji. 'The investments were not large, and the opportunities seemed interesting. It was business in which we could take leadership, so we just hired him. Fluid power was a freak thing. It was not a planned diversification.'

Rao, then thirty-one, received a budget of Rs 3 million—a third of Western India Vegetable Products' profits—and a seat at the community desk at Hasham Premji House. As an acknowledgement of his seniority and because he was Desai's friend, his seat was at the head of the table. Rao co-opted a management trainee, Lajmi's classmate V Sampath, to plan the new business, Wintrol.

Premji wanted this fluid power business to come up in Maharashtra, but Rao was wary of the rampant labor and power issues in the state. 'It was a terrible place for any industry, especially precision engineering,' Rao says. He zeroed in on Bangalore, where heavy engineering industries had already created a pool of professionals. His first hire was a designer, an engineer from Telco, Pune.

❖❖❖

Premji's plans for Western India Vegetable Products did not stop at professionalizing the management: his masterstroke lay in professionalizing the board of directors and stacking them with the kind of independent-minded, richly experienced professionals who were anathema to the regular Indian family-owned businesses. His aims were twofold. First, a competent board, he believed, could guide Western India Vegetable Products towards achieving its ambitions. Second, it would encourage fair corporate governance, thereby protecting shareholder interests—something few Indian promoters took into consideration at the time.

Among the early inductees was Nalin Thakor, the formidable head of employee relations at ESSO Standard Refining Company, who quit the company just ahead of its nationalization in 1974. (The former American oil giant is now Hindustan Petroleum Corporation Ltd.) One of his reportees at ESSO, Yasmeen Chinoy—a master's degree–holder in psychology from Smith College, Massachusetts, who had worked on the company's HR policy—introduced Thakor to her fiancé Azim Premji. The two men hit it off almost immediately. In 1975, Thakor joined the Western India Vegetable Products board. 'It is in the interest of the company to have professionals on the board,' Premji told the Western India Vegetable Products directors with characteristic firmness.

Thakor wrote the first HR policy for Western India Vegetable Products, and helped Premji rearticulate the company's beliefs, initially published as 'Wipro Beliefs' in 1971.

Even as new currents began to swirl about the formerly still waters of Western India Vegetable Products, Premji strove to strike a balance. 'Azim stuck to his ideas, belief systems and family values without getting swept away by the American influences brought in by professionals like Thakor. He married American practices with the local ones,' reflects Desai. 'You have to be passionate about your job, but you should be compassionate too.' For Desai, this remains Premji's abiding quality.

As 1975 drew to a close, the old guard at Western India Vegetable Products seemed to be on the retreat. NP Vansia, who had presided over Amalner since 1945, made way for Desai, who took over as factory manager. The previous year, Sekhar had become the company secretary after Vansia's son Kishore resigned from the post. Nagjibhai Shah moved to Bombay from Hasham Premji's Calcutta office, where he had coaxed profits out of the bleeding commodities trade in less than five years. While Parikh handled purchase, Shah took charge of commodities —the fulcrum of Western India Vegetable Products' profitability. All through, Premji worked on bolstering Western India Vegetable Products' solid network of distributors and retailers for Sunflower and 787, the company's laundry soap brand. 'I remember spending long hot days after long hot days for weeks and weeks, walking the streets and talking to retailers,' he would say years later. He hit every small town where Sunflower had a presence and canvassed everyone—from wholesale distributors to shopkeepers—to push his brand of vanaspati.

By the end of 1975, as the government eased controls on the vanaspati industry, the company began 'organizing in a massive way for consumer marketing'. Premji explained his plans for a consumer brand to the board, and Hindustan Thompson Associates (HTA), one of India's largest advertising agencies at the

Western India Vegetable Products was on the rise. From the cramped premises on Ghoga Street, it moved to the fourteenth floor of a new building on Nariman Point, the beating heart of Bombay. Premji's vision was expanding, so was his team. Soon afterwards, the company formally registered itself as Wipro. No longer would it be limited by its name.

ABOVE
Nariman Point in 1975 was the most coveted business address in Bombay.

LEFT
Bakhtawar in Nariman Point, Bombay, Wipro's new address in 1976.

time, was entrusted with the critical advertising campaign.

Meanwhile, the Karnataka government allotted land for the Wintrol factory in Peenya in Bangalore. 'With zero experience in engineering, let alone precision engineering, we decided to invest time, energy and money in building the technology and engineering ourselves,' Premji remembers. 'The simpler and easier option would have been to get the engineering and technology from a global partner.' But, after a scouting trip around Europe, Rao and Premji decided they needed to take end-to-end control of their product. Going against conventional wisdom, they put down money in building the plant and creating the technology ground-up, no matter that each investment decision dug deeply into the fledgling company's precarious reserves.

Although the financial outlay here was comparatively small, the Wintrol model set the tone for future expansions.

❖❖❖

In early 1976, the expanded Western India Vegetable Products team moved out of the poky premises at Ghoga Street in Bombay and into the fourteenth floor of Bakhtawar, a new building in the tony Nariman Point. The new registered office was symbolic of a company on the ascendant, but validation also came from the enthusiasm of agencies such as HTA.

'Our business was worth peanuts [to HTA]. It was Premji's personality, his presentation of plans that swung the deal,' recalls Lajmi. Premji insisted that HTA's national head, Subhas Ghoshal, work on their campaign. Riding high on his 'Made for each other' mega-campaign for a leading cigarette brand, Ghoshal actually agreed. The first Sunflower consumer advertisement rolled out in 1977 with the tagline '*Shuddh ghee ke baad pehli pasand* (The first choice after pure ghee)'. Premji worked closely with HTA on both advertising and brand packaging to consolidate the Sunflower brand identity.

The moment was of immense significance. As Jagdish Sheth, Charles H. Kellstadt Professor of Business at Emory University's Goizueta Business School, explains, brands are an asset quite independent of the business, creating additional shareholder value. A long-time consultant who became an independent board member of Wipro, Sheth believes the move to a packaged, consumer-facing avatar marked Sunflower's transition from a mass-market product to a more premium position.

Notwithstanding these changes, in absolute terms, Western India Vegetable Products was far from an emerging heavyweight. At the end of 1975–76, Western India Vegetable Products' profit after taxes stood at just Rs 2.4 million. The sky was still the limit, and Premji, evermore confident in his talent-spotting abilities, continued his search for the right people to power growth. None of his hires over this period fit a mould: each was a unique individual, bringing his own set of skills to the role.

Consider Dileep Ranjekar, who joined Western India Vegetable Products as the factory personnel supervisor in 1976. A sports captain and mess supervisor in college, the Tata Institute of Social Sciences graduate mentally dismissed the quiet Premji as the 'tie-wearing son of a businessman (*Seth ka beta* tie *lagake baitha hai*)', but quickly revised his opinion once the interview got underway.

Ranjekar knew little English. In most companies, this would have been a serious negative, but Premji stationed him in Amalner and, on his fourth day on the job, deputed the rookie to negotiate workers' wages with the assistant labor commissioner in Aurangabad. Ranjekar repaid the trust by working out a settlement.

'Over time, the workers became friends. I'd come to the factory at 8 a.m. and stay until midnight. The expectations were high, but I had complete freedom,' he reminisces. 'I had to learn everything about the factory work in order to recruit people. I made independent decisions, identifying problems and eliminating them as I saw fit. I was never required to do anything [ethically] wrong, and I instituted good practices.'

❖❖❖

In Bombay, Premji continued his talent hunt. Ram Agarwal, then employed at Glaxo, was put through an eleven-hour interview with the managing director. 'By the end of the day, I think he knew more about me than I knew myself,' laughs Agarwal, who went through two subsequent rounds of interviews and finally took a 15 per cent pay cut to join. Like many others before and after him, he was drawn in by Premji's engagement, ambition and uncompromising values.

From early on, Premji positioned himself as a facilitator of growth, setting up professionals in particular roles and then moving out of their way. His hires were quick to appreciate the unusualness of this approach. Shah remembers, 'Every April, we would decide together the quantum of manufacture that financial year. I had to ensure the plant received enough raw material. Premji gave me a capital and a budget, and then I had full liberty on purchase decisions. The price I paid for the oil was my problem and the price at which vanaspati was sold was

ABOVE, LEFT
Dileep Ranjekar (seated third from left; on extreme right, playing table tennis), personnel manager at the Amalner factory in the 1970s and 1980s, with colleagues. Camaraderie was an important part of the factory life.

the marketing team's problem. This made one not an employee but an entrepreneur.'

Premji's egalitarianism revealed itself in other ways too. For instance, the conference room was fitted out with a round table, despite its inconvenient shape and size, because it precluded the idea of a head of the table. 'You couldn't carry anyone else's bag. There were no call bells in the factory. Slowly, we discontinued peons,' adds Ranjekar. 'But the most important was the freedom for people to speak their mind. What they said might be contested, but it would not be held against them. These were very important differentiators. We began attracting people who were aligned with this kind of thinking, not because they didn't have alternative opportunities.'

❖❖❖

Within Western India Vegetable Products, the world was ordered, inflexibly, in black and white. In a politically fragmented India that had just emerged from Emergency rule, corruption was rampant, but Western India Vegetable Products insisted on complete integrity in all its practices. Ram Agarwal remembers the blowback on their refusal to appoint dealers recommended by a Madhya Pradesh minister: there were forty-eight raids on Western India Vegetable Products properties, topped by a charge of adulteration. Newspapers ran headlines like, 'Sunflower Found Adulterated'. Despite the in-house panic, Agarwal says, Premji would not even consider the possibility of bribing, not even when an arrest warrant was issued against him, Agarwal and a local distributor.

'Fight,' Premji flatly told Agarwal. Diwali, peak season for vanaspati, was then just a few days away. Agarwal decided to withdraw supplies from Madhya Pradesh, where Western India Vegetable Products commanded a 40 per cent market share. The huge shortage alarmed the administration. An anxious district collector called Western India Vegetable Products, and was politely told that they could not possibly send 'adulterated' vanaspati. 'Two days before Diwali, they withdrew all cases, charges, FIRs. Only one case continued, but even that was eventually dropped. The industry norm was to pay the bribe, but we would not,' says Agarwal.

Maintaining this stand was no mean feat, especially as the profitable plant itself was facing difficulties. Desai quit Western India Vegetable Products at the end of 1976, and a long-term replacement proved hard to come by. Without a strong administrator at the helm, Amalner faced sporadic strikes—mostly involving a handful of workers unhappy with management decisions—and cases of oil pilferage. For a while, the factory threatened to slip into chaos.

Wintrol, meanwhile, had had a slow start. It went into production in 1976 with hydraulic cylinders for machine tools and industrial applications. But Premji had bigger ambitions. It was time to revisit the plans he had shared with Lajmi during his interview in 1973, about something 'hi-tech, something based on electronics or computers which has a lot of future'.

❖❖❖

The Western India Vegetable Products nomenclature transitioned to Wivpro, for a short while, and then to Wipro Products Limited in 1977. The old name had been an impediment for Wintrol; with the company scoping out every possibility for diversification—from scooters to seafood—it was time to look at the future.

And when it presented itself, Premji wasted no time in seizing it. At a dinner with an IIM Calcutta professor Ramu Iyer, he met Ashok Narasimhan, one of the Tatas' youngest finance controllers. Following an engaged conversation around business and information technology, the two met several times in Bombay, and a few months later, Premji asked Narasimhan to join Wipro as general manager of finance.

Struck from the very first meeting by Premji's openness and willingness to learn, and promised a free hand with the new diversification, Narasimhan did not have to think too hard about taking up the offer. But before that, he found himself standing before industry doyen JRD Tata, nervously explaining that he did not really want to handle the in-house vanaspati business and was moving to a small vanaspati company for a different challenge.

Hired in November 1977, Narasimhan's first decisions included hiring DA Prasanna from the elite Tata Administrative Service, a leadership program by the Tata group. Prasanna worked to create a corporate set-up for Wipro, with clear HR and financial arms.

By the end of 1978, Amalner, however, needed more attention. Oil pilferage became so rampant that Wipro had to bring in a detective agency to track the culprits. The vanaspati business—still the company's whole and soul—was on the brink of making losses.

But the very next year, Narasimhan would chart a course to take Wipro into its future. And the irascible PS Pai would join as the factory general manager Amalner and, as Ranjekar describes it,'turn the consumer division into a nation in itself'. ◆

1979–1990

A moment comes, which comes but rarely in history,
when we step out from the old to the new;
when an age ends; and when the soul of a nation
long suppressed finds utterance.

Jawaharlal Nehru

PS PAI

MS RAO

SRIDHAR MITTA

ASHOK SOOTA

ASHOK NARASIMHAN

DA PRASANNA

Chapter | **4** | 1979–1990

A Large Canvas of Opportunities

'Do something,' PS Pai said, conversationally, to the unsuspecting visitor. 'I will give you the company car. Take a ride in that car. It will stop on the bridge over the river. You can then get down and jump into the river from the bridge.' The food and drugs inspector had only been following the norm of the day by demanding a bribe at the Amalner factory. Pai's unambiguous response ensured it was the last time anyone ever threatened to misuse the Prevention of Food Adulteration Act, 1954, against Wipro.

Pai, who'd had an eleven-year stint with Union Carbide, made his presence felt soon after joining Amalner as factory general manager in 1979. An accidental recruit—Wipro had been trying to hire his brother, who instead recommended him—he found a business in crisis, with mounting oil pilferage and a rudderless factory management. In 1978–79, Wipro's profit after taxes stood at an abysmal Rs 835,000, down from Rs 3.5 million the previous year. Even then, long-term profitability was expected to be 'consistent with the highest standard of integrity and our obligations to the customers and employees', according to the Wipro annual report of 1978–79.

Soon after joining, Pai discovered a report from an external agency detailing possible theft of oil in the factory. However, nobody was able to decide the next steps. Pai decided to fire visible signals to not only the factory workforce but also the vendors dealing with the factory: there would be zero tolerance for lack of

PS Pai was the man Wipro needed at Amalner. Firm yet kind, he amped up discipline, fought corruption and coaxed unprecedented revenues out of the vanaspati business. Pai loved the factory life. But once production was streamlined, Premji brought him to Bombay to head Consumer Care. The profits of the division would go on to fund Wipro's ambitious future.

ABOVE
PS Pai (second from right) at a settlement with the workers' union in 1980.

LEFT
Dr Gulbanoo Premji, Chairman from 1966 to 1983, with PS Pai in Amalner.

integrity. He conveyed clear and firm decisions to the senior management, with sufficient time to implement a strategy that led to the separation of a half-dozen employees in the oil-receiving and related sections of the factory. This earned support from the workers' union too, which helped set in place a series of actions for the next decade or so. A powerful minister from the ruling party was dealt with the same iron hand when he asked for funds for his political party.

This firm handling, coupled with several positive actions in the manufacturing set-up and tightening of processes, led to profit after taxes rising again to Rs 6.5 million in 1980 and crossing the Rs 10–million mark in 1981.

❖❖❖

'I saw the passion, honesty and intense desire in Premji to succeed under any circumstances,' Pai would say about his first encounter with the then managing director. Premji's intensity would rub off on the people he recruited, creating a similar ambition in everyone who worked in Wipro in these early years.

If Premji's skill for talent acquisition shaped the ecosystem, his insistence on profitability instilled tremendous financial discipline throughout Wipro. He knew the right people and processes were important for Wipro to realize its goals and he paid a lot of attention to Human Resources and Finance. Premji's hunger for excellence and performance was, unquestionably, Wipro's driving force. But the hand steering Amalner after 1979 became Pai's. His sense of fairness was as strong as his likes and dislikes, his camaraderie with the workers as clear as his impatience with greedy officials. His sense of ownership was absolute. 'When he would see things that were not in the overall interest of Premji [and Wipro]—including Premji's own views—he would have a problem. And he would immediately point it out in the strongest possible manner,' recalls Dileep Ranjekar.

Possessing a rare gift for languages—he was fluent in nine—and relationships, Pai knew how to get the best out of people and the business: processes had to be set, raw materials optimized and a cultural shift instituted to maximize operating efficiencies.As Ranjekar handled the HR challenges, twenty-six-year-old Suresh Senapaty, the audits and systems coordinator, was sent over to manage the finances of the factory. Keen on a job abroad, the young chartered accountant regarded Wipro as a short halt. Senapaty moved to Amalner in June 1981 to carry out his audits. A few months later though, when Senapaty's work in the factory made him a candidate for the Corporate Office, he flatly refused to move to Bombay.

Earlier, Pai too had not been keen to move out of Amalner. Halfway into his promised three-year stint there, Premji had brought him to Bombay to lead Wipro's consumer

From Vanaspati to Soaps

By the early 1980s, the big names in India's fast-moving consumer goods (FMCG) market—Hindustan Lever Ltd and Tata Oil Mills Company (TOMCO)—had been lulled into a sense of complacency. In 1981, HLL commanded 69 per cent of the toilet-soap market, despite focusing on exports to work around the draconian Foreign Exchange Regulation Act (FERA), which capped foreign equity participation in local operations at 40 per cent. The 1973 act looked to encourage Indian industry, but by 1981, TOMCO, the second biggest player in India, had cornered only 19 per cent of the market. That same year, JRD Tata said that TOMCO had to move away from the soap market, admitting that they had 'failed to make any real dent in the dominant hold over the market ... by our main competitor'.

Wipro's growth in the soap market was slow. It was 1995 before it could corner 3 per cent of the pie. But HLL sat up and took notice of Santoor—launched in 1986—as early as 1990. Shunu Sen, a top marketing executive of HLL, confessed to Premji that, 'Levers has started taking Santoor very seriously.' Apprehending possible HLL aggression, Wipro's Consumer Care division went all out to protect Santoor's market share and, in time, went on to use its brand identity to forge a deep connection with the everyday woman, particularly in southern India, where it had built a robust distribution channel.

products business that was formed to pursue ambitious plans. Ranjekar had moved three months before Pai, and a reluctant Senapaty eventually followed a few months later. The two of them went on to be regarded as Pai's trusted lieutenants in the Bombay backrooms.

❖❖❖

A large part of the credit for turning Amalner around and instituting processes that converted efficiency to profitability goes to Pai. During the year under his direct watch, vanaspati production in the factory stopped only after fulfilling the day's quota of 125 tonnes, achieving a record production of more than 54,528 tonnes during 1981–82, a record that would not be broken. The sales force complained about inconsistencies in various batches of the product, but Premji, conscious of the difference Pai was making, stood up for the factory.

'Pai was superior in operations,' Premji confirms. 'He did a very strong execution job. And he brought in a very strong commercial orientation to the business.' Ranjekar elaborates, 'His strengths were analyzing problems, identifying solutions, having the guts to implement the solutions and doing all the strategic stuff to make the solution acceptable to all.'

Once Wipro's sales team accepted the variations in the different batches of vanaspati they were expected to sell, they set about putting in a network of distributors in India's small towns and cities around Maharashtra and parts of central India. On the shoulders of the early sales professionals, Wipro created a consumer products business that challenged established hegemonies (see: From Vanaspati to Soaps) and grew the brand into a household name. Pai was with the sales team every step of the way, charming stockists and retailers alike during his extensive travels.

As fresh graduates of India's top business schools marketed vanaspati in India's small towns, as veteran members of the sales team took overnight trains to chase down orders, as factory officials refused point-blank to pay bribes, Wipro grew into an organization that fostered ownership and allowed for the creation of a strong bulwark of values. Without these fundamentals in place, the best of intentions and policies would have failed.

❖❖❖

Come 1981, Wipro made further inroads into the Indian kitchen. It introduced the flexi pack for vanaspati, beating HLL at it by four years, thereby gaining more credence as a consumer brand. However, it was easier to persuade the householder to adopt the new pack than the retailer or stockist—the trade was tremendously resistant to packaging that seemed hard to tamper with and easy to damage. R Ramamoorthy, who had risen from his job as a typist to head the sale of bulk packs of vanaspati, remembers balancing his 45 kg self on a flexi pack to emphasize to the stockist that it was as tough as a jar or a tin.

Over the next couple of years, looking to exploit the no-tax-on-export-profits regime, Wipro ventured into exporting leather shoe uppers—Clark's and K Shoes would soon become clients. More significantly, the company also began manufacturing bath soaps, or 'toilet soaps' as they were called in India. It made its debut with Bubbles, a well-received soap for children, but ran into trouble over the name: a company with a similar-sounding detergent filed a lawsuit and, within a year of its launch, Wipro had to withdraw the product.

But the setback only caused the consumer products business to double down on researching its next product, and, in August 1986, Wipro launched Santoor, a sandal-turmeric soap that is now India's second-largest soap brand. Soon, Wipro cornered part of shampoo bars (known in India as hair-care soap) market. When a workers' strike in the manufacturing plant of the leading competitor's brand affected their supply, Wipro swooped in to fill the gap with Wipro Shikakai.

Under Pai, the division continued to be responsible for the lion's share of contributions to the corporate kitty. The profits, so hard to come by in a capital-intensive, low-returns business, were essentially the fuel for Wipro's growth engine.

❖❖❖

Government policy was the prime reason Premji decided to diversify out of the vanaspati industry, paving the way for Wipro's transition.

Through the late 1970s, the central government leaned heavily on a wide variety of foreign companies in an effort to encourage domestic enterprise. Finally, in 1977, asked to meet impossible conditions for their continued presence in India, a number of foreign companies—including IBM, which had a near monopoly in the Indian technology market—shut down their operations in the country.

Public sector units had a strong presence in India's tech sector. The Electronics Corporation of India Ltd (ECIL), established in 1967, was the largest systems supplier in the Indian market. The National Informatics Centre (NIC) and the Computer Maintenance Corporation (CMC) came up later in the 1970s to further the use of computers in governance and maintenance of the same. The time was ripe for new players to

TOP
As Wipro Infotech expanded its factory capabilities, it entered into an agreement with Epson, Japan, in 1984 to manufacture computer peripherals.

ABOVE
Wipro Infotech's hardware-manufacturing facility, Mysore, 1980s.

What Wipro lacked in experience, it made up in ambition. The company incubated its 'electronics project' at the premier Indian Institute of Science and hired talent from elite schools and companies. In his people, Premji wanted diverse personalities and interests as well as a commercial orientation.

emerge, and Wipro was waiting in the wings (see: Shaping IT for Years to Come).

'The IT business was a planned diversification,' says Premji, who saw the opportunity he had been waiting for taking shape. However, Wipro lacked experience with electronics and technology, and there was a dearth of talent in the field. 'We found that the industry was dictated by techies who didn't understand business,' says Premji. 'In Ashok Narasimhan, we found a differentiating factor—a person who understood technology and who could understand business. He was bright and brought a very strong commercial orientation.' The former Tata man, who began drafting a business plan for Wipro's new venture from the very day he joined, worked in an almost start-up-like atmosphere to bring together the right team and develop the right approach for the future.

What Wipro lacked in experience, it made up in ambition. Premji and Narasimhan incubated Wipro's 'electronics project' at the Centre for Science and Industrial Consultancy of the prestigious Indian Institute of Science (IISc), Bangalore. In August 1979, they also recruited the first member of Wipro's Infotech (WIT) division—this was the first recorded use of the now-ubiquitous abbreviation of information technology—from IISc. A master's graduate in engineering, Victor Jayakaran worked out of a small room at the institute's Digital Lab.

Two months later, Wipro applied for a license to 'develop, manufacture and market minicomputers for the commercial data processing segment' and 'export ... software products'. By May 1980, Narasimhan and Premji had persuaded Dr Sridhar Mitta of ECIL to take up the challenge of building an R&D team from scratch. And by December that year, they had received their license. 'We put together a very strong team. We built R&D from scratch by hiring from ECIL, ISRO [Indian Space Research Oganisation], defense. The young people did a remarkable job. There was very strong leadership at that point of time in Sridhar Mitta,' Premji says.

While Narasimhan and his team threw themselves into the business side of things, Mitta had the unenviable job of putting together a team and the technology for Wipro. The IITs and ECIL were his favorite hunting grounds. Among those he wooed away from ECIL were BV Venkatesh, who would go on to become Wipro's first sales manager; A Lakshman Rao, Wipro's first software professional; and A Sadashivam, who headed hardware production. Eight others from ECIL joined Wipro's factory and its Testing and Development divisions.

WIT's first independent office was a small room on Dickenson Road in Bangalore. The earliest recruits still remember sacrificing several pairs of trousers to the protruding nails that held together the rickety rented chairs. But more than the nails, they were inhibited by Mitta's presence. They heaved a sigh of relief when Sadashivam coaxed the boss to move into a tiny cabin.

❖❖❖

'Ashok, none of you has seen a computer company; none of you has seen a computer being manufactured. So, let's go to the US and see it,' Mitta recalls telling Narasimhan. To prepare the ground, he took Premji and Narasimhan around ECIL—and, while at it, poached one more of his former colleagues.

Shaping IT for Years to Come

The foundations for India's IT industry were laid when the Indian government cracked down on multinationals, leading to IBM's exit from India in 1977. The very next year, a new government under Morarji Desai allowed private companies in India to start making minicomputers using imported microprocessors. Among those who took up the challenge were Delhi Cloth Mills (DCM) and the Tatas. DCM computerized its in-house payroll functions in the 1970s and ventured into computer manufacture in 1979. The Tatas first used computers for data processing in their steel and automobile industries, and went into computer manufacture with Burroughs in 1975. They shut down after four years and later entered into a joint venture with IBM in 1992.

The third player to emerge on the scene was HCL, founded in 1976 by six former employees of DCM. Their first product was a teledigital calculator. Its profits were channelized into their hardware manufacturing enterprise. They went on to prove themselves as innovators, adopting the latest hardware technologies, sometimes before companies in the West, and staying on top of the rapidly changing industry, including the personal computer revolution in the mid-1980s. Later, they branched out into software services. Infosys, set up in the next decade, in contrast, focused on software services from day one.

TOP
Lee Cole (center), Sentinel's key business development executive, with Vallab Kulkarni (left) and M Divakaran, two of Wipro Infotech's early recruits.

ABOVE
A Sentinel ad in *Computerworld*, 1979.

Sridhar Mitta used his old boys' network to set up a US tour for Premji and Ashok Narasimhan. They visited HP, Digital, Intel and Data General before zeroing in on Sentinel, a small company in Cincinnati, Ohio. The specs for their OS matched Mitta's requirements closely and Narasimhan struck a hard bargain for the software, including the source code.

Wipro decided that their first foray into technology would be minicomputers. While the government forbade the import of hardware—Mitta's R&D team would have to build it from scratch—no government policy existed for software. Wipro rejected suggestions of using pirated software (the popular option then), and Premji greenlit a shopping trip to the US. On their radar were: Sentinel in Cincinnati, Ohio; HP, Digital Research and Intel, all in California; and Data General in Austin, Texas.

Mitta found that Sentinel used an Intel 8086 16-bit processor and Multibus architecture, like Wipro wanted. He spent two weeks there to familiarize himself with the system. Narasimhan, on his part, drove a hard bargain for Sentinel's Data Base Operating System (DBOS), including the source code. Sentinel did not think a market existed in India and obliged. However, India had no provision for the legitimate import of the Sentinel technology. Eventually, Wipro was allowed to import the software, a first, under the category of 'design and drawings'.

Industry members, savvy technocrats and curious visitors alike did a double take when they saw the Wipro display at the annual exhibition held by the Computer Society of India in Delhi in February 1981. The sales team was bombarded with the question, 'But where's the computer?' Wipro's Series 86, India's first-ever multiuser minicomputer, was just a desk with terminals: all the hardware was built into the desk. It was a glimpse into the possibility of a radical world beyond mainframes.

The previous night, time had come to a standstill for the engineering team, as they realized they had to reprogram a read-only memory chip for the multiuser configuration to work. With few contacts in the city, they were scrambling till a former IIT Delhi graduate on the team called his professor in desperation. He granted them access to IIT's computer lab. The team returned to base at 3 a.m., merely hours before the exhibition opened, inserted the chip and found, to everyone's intense relief, that the multiuser configuration fired up.

❖❖❖

Engineers and salespeople at the Dickenson Road office became accustomed to a light-eyed man working furiously to teach himself the Data Business Language of the Series 86. TS Krishnamurthi, founding partner of data-analyzing firm Alpha Systems, was WIT's first-ever customer in June 1981—paying a whopping Rs 1.48 million—but he was determined to become familiar with the system ahead of delivery in December. Once the system had been installed at his office, Krishnamurthi returned the favor by allowing Wipro engineers to do their product-testing after hours. Alpha Systems would come back to be the first customer for several of Wipro's subsequent products.

The breakthrough sale, though, was initiated in a meeting early in 1982 with Vittal Mallya and his son, Vijay, who ran a sprawling business empire encompassing breweries, distilleries and processed-food companies. Credit for landing the account went to Narasimhan, the suave Doon School alumnus who moved in the same social circles as the younger Mallya. 'But Vijay said he didn't know anything about computers, and he would get the CIO [chief information officer] or CTO [chief technology officer] of Hoechst AG, their German associate, to come down and take a

LEFT
Wipro Infotech employee Muthaiyan at work on the first 68K platform hardware, based on Motorola's 68K processor, during a visit to the US in 1985.

LEFT

Ashok Narasimhan (extreme right) and Sridhar Mitta (second from right) make a sales pitch to Vittal Mallya (third from left) and his son Vijay (second from left) of McDowell & Co. in 1982. This would be Wipro Infotech's first big deal.

RIGHT

Wipro Infotech's Series 86 was a fast-selling computer catering to the needs of large and medium-sized organizations.

LEFT

The McDowell account opened doors to the enterprise segment for Wipro. HTA designed an ad campaign around it, shot in the McDowell office in Madras.

call,' Narasimhan remembers.

The Wipro team, then operating out of a basement and a room on Dickenson Road, was aghast at the thought of meeting their prospective clients in their own cramped quarters. In a mad rush, they booked a room at an prominent hotel for the meeting. It went well, but six months passed with only sporadic conversation about the number of machines and exchange rates.

AV Sridhar, who left Delhi Cloth Mills (DCM) to handle sales for Wipro in 1981, recalls frantic attempts to close the order before the end of March 1983 and wrangling with Vijay Mallya at yet another meeting. 'After making us wait for hours, Mallya suddenly demanded two more computers. Then, he said he was going to New Delhi and would sign the order on the flight! I flew with him to Delhi, he in business class, and I, in economy. Finally, at the Delhi airport, as I explained that excise duties would go up if I didn't get the order to the factory by 31 March, Mallya signed the papers, resting his leg against the baggage carousel,' Sridhar says.

The deal, worth Rs 25 million, placed Wipro firmly front and center of India's IT industry, particularly in the enterprise market.

❖❖❖

Wipro's reputation received another boost in 1983, when it secured a prestigious World Bank-funded project for the Calcutta Metropolitan Development Authority. One of its rivals for the bid was HCL, represented by Sudip Banerjee. Wipro won him over as well. 'The Wipro minicomputer was cleared by international consultants because this was a World Bank project—so I knew it was a good product I wanted to work with,' Banerjee says, explaining why he jumped ship.

The Hasham Premji trading firm was the primary Premji company in Calcutta, with computer engineers and salespeople jostling for space in a corner. The office was on the twentieth floor of one of Calcutta's first high-rises. The lift went up only to the tenth floor—a fact that bothered everyone except Premji, who would urge his colleagues to look out and admire the view on almost every visit, hardly out of breath after having walked up ten flights.

Along with regular visits to each zone to boost the sales force, Premji instituted a system that placed customer need at the center, so much so that many graduates of India's elite institutes of learning, who were sent to service any problems, joked that they were being 'shipped off with a Wipro computer!' No call from a customer was too late, too far, or too complicated for the Wipro team to handle.

❖❖❖

Wipro considered its people its greatest assets, and held them to the highest standard of integrity and conduct.

As Wipro grew, Premji took it upon himself to inculcate these values—first articulated in 1971—to his people. All new employees received a statement of beliefs and objectives upon joining. On his regional tours, Premji would meet new employees and conduct a session on Wipro's beliefs. By 1983, these sessions were held annually in each location. Each regional head would brief the recruits on the business, and then Premji would take over to give a broad overview of Wipro, followed by a discussion on the company's values.

Deeply inclusive, as the culture of Wipro was, these town halls were spaces for all sorts of questions. S Janakiraman of WIT still remembers the first session he attended in 1984. 'A campus recruit stood up and asked, "Mr Premji, you own Wipro. When are you giving us some shares?" We didn't even know there was something called shares,' chuckles Janakiraman. Later, he remembers, Premji would tell ranks of bemused techies all about Santoor and the waves it was making in the consumer market.

❖❖❖

Through the 1980s, Wipro Infotech rode the market, sometimes responding to India's policy reforms and frequently anticipating them (see: Public Policy and Information Technology). Within two years of getting into the information technology industry, Wipro began to make software. On 1 January 1983, Wipro Information Technology Ltd (WITL) became a subsidiary company focused on R&D and systems engineering, while Wipro Systems Ltd (WSL) was incorporated on 14 July 1983 to make software products for the export market.

In 1984, Rajiv Gandhi became the prime minister of India after the assassination of his mother, Prime Minister Indira Gandhi. The young, pro-technology leader is among those credited for the growth of India's information technology industry and the telecom revolution. The 1980s witnessed industrial deregulation, privatization of the telecom sector, greater representation of industry interests in policymaking, major computerization of the public sector and the emergence of an export-oriented software industry.

Narasimhan spearheaded the change of track to software products, moving to head WSL. Premji brought in Ashok Soota to take charge of

TOP LEFT
Wipro's Series 386 story fired the cognoscenti imagination like few other tech launches. Computer magazine *Dataquest* gave it the pride of place on the cover.

ABOVE
Several members of the team that built Series 386 stayed on in Wipro Infotech, helping the business achieve multiple technological firsts.

LEFT
Wipro Infotech's third big hit was touted—and rightly so—as the biggest evidence of its formidable technological capability.

WITL. Soota had the right credentials for the role—he had worked for several years with the DCM group, and had a strong experience in managing operations and factory, skills a new business like WITL was in desperate need of.

Premji's decision to enter the IT industry was paying off. 'We thought that IT had a better, quicker, higher growth future [than the industry Wipro was in]. ... Everyone in the business was optimistic in spite of the fact that they were not making money, and that's a good sign. We started making decent money in terms of our revenue and investment in year two or three. It was remarkable, unprecedented,' Premji recalls.

The next major product for Wipro's R&D team was Series 386, the world's first minicomputer made with an Intel chip. Wipro's cutting-edge ambition was becoming an identity. At IIT Kanpur for a campus recruitment drive, Mitta was confronted by a twenty-two-year-old graduate, MV Govind, who demanded to know if Wipro was looking to build 'the 386 machine'. Pleased with the answer, he allowed himself to be hired and went on to manually design the printed circuit board even before Mitta landed in Bangalore with the Intel chip.

Wipro's first order, a few years ago, had been assembled in a three-bedroom apartment in neighboring Mysore. Now, they had a state-of-the-art, albeit slightly disorganized, factory in the small town. Because of the budgetary peculiarities of their clients, they often received a bulk of their orders in the last month of the financial year, as was the case with the UB order. Accounting processes needed an overhaul. The too-big-too-fast scaling up led to poor inventory management, order processing and dispatch. But it was clear the IT business was beginning to bring in the revenue.

In 1987, Series 386 was launched to universal acclaim. Its resounding success catapulted Wipro to the next level. Intel CEO Andy Grove wrote a letter of congratulations to the Wipro team. Backed by its unparalleled after-sales service, Wipro's robust technical capability cemented its position at the very top of the hardware industry.

❖❖❖

By the mid-1980s, Wipro developed something akin to a federal structure. Each business unit had its chief executive, and an independent P&L, while the Corporate Office pooled the profits generated by each business to disburse for necessary expansions. The corporate finance team brought rigor to the process by insisting on zero-based budgeting and strict monitoring of profit and loss for each functional unit. HR ensured shared values and beliefs across businesses—an effort helped by, as Ranjekar says, the fact that 'till 1992, Premji interviewed all campus recruits'.

But it was not just the campus recruits who were put through Premji's grilling. Som Mittal came to Wipro for an interview in 1989 after fourteen years with Larsen & Toubro, Escorts and Denso. Seated across from Premji, he recognized the man he had seen walking up thirteen flights of stairs just minutes earlier. 'The interview started at 9.15 a.m. and, except for a forty-minute break, went on till 4 p.m.,' Mittal remembers. 'It was a one-on-one. Mr Premji had a long list of questions and, every one and a half hours, he would say, "I don't have a fit on you."'

Mittal was already a general manager at Denso. The Wipro salary offered to him was not spectacular and the position was almost the same, so he was not terribly keen on the job. 'When I reflected back on it, I realized I'd never been through an interview like this. [I thought] if the man spends so much time with me as a person, then there must be something different in this organization,' Mittal says. 'It wasn't about joining a sunrise industry or a start-up, but this whole experience of decision-making. I don't remember what he asked me or what he didn't, but he was weighing my value system.'

Soon after, Mittal joined Wipro Infotech. 'Mr Premji had a belief session in Bangalore for the new employees, maybe fifteen of us. He addressed us for an hour and didn't mention Wipro even once. He didn't speak one word about the business or any expectations he had from us as employees. He simply described his own values and ethics and what they meant, and what values mean and what they don't.'

❖❖❖

But back to 1983 and the newer ground Wipro aimed to cover. 'Narasimhan's focus was sharply on product software,' says Jayakaran. 'He felt if we got even 1 per cent of the world market, we'd be okay.'

Borrowing a few promising people from WITL, including Jayakaran and R&D manager Prakash Mutalik, Narasimhan set up WSL. By then, an office was already in place on MG Road in Bangalore. Wipro occupied three floors of the building in those initial years. But, much to the chagrin of the team, Bangalore stubbornly called it 'The Times of India building', after the English daily occupying the floor below.

'We would punch in at 8.30 a.m., troop out for a second breakfast an hour later, browse through the nearby

My congratulations on the launch of your Multibus II-based supermini computer ... [it] is a blend of a powerful bus and microprocessor (80386). I anticipate it will be a great success ... we will continue to work closely with you in future ... to strengthen our relationship with Wipro.

Andrew S Grove,
Intel

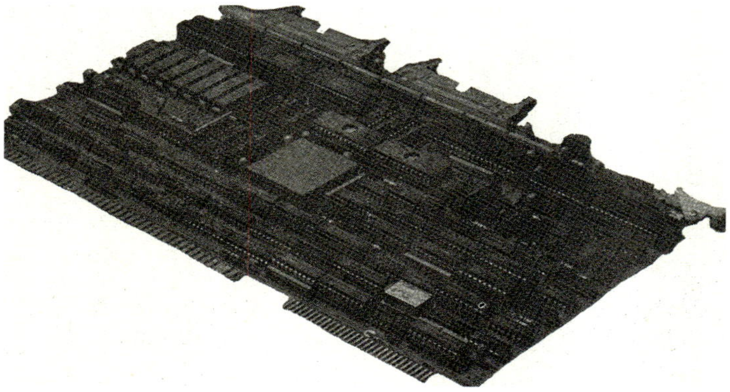

ABOVE
Wipro's Series 386 was one of the world's first minicomputers made with the Intel 80386 chip.

ABOVE
Intel's Vinod Dham (center, with briefcase) with Sridhar Mitta (third from left) and the rest of the Wipro Infotech R&D team soon after the resounding success of Series 386.

LB bookstore, mentally spending our Rs 45 monthly book allowance, and then, on most days, we'd go and window-shop at a home electronics store, dreaming about the kind of home entertainment system we'd get when we made money,' laughs Girish Elchuri, one of the first campus recruits at WSL. Elchuri, too, was an IIT Kanpur graduate, won over to Wipro by recruiter Laxman Badiga's 'six suitcases full of audio-visual equipment for a presentation to students' and the chance to get back to southern India.

The anecdotes, however, obscure the uphill task they faced. Jayakaran, Mutalik, Elchuri and the rest of their team were developing software almost blind. Without access to reference material, they had to fall back on hand-drawn sketches of what the screen looked like in similar products for guidance. Volumes from the nearby bookshop, manuals brought in by colleagues returning from the US and sheer intuition drove them on.

❖❖❖

The software business's need to be close to the customer took Wipro to the US. A five-bedroom house in Monterey, California, served as their first office and doubled up as a dorm, with members of the sales and service team claiming a room each to live and work out of. But it was far from an easy life. 'We had to make enough money to sustain ourselves in the US,' says Elchuri. 'We'd go to the extent of placing our software packages—everything from word processors to accounting software—on the open

Public Policy and Information Technology

In the 1970s, the government's policy on computers was marked by an emphasis on self-sufficiency. It set up the Electronic Corporation of India in 1967, the National Informatics Centre in 1975 and the Computer Maintenance Corporation in 1976. In the 1970s, ECIL's mandate shifted from their initial focus—to provide systems for nuclear energy and defense facilities—to developing indigenous computers. CMC was launched with the sole purpose of maintaining IBM computers following the company's exit in 1977. Later, it reinvented itself as a software services company. NIC was tasked with creating computer solutions for government departments.

Overall, government policy remained restrictive towards the private computer industry till 1978, when private players were allowed to make microprocessor-based minicomputers. The next milestone came in 1984, when the Rajiv Gandhi government announced the New Computer Policy. It created an environment for Indian companies to produce computer hardware and peripherals without restrictions, with the larger goal of popularizing computerization, promoting exports and encouraging private enterprise. To that end, the government issued as many as 151 licenses for the manufacture of micro/minicomputers by January 1985.

Perhaps not surprisingly, labor unions across the railways, banking and postal services opposed the idea of computerization. But the tide was inexorable. Following a trial run in Delhi, railway computerization had immediate impact across the country, cutting short the long queues for booking tickets. Computerization also triggered the first phase of the Telecom Revolution, with microprocessor-based calling booths springing up in every corner of India, making long-distance calls both affordable and easy.

LEFT
Srikanth, Ashok Soota, Ashok Narasimhan and Sridhar Mitta at Monterey Bay, California, USA, during Soota's first visit to the Bay Area.

ABOVE
Wipro Systems Ltd entered the US market in 1986, with the first employees working and living out of a five-bedroom house in Monterey, California.

After setting up Wipro Infotech, Narasimhan turned to product software. But the odds were huge. The first recruits of Wipro Systems had little by way of references or guidance. Their only sources were books, manuals and their own intuition.

In 1987, *Time* magazine wrote: 'India's ingenuity in software designing really came of age last March with the US launch of InstaPlan'. Harvard Business School was one of the early users.

RIGHT
InstaPlan, marketed in the US through a collaboration with Xyton Inc., was a resounding triumph by 1987.

FAR RIGHT
Wipro tried to use InstaPlan's US success to boost the sales of its software products in India. The products were compatible with almost all makes of computers available in India in the late 1980s.

shelves of Kmart.'

But sales were slow; names like Microsoft had already staked out their turf. Elchuri, therefore, also developed solutions for various clients, working on their software to keep the lights burning at Monterey.

Despite the huge odds, WSL managed to make world-class products through the 1980s. The big-ticket win was InstaPlan, a project-planning software. In 1987, Time magazine wrote, 'India's ingenuity in software designing really came of age last March with the US launch of InstaPlan.' Harvard Business School was one of the early users. 'Till then [InstaPlan], we used to go and meet customers and build products based on what we thought they required. Whereas for InstaPlan, we had Gary Cole, a product management guy who knew exactly what they wanted,' remembers Jayakaran. With a world-class brochure and aggressive, almost door-to-door marketing, InstaPlan made its mark.

But InstaPlan was an exception. Wipro's reading of the software products market had not taken into account the widespread piracy. Narasimhan's decision to quit Wipro and relocate to the US towards the end of 1988 dealt another blow. It was time for a reorganization.

While WSL was struggling to find its feet, WITL registered robust growth, fighting hard in a competitive space. The 1989 annual report sums it up by listing the product range: 'Personal computers, minis and superminis, engineering workstations, mini super computers, online transaction processing [OLTP] mainframes and dot matrix printers.'

It had landed several major government accounts, like the railways and banks. Besides, it made satellite-tracking devices for ISRO and developed ruggedized systems for military tanks. It also became the first-ever computer company to win the national R&D award for the electronics industry in 1989.

The previous year, as a sign of its growing expertise and confidence in allied areas, WITL had launched the Peripherals Systems division for the manufacture of printers and ancillary systems. Ram Agarwal headed the division till 1990, when Mittal took over. WITL also tied up with Seiko Epson to make dot matrix printers during Agarwal's tenure, partnered to manufacture engineering workstations under license from Sun Microsystems, worked with Tandem Computers

RIGHT
Chief Executive MS Rao (seated, center) with the R&D team for Wipro Fluid Power, Peenya, 1989.

BELOW
With sophisticated manufacturing capabilities in its Bangalore factory, Wipro Fluid Power had a valued customer base that included BEML–Komatsu, Telco–Hitachi, Ingersoll–Rand, Escorts–JCB and SAIL.

At the company's first outpost in Bangalore, Wipro Fluid Power emerged as the largest Indian manufacturer of hydraulic cylinders by the end of the 1980s. They based their products entirely on in-house research and design and introduced the CETOP European standards in the country.

ABOVE
Factory workers at Wipro's Fluid Power division testing the longest crane hydraulic cylinder at the Peenya factory in Bangalore.

for OLTP mainframes and made mini supercomputers with Convex Computer Corporation. While each of these served its business purpose, they also enabled knowledge sharing.

In an interview to *Span* magazine in 1990, Soota, then WITL president, explained the growth with characteristic élan: 'Our main priority at Wipro is not merely to become number one. We aim for excellence in our products and technology and aspire to give our customers the best value for their money. We are in a position to walk away from orders that do not mesh with our plans.'

❖❖❖

If Soota was able to walk away from orders, much of the credit goes to the Consumer Care business: it provided WITL the luxury of turning down work that did not fit with their goals. 'Our ambition was not so grandiose that we couldn't fund it through internal accruals,' asserts Premji. 'And we turned Consumer Care into a very profitable business.'

Wintrol, the older diversification, however, was captive to the cyclical nature of the business. Its main thrust in the 1980s lay on hydraulic cylinders with automobile applications. Although hydraulic cylinders were an indispensable part of excavators, road-diggers, cranes and tippers, the demand for these was derived from the push in building road infrastructure and other construction.

While the division's profits were not something to write home about, two things stood out. The first was a decision to develop in-house R&D, instead of borrowing foreign technology. 'Our independence gave us considerable flexibility in product design as we were not locked into the foreign collaborators' rigid specifications,' says MS Rao. The second was the emphasis on quality. Between 1985 and 1988, Wipro Fluid Power (WFP), as Wintrol was renamed in 1982, was the first company to introduce Comité Européen des Transmissions Oléohydrauliques et Pneumatiques (CETOP) standards in India.These were European standards for fluid-power applications, approved by the International Statistics Committee.

In 1979, JC Bamford Excavators (JCB) struck up a collaboration with the Indian engineering group Escorts to manufacture cylinders for mobile application. A British company, JCB had an impeccable reputation as a manufacturer of equipment for construction, agriculture, waste-handling and demolition. WFP was already supplying cylinders for crane and forklift applications to Escorts. With Escorts–JCB coming up, it was quite natural that WFP pitched to be a supplier right after the joint venture got off the ground. The British buyers representing JCB, however, ruled out Wipro. 'They said, "Hydraulic cylinders are hi-tech stuff, and we make them in-house in Rochester in England. We can't have some Indian company manufacturing that,"' Rao remembers.

But transportation costs pushed for greater indigenization of the manufacturing process, and WFP got an opportunity to develop some cylinders for Escorts–JCB around 1983. The previous association with Escorts stood in good stead. While the manufacturing process was on, Rao ran into the Indian executive in charge of the JCB plant, who gave him a timely warning. 'He pointed out that in India, the machines [like dirt-diggers] were used twenty-four hours a day by contractors, and said, "Let your designs be robust,"' recalls Rao. He accepted the advice. 'We delivered one set of samples for them, they tried that, found them okay in India, and they sent them to the UK [for testing]. We got a small order, gradually built it up and then we got bigger orders. Then they decided to replace the imported ones with our cylinders. For British manufacturing, they made cylinders there in their in-house plant. For all the manufacturing in India, they bought from us. We were the only suppliers.'

WFP stepped into the 1990s as the largest Indian manufacturer of hydraulic cylinders. In keeping with the Wipro way of working, it was known for customer-orientation and quality.

❖❖❖

Premji, by now, had moved into the role of facilitator and enabler for the various divisions: pushing sales here, chalking key strategies there, mapping the terrain. Even social exchanges with his industry peers—a drink, a dinner or a shared car ride from the airport—would generate memos to let the management know what the competition was up to.

However, when it came to the larger identity of Wipro and what it stood for, it was a different story. Premji was both creator of and custodian for this identity. He had shaped a modern corporate entity that was starkly different from its competitors. Few companies in the private sector could boast of Wipro's pension plan, home loan scheme, skilling program or schemes like the Wipro Equity Reward Trust (WERT), one of India's first stock-option plans.

But even as the Wipro values were being refined, there was a bit of a culture clash between the old and the new businesses. One of the notable campus recruits of the time, Vineet

Our main priority at Wipro is not merely to become number one. We aim for excellence in our products and technology and aspire to give our customers the best value for their money. We are in a position to walk away from orders that do not mesh with our plans.

Ashok Soota, in an interview to *Span*, 1990.

FAR LEFT
Wipro's Landmark II, launched in early 1989.

LEFT
Computers Today featured (from left) AL Rao, Sridhar Mitta and Ashok Soota on its cover in March 1989, marking the launch of Landmark II.

Agrawal, recalls, 'We were a Rs 1,000 million company when I joined in 1985. We had only two products: vanaspati and laundry soap, which was a byproduct of vanaspati. Consumer Care was then worth Rs 900 million, [IT] hardware was worth Rs 50–100 million. Wintrol was about Rs 20 million.' Inevitably, the divisions started asking which business was more valuable for Wipro.

Agrawal was put to work on the Santoor launch in 1986, and he traveled all across northern India to sell the soap. Pai's men fought from the trenches. They hopped on to trains, went deep into India's heartland and ensured their toil reflected in the bottom line. But their counterparts in the computer business traveled by air—no client could wait overnight for his machine to resume processing payroll or bank operations—walked late into the office after a late-night brainstorming session and, generally, worked in a way far removed from the factory floors and chaotic markets of a consumer care business. Pai, deeply skeptical of this new way of working and the future of the new business, would not even allow the IT team to give clients the telex number assigned to Consumer Care.

❖❖❖

Old school, intransigent, a bit of a martinet, larger-than-life—the legends about Pai swirl around Wipro decades after his retirement: How he stormed out of a meeting because Premji was a minute late. Or, the day he sent someone to check on a top executive who was frequently absent on Mondays. But his legacy overrides the legends—not just of profits, but of the people he groomed, the future leaders of Wipro. Among them were Senapaty, Ranjekar and Agrawal, whose values resonated deeply with the Wipro ethos, molding Wipro's culture for decades to come. It is on this common ground of values that Pai had met Premji. It was this common ground that gave Premji the ability to bring together a group of widely different people and then step back, so they could find their entrepreneurial way forward.

Though the old business remained the largest part of Wipro, Premji's faith in his 'planned diversification' was vindicated soon.

In 1989–90, Wipro—describing itself as a 'diversified integrated corporation'—had chalked up Rs 87 million in profit after taxes. Together, WITL and WSL contributed Rs 41 million, close on the heels of the other divisions clubbed under Wipro Ltd, which made a profit of Rs 46 million after taxes. Things were changing. Indeed, India was gearing up for a big change. And Wipro was about to leap into that tide. ◆

LEFT
Sridhar Mitta (third from right) accepting an award instituted by the government of India for research and design in 1991. Wipro was the first Indian computer manufacturer to be so recognized.

1990–2005

Conquer the world by intelligence, and not merely by being slavishly subdued by the terror that comes from it.

Bertrand Russell

NEW YORK STOCK EXCHANGE
WIPRO
Applying Thought
WIPRO
WIT
LISTED
NYSE
WIPRO
WIT
LISTED
NYSE
NYC

Chapter | 5 | 1990–2005

Poised for Global Leadership

It was nearly 8 p.m. in Bangalore. As high-mast lights banished the darkness, excitement grew to a fever pitch among the Wipro people gathered at the spot, from technologists to sales personnel.

In New York, it was a crisp autumn morning. A vibrant banner featuring a rainbow flower hung down from the Corinthian columns of the New York Stock Exchange. Inside, international media and corporate America waited alongside analysts and visiting delegates. At 9.30 a.m. eastern daylight time, Premji stepped away from his conversation with Richard Grasso, chairman and chief executive of NYSE, to ring the exchange's opening bell. On 19 October 2000, Wipro listed on NYSE for its American depositary receipt (ADR), a US bank certificate representing the shares of a foreign company.

As onlookers burst into cheers, Premji turned to speak to the Wipro employees in Bangalore on a giant screen. A year earlier, Infosys and Satyam had enrolled on NASDAQ, the favored list for technology stocks. Wipro had chosen NYSE because, as Premji explained that day, it was home to most of the Fortune 100 companies. Listing on NYSE, he said, would accelerate Wipro's brand globally. It would build recognition with customers and potential partners around the world, and attract a multicultural employee base.[1]

Wipro's American depository shares (ADS) sold at $44.59, enjoying a premium over the offer price of $41.38 that day. In India, the company's stock prices rose by 16 per cent to close at Rs 2,223 on the Bombay Stock Exchange.[2] Later that day, Premji rang the NYSE closing bell with the multinational conglomerate GE's legendary chairman Jack Welch by his side.

Wipro's American depository shares sold at $44.59, enjoying a premium over the offer price of $41.38 on 19 October 2000. In India, stock prices rose by 16 per cent to close at Rs 2,223 on the Bombay Stock Exchange. To close the day, Premji rang the NYSE bell with GE chairman Jack Welch by his side.

BELOW
From left: CFO Suresh Senapaty, Founder Chairman Azim Premji, NYSE chairman Richard Grasso and Wipro Technologies CEO Vivek Paul, during the Wipro ADR listing

Dileep Ranjekar, chief of HR at Wipro and master of ceremonies for the evening, paused at the podium in Bangalore. As thousands of young men and women whooped and clapped, Ranjekar produced a shrill whistle or two himself. In that carnivalesque atmosphere, with live music and bright lights, he teamed up with Ramesh Emani, chief technology officer at Wipro Ltd, to narrate the story of Wipro's growth through the 1990s: how Wipro had made the most of a changing world and taken on a new identity to pursue global opportunities. How, at $40 billion in February 2000, Wipro was the highest-valued company in India.[3] How this listing, among America's corporate glitterati, was a stepping stone to the exciting future that lay ahead.

❖❖❖

Between December 1989 and June 1991, India had run through three prime ministers and as many finance ministers. With each change in government, the country inched closer to an economic precipice brought on by decades of reckless spending in foreign exchange. By the time PV Narasimha Rao took office in mid-1991, only drastic steps could have averted the collapse. Accordingly, within a month, his finance minister, Manmohan Singh, introduced a staggered series of measures that came to be referred to as liberalization. In the long run, Singh's market reforms would be considered a savior for the Indian economy, but initially, the policies were regarded with apprehension throughout the country.

Wipro Consumer Products (WCP) was no exception to the general mood. Despite benchmarking against a multinational for much of its life, WCP leaders were only too aware that Singh's policies could upend business as they knew it.

WCP had opened the decade on an upbeat note. By 1991, Santoor, the soap brand of the company, was reaping the advantages of a focused advertising campaign that, for the first time in the Indian market, successfully marketed the benefits of 'younger-looking skin'. Launched in 1989, the four-ad series, created by FCB Ulka, featured a woman who is mistaken for a college girl, till a child bursts into the scene, addressing her as 'mummy'. The ads struck a chord and, within a couple of years, Santoor's sales doubled, crossing the 10,000-tonne mark, no mean feat in a market dominated by Hindustan Lever Ltd (HLL).

It was especially welcome, given that the vanaspati market was shrinking. Although both Sunflower and Camel, the house brands, had begun the decade as market leaders, it became increasingly clear that the business needed to recalibrate.

Led by PS Pai, WCP tried several strategies. Besides brand extensions for Santoor, it launched Wipro Baby Soft, an infant-care range that sought to bust the Johnson & Johnson monopoly. The company also looked to capitalize on the skincare soap segment, which Santoor had opened up, with brands such as Spring and Milk & Roses, but neither achieved any level of success.

'We thought we could be a multi-brand company,' says Kumar Chander, who quit Hindustan Lever in 1992 to join Wipro as an area manager, encouraged by market feedback on the MNC's aspiring rival. 'But by the mid-1990s, we felt the need for growth. And we thought we should go for a category we understood.'

WCP grasped the huge challenges of building consumer brands from scratch. Consequently, the team began

WCC's earliest acquisitions

If PS Pai is something of a Wipro legend, a part of it could be attributed to his exemplary control over outlays and efficiencies. On his watch, Wipro Consumer Care was a tightly run ship, producing the maximum permissible quantities of vanaspati daily, manufacturing the most economical soap bars, and spurning advertising to push the Santoor and Shikakai soaps through Sunflower distributors. His costs were low and his earnings stable, even as soap replaced vanaspati as the top earner in Wipro Consumer Care over the course of a decade.

Thus, when Vineet Agrawal, designated Pai's successor in 1995, took charge of Wipro Consumer Care in 2002, the Wipro Consumer Care coffers were ready to power the business's expansion plans. In a remarkable departure from the growth path Wipro Consumer Care had followed so far, Agrawal made two quick acquisitions in 2003: Chandrika, a hand-made soap, and Glucovita, a glucose energy powder.

In a scenario where most soap brands were owned by MNCs and therefore unavailable for acquisition, Chandrika, a sixty-year-old family brand, began evoking a great deal of interest from prospective buyers in the early 2000s. Wipro, which had first expressed interest in the brand a few years earlier, also zeroed in and, after all the fabled thrills of the chase, closed in on the long-term manufacturing and marketing rights for India and the remaining SAARC markets (Afghanistan, Bhutan, the Maldives, Nepal, Pakistan and Sri Lanka).

Glucovita, by contrast, was an uncomplicated Rs 50 million purchase from HLL; the MNC had decided the brand no longer fit its needs. Agrawal, on his part, hoped the acquisition would help open doors to Nepal, where the glucose energy powder was popular.

Unlikely as it seems, these humble acquisitions guided Wipro Consumer Care's growth trajectory over the next decade.

LEFT AND BELOW
In a cheeky play on an arch-rival's positioning as the film stars' soap of choice, Santoor ads featured top actors in peripheral roles, while keeping the regular woman—the target audience—front and center.

After the positive impact of the 'mummy' ads, the challenge for Santoor lay in keeping its communication fresh without diluting the core message. The Wipro Consumer Care leadership worked closely with its creative partners to pull it off. By 2018, it was the second highest-selling soap in India.

exploring alliances with a number of global brands in the areas of food and personal care, seeking to exploit the vast distribution strength carefully nurtured by Pai and his team. Among them were Sodial, Borden and Kraft for dairy products; Cargill for salt and citric acid; Kao Corporation for detergents; Schwarzkopf, Maybelline, L'Oreal, Revlon and Wella for haircare; and Hershey's, Quaker Oats, Sara Lee, Glaxo, Lipton and Heinz for food products. Despite long correspondences and visits to the headquarters of each brand, none of them came through.

By this time, the glow of the Santoor ad campaign was wearing off, and sales plateaued again. 'We began doubting ourselves,' says Vineet Agrawal, today the CEO of Wipro Consumer Care & Lighting. 'Had we boxed ourselves in with the sandal-turmeric combination? Was the "mummy" theme too limiting? Was the focus on a married woman alienating others? Could Santoor cross the next psychological milestone?'

Vanaspati sales, the Wipro mainstay for close to fifty years, were also slipping. Global brands ushered in by liberalization were settling down in the supermarket shelves. WCP found itself at a crossroads by the mid-1990s. In this challenging situation, Pai was asked to take charge of Wipro Lighting as well.

The lighting business was a purely opportunistic response to an anticipated spike in demand for office infrastructure post liberalization, and the play was spot on. After a partnership with GE Lighting failed to materialize, Wipro decided to set up the business on their own. By then, the team knew enough about this growing industry. Consequently, Wipro Lighting came up in 1991 with Varun Nijhawan as its chief executive. But when Nijhawan died unexpectedly in 1996, Premji, in consultation with Ranjekar, asked Pai to take charge of yet another consumer-facing business, banking on his superlative record with operations and efficiencies to rev it up. In 1997–98, the business was formally renamed Wipro Consumer Care & Lighting.

However, the bigger questions persisted. What exactly was the WCP business, and what should it be in a globally charged environment? And, critically, would Wipro's IT fame overshadow its credentials as a consumer products company? Wipro brought in multiple renowned consultants—Sumantra Ghoshal from INSEAD Business School in France; Rajeev Batra from the University of Michigan and Jagdish Sheth from Emory University in the US—for their views. These sessions, for the most part, reinforced management strategy. Briefly, it was debated if every product would bear the prefix 'Wipro' for the sake of a unified brand identity. But it was decided the consumer brands would remain as they were.

Recognizing the success they had achieved with Santoor, WCP doubled down on the brand. Following complaints on quality, they rejigged the total fatty matter (TFM) component, tweaked the perfume, improved the color and designed a new wrapper. The relaunch called for a new ad campaign as well. Working with Ulka's Ambi Parameswaran, Agrawal oversaw a slight but significant modification of the old theme. The Santoor woman stepped out of traditional family settings like weddings. There was more to her identity than being a mother. The script played out in two scenarios, a musical instruments store and an aerobics class.

'It was a huge leap for our Santoor woman; we were very worried about it,' says Agrawal. 'To hedge our bets, we decided to run the music shop ad in southern India, where we were stronger, and keep the [comparatively edgy] aerobics ad for the north. The ads released in November 1994, and there was absolutely no impact on sales till March–April 1995. And then we made two decisions: we'd run the aerobics ad in the south and focus our ad budget on a few strongholds, not pan-India.'

Agrawal's gamble paid off. On the back of the campaign, Santoor broke the 15,000-tonne mark in 1997–98, becoming a Rs 1,000 million brand. In 2000, for the first time, Santoor overtook Sunflower vanaspati in revenue, becoming the undisputed driver of WCC's fortunes. It has kept growing since. In 2018, Santoor beat Hindustan Lever's (HLL) Lux to become the second-highest-selling soap in the country.

❖❖❖

Even as WCP was figuring out how to deal with changing global realities at the turn of the 1990s, MS Rao, at the helm of Wipro Fluid Power, was a step ahead. But not without some initial challenges.

In the mid-1980s, WFP had bagged a small order from the Swedish hydraulics company Hydrauto. Five years later, WFP was still trying to fulfill the commission. 'In 1990, after we finally dispatched the order, we learned that it didn't meet their quality standards,' says Sunil Rajagopalan, Rao's first business school recruit who took up charge of sales in 1985.

The setback woke up WFP to the fact that its leadership position in India would not really mean much in a

In the 1990s, Wipro Fluid Power zeroed in on exports as the best way to educate itself. It signed deals with companies in the US, Japan and Sweden, hoping experience with foreign technology and discipline would help it sharpen its competitiveness on a global scale.

ABOVE
The material handling unit of Wipro Fluid Power at Hindupur, Andhra Pradesh—the second factory after Peenya in Bangalore—set up in 1996 to cater to an expanding market.

RIGHT
Anurag Behar (seated, center), who took over as CEO of Wipro Fluid Power in 2004, and Sunil Rajagopalan (seated, left), the head of business development, at Kubota's Tsukuba plant in Japan in 2004.

flattening world. The only option, then, was to improve its game. 'Both Premji and I became convinced that exports were the best way to learn,' says Rao. 'The demands [of the export market] were so high, it would bring us the discipline we needed on the quality front.'

Alongside, WFP leveraged its experience in the manufacture of mobile hydraulic systems—used in construction, agriculture, forestry and the like—to seal strategic manufacturing, marketing and distribution deals with global brands. In 1991, it signed up with Eaton Corporation in the US to be the sole distributor of their steering system valves. This partnership came in unexpectedly handy when Rao and Rajagopalan began exploring exports to Japan a couple of years later. The US company had a Japanese joint venture called Sumitomo Eaton Hydraulics Company (SEHYCO). Based on Eaton's experience, SEHYCO agreed to represent WFP and helped generate business among their clients.

As with the Swedish experience, WFP's first visit to the biennial International Fluid Power Exposition in Japan in 1993 was an all-round reality check. 'We got a tremendous response at the fair. As follow-up, we visited Komatsu Forklift and realized they needed 75,000 actuators a year. We made 25,000 annually,' Rajagopalan says wryly. ' Our presentation had been in English. And the Japanese, being not so conversant in the language, thought we manufactured 25,000 cylinders a month.'

Rao and Rajagopalan worked hard to keep relationships alive with possible Japanese clients. When a potential customer demanded a sample, they shipped out one of their best products to the country. 'A month later, we visited them. They'd stripped down the cylinder to show us tiny patches of rust in the piston rod. I asked them, "What did you do to the cylinder?" They said, "Nothing." They'd simply left it exposed to the elements on the factory roof for a month. And they'd run tests and found that the welding, heat treatment and chrome plating—three crucial processes in the construction of any actuator—were not good enough,' remembers Rajagopalan.

This insight into their shortcomings pushed WFP to take advantage of a Japanese government-funded program to hire a hydraulics expert, Tadashi Satake, for two years, in 1996. His inputs on manufacturing, technology and quality proved to be so useful that Rao persuaded the Corporate division to retain him on the Wipro payroll for a third year.

Besides improving quality standards and boosting the WFP image in the island nation, the Japanese association gave WFP a significant technological advantage in helping them retain long-term accounts like JCB. 'They knew no one could give them the international quality that we could,' says Rajagopalan.

Further working its connection with Japan, WFP tied up with Kawasaki to distribute its hydraulic aggregates to the Indian earthmoving and construction equipment market; the relationship would morph into a joint venture in the succeeding decade. The next year, in 1997, WFP began manufacturing valves and manifolds under an agreement with Sun Hydraulics.[4] Much like Wipro

Premji's oldest diversification was also the smallest part of his expanding corporation. Wipro Fluid Power was in a slow-moving, cyclical business, tied down by the vagaries of the economy. But Premji didn't believe in holding it to a different standard. In 2001, its twenty-fifth anniversary, he said WFP must grow much faster than the current rate.

ABOVE
Wipro Fluid Power's Peenya factory, the corporation's first outpost in Bangalore.

Information Technology Ltd (WITL), WFP was on its way to becoming a one-stop shop for cylinders, pumps, valves and motors, which Indian clients had previously imported.

As exciting as these developments were for the insider, for the outside world, WFP continued to be the smallest part of the expanding Wipro corporation. In 1995–96, its revenues were Rs 566 million, barely 5 per cent of the combined revenues of Wipro Infotech and WCP. The exports market, which Rao and Rajagopalan had worked so assiduously to cultivate, was hit soon afterwards by the 1997 Asian Financial Crisis. The silver lining appeared at home the next year, when the Indian government kicked off the National Highways Development Project, pushing up the demand for earthmovers and excavators.

That WFP was a slow-moving, cyclical business, inextricably tied to the ups and downs of the economy, was an undeniable fact. But its growth was perhaps further limited by its self-imposed narrow focus. While Premji dismissed consultants who urged him to hive off his smallest division—especially in view of the exponential growth predicted for software services—he did not believe in holding WFP to a different standard from his other businesses. In its twenty-fifth year in 2001, as WFP crossed the Rs 1,000 million revenue mark, Premji urged WFP to buck up. 'We need to look for avenues of rapid growth. We must grow a lot faster than what we're doing,' he said at a WFP conference.

As Rao retired in 2004, Premji asked Anurag Behar—fresh off a stint at Corporate where he handled innovation, brand and quality—to weigh in. As Behar remembers, 'My mandate was very simple. Go there, assess the business and either sell it or grow it.'

❖❖❖

Wipro's technology businesses accounted for more than a quarter of the corporation's revenues as 1988 drew to a close. But with the buzz around liberalization growing stronger, Premji, Ashok Soota and Sridhar Mitta considered their choices. Ashok Narasimhan announced his departure; he was set to move to the US. More than any other Wipro entity, WITL and Wipro Systems (WSL) could expect to be directly impacted by the lowering of entry barriers. If the likes of IBM entered the Indian market, would WITL's impeccable record still count with customers? And what exactly was WSL anyway, after six-odd years—some valiant efforts to break into the software products market and one hit in InstaPlan?

'We had to be looking out and also looking in with a different lens because of the intensity of competition building up from companies vying to enter India,' says Premji. Interestingly, this translated not into a single, unified approach towards transition but a three-pronged response—dramatic redefinition of business, repositioning of an existing division and consolidation of a successful strategy—that paid off spectacularly.

The most drastic turnaround, without question, was the shift from products to services. It began with the realization that product software, the mainstay of WSL, had not been the right focus. What followed 'was perhaps the most deliberate decision Premji has ever taken. I have no idea how many hours he put into it,' says Soota. 'He necessarily wanted to get into services. It was looked down upon [at the time]; it hadn't made much of a mark. But we could leverage the existing businesses. And because we could bring the work to India, the margins were very good. Later, they came down to 60 to 70 per cent, but initially, they were as high as 80 to 90 per cent.'

To initiate the change, Premji hired Venkat Mohan, an IIT-trained engineer with an MBA from Harvard and consulting stints in the US with McKinsey and Young & Rubicam. He was joined by Kannan Jagan, from Tata Consultancy Services (TCS) Europe, and Emani, an Infotech man.

'My understanding was that Venkat had been brought in to fix the IT export business, which could be product or non-product,' says Emani, a techie who switched businesses because he believed software, overlooked at hardware-focused Infotech, would get its due at Wipro Systems. 'I spent seven months in Europe in 1989, cold-calling companies, telling them, "We're India, we're cost-effective, we're quick, we're an opportunity."'

Meanwhile, business came looking for WSL. In a meeting with the government of India, as part of his emerging markets strategy, GE's Welch was surprised by a proposal to explore software development in the country. Led by the then prime minister, Rajiv Gandhi, there was a concerted official effort to tap the possibilities of this fledgling industry. Within a month, after Welch's executives surveyed the emerging companies, Wipro Systems bagged a $1 million deal for five projects.

Government policies helped too. The central Department of Electronics set up software technology parks with satellite communication links. The Ministry of Finance waived taxes on export earnings of software companies and dropped import duty

ABOVE
The Nortel headquarters in Brampton, Ontario, Canada, 2004. Then Bell Northern Research, the telecommunications giant was one of the first to give a long-term R&D contract to Wipro Systems in 1990–91.

LEFT
At the inauguration of the first India Development Center at Wipro's 88 MG Road office in Bangalore in the early 1990s. From left: Bakhta, DA Prasanna, V Chandrasekaran, Ashok Soota, Sridhar Mitta, AL Rao, Subroto Bagchi and Sridhar Ramasubbu. Wipro was one of the first to come up with the concept of an offshore center for global clients.

ABOVE
Wipro Infotech employees Lakshmi Vaidyanathan and Narasimhan S Raghavan at a lab for Fujitsu, Japan, at Wipro's Madras Development Center

on computers and tools used for software exports. The devaluation of the rupee also made it easy for Indian companies to bid at competitive rates. Even the time difference between the US and India was an ally in the fast and efficient delivery of IT-enabled services.

❖❖❖

That the US was taking notice of this nascent outsourcing phenomenon became apparent in April 1989, when the US radio broadcaster PBS aired a two-part documentary called Third World Software, featuring, among others, Soota and Mohan. Among its audience was Diju Raha, vice president of International R&D at Bell Northern Research (BNR, which later became Nortel Networks), a Canada-based telecom company then aiming to touch $30 billion by 2000. Inspired to globalize their talent pool for a cost advantage, Raha tracked down the producers of the show for the raw footage and found that he had been beaten to it by none other than the Central Intelligence Agency (CIA). The US government's foreign intelligence service found it highly suspicious that countries such as India were producing software.

Raha met Mani Subramaniam, who took charge of WSL after Mohan and Jagan quit in 1990. Soon, Emani, the only person with experience of big client accounts, had another serious client in his portfolio, this time with an R&D focus. 'They wanted a total environment for the project, including a dedicated communication network between Wipro and BNR,' says Emani. ' We marked off a small area on the third floor of our MG Road office in Bangalore as a BNR Lab, with its own security.'

A few years into the relationship, senior BNR executives arrived at the lab for a meeting with Premji. 'Once it was done, someone checked if Premji had signed himself in at the reception register, and he had,' recalls Emani. 'Raha couldn't stop talking about it to his entire top management. He said, "The owner follows the rules, this is how we know we can trust India!"'

There was some heartburn at Wipro Infotech over the BNR account: some quarters felt that, as an R&D deal, it rightfully belonged to WITL. But Mitta had no time to lose sleep over it; he was too busy prying out an opportunity from a seeming crisis. 'During the annual planning exercise for Wipro R&D in 1990, we were worried about what IBM and Digital could do to us,' says Mitta. 'But then, it dawned on us that if the door was open for these companies to come in, it was also open for us to go out.'

Banking on the prodigious reputation of Indian software skills as well as a paucity of programmers in Unix—an emerging operating system (OS) in the US—Mitta decided to reposition his R&D division 'as a provider of product design services in Unix-related areas to global computer companies'. The idea met with resistance, most notably from Premji, who pointed out that it was WSL that was mandated to deal with foreign markets. But Soota and Mitta argued that WSL was catering to the IT departments of international businesses, while their venture would offer hardware design, OS and networking technology to the R&D and engineering departments of global companies.

And thus began one of the most audacious gambits of the Indian software services industry: selling technological brainpower to the world. To that end, Mitta mined all his contacts among Wipro's fundamental tech providers. Starting with Intel, within a very short period of time, Global R&D's Lab on Hire, as the division came to be called, went on to notch up clients such as Sun, Stratacom, and then Cisco—when they bought Stratacom—VLSI, Tandem, NCR, Novell and others.

Wipro-GE: The Perfect Partnership

By 1989, Wipro Infotech was on a strong footing, while Wipro Systems was undergoing a well-timed rehaul. Although both seemed to be in tune with the times, the businessman in Premji was not happy that the quick-changing nature of technology threatened to upend his businesses every three years. The search for a more stable, future-proof business led Wipro to medical equipment, a sector with massive potential in India. 'Healthcare systems were quite IT-oriented even then. And we had the right competencies,' says Premji.

After a couple of false starts, they learned that GE—with revenues of $50 billion, much bigger than Wipro's Rs 1,864 million—was looking at India as part of its emerging markets strategy. The Asia initiative was triggered by the plateauing of developed markets in the US and Europe.

On the ground, the front person for GE Medical Systems was Chuck Pieper. 'I had to find a team [in India] that could give us 80 per cent of the functionality of Japan at 50 per cent of its cost,' says Pieper. After he vetted ten businesses, the shortlist came down to two: Wipro and its rival computer business in the national capital. On the eve of the GE team's visit to Bangalore, however, Wipro leaders learned that the GE team had been so impressed with the Delhi-based company that they cancelled their trip south.

Premji, a long-time GE observer, stepped in. He wrote to Welch about the centrality of integrity at Wipro. Within hours, the GE team reinstated their trip.

On arrival, Pieper was immensely taken with Premji. 'We chose Wipro for a variety of reasons, but mainly because Pieper fell in love with Premji, with his quiet charm and his engineering capability,' says Welch. 'Premji was the perfect partner.'

Wipro and GE signed the MoU for a 60:40 joint venture in November 1989. Thirty-odd years and many ups and downs later, the joint venture still thrives and is mutually beneficial, primarily because, as Premji says, the chief executive puts the interests of the partnership first, rather than either Wipro or GE. Besides multiple other exchanges, Wipro drew a great deal of top-level managerial talent from Wipro-GE, including Vivek Paul, Anurag Behar and TK Kurien.

BELOW
Azim Premji with DA Prasanna (center), managing director, Wipro GE Medical Systems, and Jack Welch, chairman and CEO of GE, during Welch's visit to the Wipro campus in 2000.

CLOCKWISE FROM ABOVE

Aerospace scientist and later president of India (2002–07) APJ Abdul Kalam (left) with Azim Premji at the Wipro GE Medical Systems campus in September 2000.

The Wipro GE campus in Whitefield, Bangalore. The three-decades-old joint venture has a series of radical innovations in medical diagnostic equipment to its credit.

From left: Ramesh Emani of Wipro Systems and Ashok Soota of Wipro Infotech with Alan Blumenfeld, CIO, GE Medical Systems, USA, and Marc Onetto, Global CIO, GE Medical Systems Worldwide, at the inauguration of Wipro GE Development Center in the early 1990s.

Wipro set up Orbit 1, an R&D center to support Sun. It was the first time ever that Sun allowed support services to operate away from its own premises. '(It) was pretty easy for us ... (because) Wipro was a company we knew and trusted.'

Scott McNealy, co-founder of Sun.

FROM TOP
Scott McNealy, chairman and CEO of Sun Microsystems.

The SPARCstation 1, launched in 1990 under the Wipro–Sun partnership, promised advanced, multifunctional performances at affordable prices in the desktop market segment.

Among the unconventional elements of the business was the man Wipro chose as Lab on Hire's face in the US: Subroto Bagchi. A political science graduate with an unlikely career graph, his job was to introduce India to Silicon Valley. At Sun Microsystems—the most coveted client for Soota, who had sold Sun workstations—Bagchi responded to an executive's admission of his ignorance about India by drawing a world map on his whiteboard and locating India on it. On such beginnings was based a years-long relationship that included a dedicated R&D support center called Orbit 1, the first time ever Sun allowed such a service away from their own locations.

'[Orbit 1] was pretty easy for us ... [because] Wipro was a company we knew and trusted,' says Scott McNealy, co-founder of Sun, referring to the decade-old association. 'I must say, Mr Premji put a wonderful culture together and won us over, immediately, effectively and continuously. Just wonderful ethics, technical excellence, very competent executives and real customer-partner focus,' he says, crediting both personality and technology for the durable partnership. Wipro's engineers were just as competent as their US counterparts, and the company's culture had the right tone set at the top. 'That permeated throughout the company and made it very, very comfortable and easy for us to partner,' he says.

Wipro faced scores of obstacles as it tried to build its business abroad. Sridhar Ramasubbu, a WITL man who switched to Mitta's team, remembers two huge knots untangled around this time. One was with the Reserve Bank of India (RBI), which blacklisted Wipro over incomplete paperwork on the deal with Sentinel. As more Wipro employees went to the US, foreign exchange became an enormous sticking point till such time as Ramasubbu stumbled across the missing papers and turned them over to the central bank officials.

The US visas were an equally touchy matter—the H1B was yet to be introduced and there was pressure on the B1 (business) and L1 (intra-company transfer) visas. The way Wipro handled visas quickly became the template for tech companies looking to ship people overseas.

Closer home, Wipro set up an Overseas Development Center (ODC) for Tandem, then a $2 billion company manufacturing fault-tolerant systems for US institutions such as the NYSE.

'We were looking for a company that had experience in working with hardware, software, OS, not just applications. Wipro was probably the only company, or one of the few, that had built computers internally,' remembers MM 'Sath' Sathyanarayan, who spearheaded Tandem's worldwide hunt for offshore partners in the early 1990s. If they were one of the first US companies to consider farming out work beyond North America, the Tandem ODC was the first of its kind to be set up by any Indian company.

While Lab on Hire was the breakout star of Wipro Infotech in the international market, Soota continued to aggressively expand in the domestic market, as he had in the previous decade. Now, it was propelled by the threat of foreign majors wiping out homegrown brands. Moving on from tech alliances with Acer (for the Genius range of PCs) and marketing deals for Sun and Convex, Soota tied up with Apple in 1993. On the strength of Wipro's distribution network, the sale of Apple products went up by 70 per cent within ten months. By 2000, Wipro was the largest IT vendor in India.

Wipro had made the most of opportunities that arose when the central government's Department of Telecommunications invited private sector participation in value-added services (VAS), covering email, voice mail, data services, audio text services, video text services, video conferencing, radio paging and cellular mobile telephone. As head of the Communications division, old Wipro hand Anand Talwai found clients such as Citibank, who asked Wipro Infotech to 'architect, consult, maintain and support' their data services as they went about building their ATM network in India.

As one of the first movers in the area, Talwai's team commanded high margins with low investment, but within a few years, they felt the need to ally with someone experienced in communication services.

Consequently, Wipro Infotech tied up with British Telecom (BT)—then the world's second-largest telecom company, with which the Communications division already had a relationship—to form Wipro-BT, with a paid-up capital of $5.14 million. This partnership went on to create multi-tenancy networks for lease to customers such as Cadbury's and Godrej to facilitate 24x7 business communication services.

However, the anticipated regulatory changes for VAS failed to materialize, straining the business, and the joint venture finally collapsed when BT cried off the telecom spectrum market. The VAS components went into a short-lived joint venture with KPN (Royal Dutch Telecom), a global telecom operator,

ABOVE
Inside the Wipro Peripherals factory in Mysore. Wipro Infotech launched computer peripherals with Epson, Japan, as part of its domestic IT hardware business.

LEFT
A Wipro employee tests computers at the hardware factory. In 1996, it was producing computers under license from the Taiwanese firm Acer as part of a joint venture.

OPPOSITE PAGE
The Wipro Peripherals factory in Mysore. In 2000, Wipro spun off its IT peripherals business into a separate company now known as WeP Peripherals Ltd.

which launched in 1999 to provide internet services.

❖❖❖

Given all the challenges and successes that occupied and lifted Systems, Infotech and Lab on Hire through this period, it is easy to overlook the directional thought that guided Wipro on to the global path of growth. Premji ensured there was a firm intellectual bedrock for his executives to draw on. As the businesses grew, he sought engagement with various management gurus and thought leaders, seeking a wider perspective and a fresh approach that would help Wipro stay ahead in a changing world.

One, for instance, was CK Prahalad, or CKP, as he was popularly known. A distinguished US-based academic with a doctorate from Harvard, he was a regular on the corporate India lecture circuit. In 1994, Premji attended an invitation-only workshop conducted by CKP and was impressed by the doyen's central idea of 'building Indian multinationals'. Premji was applying a new lens to look at is own businesses as the Indian economy was opening up to the world. His biggest takeaways from these conversations were: one, Indian business leaders were not resource-constrained but imagination-constrained. And two, Indian businesses had to aim to be world-class to gain a share of the world market.

He looked afresh at multiple elements, including valuing talent, developing markets, manufacturing capabilities, quality standards and the impact of strategy. Premji shared the gist of these ideas — CKP's and others' — with his top leaders, and, 1995 onwards, Wipro worked to a bigger vision.

'Prahalad showed us a vision of being the largest technology provider in the country,' says Ram Agarwal. But that was not all. Through conversations with these experts came clarity. This was a time when Wipro's tech businesses were expanding into many fields with varying degrees of success in them. If Wipro was looking for global leadership, it had to choose a field, and software services was that field.

CKP also distinguished between tech-only companies and others that placed thrust on competencies, which was the product of 'technologies multiplied by social organization and collective learning', he said. It was advice that Premji would take seriously.

❖❖❖

On the face of it, Wipro Finance, another of the company's diversification attempts, could be seen as Premji's unlikeliest choice: it did not have the manufacturing or R&D depth of his other businesses. But in India's liberalizing economy, Wipro Finance became Premji's biggest bet after IT.

While non-banking financial companies (NBFCs) had been around since the 1960s, catering mostly to the unorganized sector, they had acquired a somewhat dubious reputation as the lack of central oversight led to frauds. In 1992, NBFCs came under fresh government purview for greater control and operational transparency. Buoyed by the promise of reform, Wipro Finance launched the same year to tap into India's nascent financialization by offering hire purchase, leasing, merchant banking and advisory services for businesses.

'We had a couple of things going for us,' says KR Lakshminarayana, aka Lan, who joined the business in 1995. 'One, of course, was the Wipro brand credibility. We represented good governance in a field that did not have a lot of it. We also understood the tech part of the business. Plus, Wipro Infotech worked in the B2B [business-to-business] segment; we had served a variety of businesses. And then [there] was our capital efficiency; we were extremely good users of capital ourselves.'

ABOVE
Azim Premji (seated, fifth from left) with the senior leadership of the IT businesses at an annual managers' meeting in the mid-1990s.

As the old millennium gave way to the new, Wipro faced a changeover of its own. Businesses were booming and the future looked brighter than ever before. And Wipro's IT business needed a leader who felt at home in the changing world.

To lead the business, Premji picked SR Gopalan, a sharp, no-nonsense Wipro veteran. The capital for Wipro Finance came from the corporate kitty as well as borrowings from financial institutions and public deposits. Thus armed, Wipro Finance sought out high-risk, high-return areas for the deployment of capital. Primary among these were technology products such as computers, medical systems and the like—aligning with the interests of Wipro Infotech, Wipro-GE and Wipro Peripherals—and also car financing, commercial real estate and emerging sectors, such as renewable energy and pollution control.

Given that the team had been initially looking to form a joint venture with GE Capital, they found it exciting to benchmark against the American giant, which was, at that time, responsible for more than half of GE's profitability, revenue and market cap. 'In 1993, the corporate executive council did a visioning exercise. We looked at taking the company from Rs 300 million to Rs 3,000 million, largely on the back of Wipro Finance,' says Suresh Senapaty, then part of the Wipro Infotech group.

In 1994–95, Premji's newest venture seemed to be living up to all expectations: Wipro Finance accounted for a third of the group's profits at Rs 150 million and was accorded the same respect as long-established NBFCs. The very next year, its net worth rose to Rs 765 million, and in 1996–97, it launched two subsidiaries: Wipro Factors for receivables financing, and Wipro Securities for investment banking and issue-management support to new ventures. For a brief, shining moment, it looked like the dream would come true: Wipro Finance would account for 50 per cent of Premji's diversified, integrated corporation.

But it was not to be. 'We went into finance because it was an absolutely booming business. We didn't realize the complexities of collecting money,' says Premji. 'We didn't take care of our accounts receivables. We didn't do our due diligence of the parties we lent to. It was bad risk-management and execution. We underestimated the number of crooks in the business.'

Wipro Finance's defaulters ranged across the spectrum. Some simply pleaded inability to pay up. Others had the same asset financed multiple times, making repossession impossible. Some of the companies that borrowed didn't even exist, except on paper. Yet others misappropriated loans, which became hard to trace. This was by no means a problem Wipro Finance faced alone. It was a widely prevalent practice that would lead to a big crisis in the NBFC sector a few years later.

When the first of these cases cropped up, business was still booming, and anomalies were perhaps easy to overlook. By 1996–97, the defaults began impacting cash flow. But it was still too soon to give up. Indeed, the next year, Wipro Finance was renamed Wipro Prosper during a brand redesign, because 'we had plans to start a bank and an insurance service', says Lan.

These were not the only big bets. In 1997, Wipro Finance worked its tech core by launching Ezy Cash, India's first-ever prepaid cash card, along with the local unit of the US company VeriFone. A second tech-related venture was the Financial Information Systems (FIS) service, launched with the news agency Reuters, to provide instant updates on capital, money markets and foreign exchange for anyone with currency exposure.

Gopalan had hoped these prescient initiatives would generate substantial revenues for the business. However, after a super-successful year in an India still unfamiliar with credit cards, Ezy Cash became untenable when the RBI insisted that deposits with NBFCs like Wipro Finance required payment of interest. The FIS service continued, but by 1997–98, the ever-growing list of non-performing assets—the fallout of the rash lending policies of the earlier years—became impossible to ignore. 'From profits of Rs 150 million, we came down to Rs 15 million within a year,' says Lan.

Many of Wipro's competitors in the business were in the same boat. The buoyant feeling of the initial years was gone. It was a largely unregulated space with no entry barriers and inadequate hygiene. Some of the big names started defaulting on payments and it had a dominoes effect. The crisis came to a head in 1997. Thousands of such companies wrapped up business.

Perhaps, the last straw was an income-tax raid on Wipro Finance's Bangalore office in January 1998. 'It was painful. A borrower had come under the tax scanner. We were not directly involved, but we faced the raid,' remembers Lan. 'This was the time when we were thinking of going global, so it affected our image. It accelerated our decision to wind down the business.'

But unlike many others, Wipro Finance paid back all its outstanding debts. 'The write-off was something like 30 per cent of Wipro's net worth. We could have declared ourselves insolvent—it was a separate company—but we chose to pay back every paisa,' Premji says.

It was an ending no one could have foreseen, but it contained a valuable lesson: Wipro realized it had

ABOVE
The Wipro headquarters on Sarjapur Road, Bangalore. Located nearly 30 km from Bangalore's central business district, it seemed an unlikely spot for a global IT company to base itself, when construction began at the turn of the millennium. The campus was designed by Mistry Architects.

A significant moment in the story came in 1996, when Premji, scion of a storied Bombay family, shifted base to Bangalore. 'Wipro couldn't afford Bombay anymore,' he says. But the move was an unequivocal signal that this was the city from where Wipro would reach for greatness.

little appetite for a capital-intensive business in an ecosystem incompatible with its values.

❖❖❖

From a mere Rs 63 million in 1990–91, WSL's revenues grew to Rs 436.51 million in 1993–94, while Infotech chalked up Rs 3,207 million. It marked the first time Wipro's IT division outstripped the combined revenues of WCP, WFP, Wipro Biomed and Wipro Lighting, which all together made a total of Rs 2,616.4 million. There was little doubt now as to where the path to the future lay, but that road was not an easy one: it was built with grit and rigor, vision and ingenuity, bold decisions and out-of-the-box moves.

One such move was the decision to unite Infotech and Systems into a single Wipro Infotech Group under Soota and appoint Senapaty, coming off a successful run at WCP, as the CFO in 1992. His first task was to decentralize the financial structure, converting lines of business into P&L operations, much like the way WCP worked. The injection of financial discipline and some smart accounting raised the group's profile with bankers, who had till then been skeptical of the lack of tangible collaterals in the services industry.

After Senapaty became Wipro 's CFO, in 1995, and the Infotech Group merged with the parent company to maximize cash flows and promote corporate flexibility, Wipro made its first large-scale hiring of 1,400 engineers in one go. 'It was a landmark for the software services industry at that time,' says Ranjekar, who had just moved to Corporate HR from WCP. Previously, only TCS was thought to possess the depth to absorb so many recruits at one time.

A quieter, but no less significant, moment came in 1996, when Premji, scion of a storied Bombay family, shifted base to Bangalore. 'We couldn't afford Bombay anymore,' he says, shrugging and downplaying the personal cost of the decision as is typical of him.

Premji recognized that if Wipro was to be a world-class Indian company, it needed to be synonymous with quality, in processes and outcomes.

Wipro had already acquired International Organization for Standardization (ISO) certifications for its computer and peripherals factories, followed by software and support services, and Global R&D.

But Premji knew it was not enough. V Chandrasekaran, who had taken over as chief executive of Wipro Systems from Subramaniam, agreed. He felt that Wipro would benefit greatly from better processes.

Accordingly, the group's vice president, AL Rao, signed up for the Capability Maturity Model (CMM) designed by the Software Engineering Institute at Carnegie Mellon University. Wipro Systems and Global R&D were assessed at levels 3 and 4 initially, indicating standard, consistent processes. But a competitive WSL focused on reducing the rejection index of services deliverables. It went down from 5 per cent to 3 per cent and by December 1998, it moved up to level 5, making Wipro only the sixth company worldwide to achieve that rank.

It was a major moment for Wipro, and especially for Premji, who drove the effort himself. 'Otherwise, as the largest organization-wide initiative till then, it'd have never got off the ground,' he says. It validated his 1996 decision to launch a full-fledged Mission Quality, a roadmap to improve quality, inspired by GE's Welch, who had taken it up to further push profits and productivity at his company.

The name came from Subroto Bagchi, who was in charge of Mission Quality. Bagchi had zeroed in on Motorola's Six Sigma methodology. The four-phase system—measure, analyze, improve, control—could be applied to almost any function to improve efficiency, strengthen quality and positively impact bottom lines. Backed by Premji, Six Sigma found application in everything from recruitment processes—which came down from 78 days to 45 days—to collection cycles—which came down from 365 days to 120 days. The improvements impacted Wipro all round, making for fewer errors in processes, better adherence to delivery schedules and enviable efficiency upticks. Other advantages included enhanced teamwork and identification of new leaders. It also turned out to be a great marketing tool.

Taking off from the success of CMM and Six Sigma, Wipro pursued quality efforts periodically over the next decade. 'To me, all of Wipro's efforts on quality—in the early days of ISO, later, as a pioneer in Six Sigma, People Capability Maturity Model [PCMM], and still later on, in Lean—have been to make sure that we deliver on our commitments to our customers, day after day,' says Premji.

With the internal systems focused on quality and excellence, Wipro took a closer look at the image it projected to the world. Although Premji had taken a conscious lead on quality, the maverick artist-cum-brand-maestro Shombit Sengupta had a decisive role in shaping the branding. Brought on board initially by Pai for rebranding of Santoor, Sengupta announced at his first meeting that he would take up the job only if he could do an image

ABOVE
Not just the industry and clients, the Indian media, too, was taking note of Wipro's achievements. A business magazine featured Wipro on the cover in May 1998, marking the brand relaunch with the rainbow flower logo just ahead of its emergence on the global stage.

makeover for the entire company, from soap to software services, that too for a fee far larger than WCP's budget.

What followed was an exhaustive, years-long exercise that forced Wipro leaders to look within before they could even look out. Again, it was Premji's tacit support that brought around reluctant chief executives to Sengupta's proposed idea of a single Wipro story. But even the Chairman balked when the designer proposed changing the six Wipro Beliefs, articulated back in the 1970s.

'Even though they were clamoring for a logo, I explained to them that in a demand-led market like India, brand was less important than the connect between a company's value system and the consumer,' says Sengupta. 'I thought the Wipro Beliefs were the unfriendliest part of the company—they looked inward, excluding the customer completely—and suggested replacing them with four customer-focused promises.'

These were: 'human values', emphasizing sensitivity to the unique needs of customers and employees; 'integrity', promising deliveries of commitments with honesty, fairness, reliability and uprightness; 'innovative solutions' to customer needs; and 'value for money' through continuous improvement in quality, cost and speed. Once Wipro accepted this interpretation of its core values, Sengupta went ahead with designing a new logo. It was the Rainbow Flower, inspired by a rainbow Sengupta had witnessed in coastal France. The artist in him transposed this motif on to a sunflower. This composite flower conveyed Wipro's organic growth: the central disc floret lent itself to a digital interpretation; the rain-washed freshness of the petals stood for resilience and human values; and the rainbow colors symbolized integrity and renewal. It was accompanied by the legend: 'Applying Thought'.

After six months of back and forth, Premji finally accepted the package. Launched in 1998, the Rainbow Flower became an immediate talking point within the company and in the larger world. As Wipro began making its presence felt globally, the Rainbow Flower set Wipro apart as a vibrant, diversified conglomerate with an array of offerings, and decades of experience and skill.

❖❖❖

Instant name recognition, though, seemed a distant prospect to the pioneering engineers and managers who went out to win the West through much of the 1990s.

'Why-pro? What's Why-pro? From I-ndia? Between I-raq and I-ran?' Wipro's best and brightest soon became used to the befuddled responses from the other side of the phone line; they actually counted themselves lucky that their call had been answered at all. They hung on to their sense of humor, rekindled their flagging spirits and wangled an appointment to explain in person that Why-pro was actually Wipro, was from In-dia and deserved their business.

For most of them, that first call, opening up new territories, was preceded by an average of nine months of scouring Yellow Pages and industry directories, punching numbers into a phone, dealing with voicemail and staring at blank walls. 'I didn't get a single call returned in my first seven to eight months,' says Sanjay Gupta, a decided sales star at Wipro Infotech for close to a decade. 'Which was ironical because, when I left India for New Jersey in 1997, everyone was talking about Y2K.'

The 'millennium bug', as it was called, had a large role to play in the global recognition that Indian tech talent has today. Through the 1990s, apprehension grew that mid-century computing systems using the dd/mm/yy format—the first two digits of the year knocked off to save expensive space—would read 1 January 2000 as 1 January 1900. The fears ran especially high in the banking and financial sectors, where there was the dread of corrupted ledgers and malfunctioning ATMs. The fix involved a large number of tedious hours spent combing through millions of lines of code. A number of Wipro's competitors sniffed out the panic early and bagged most of the available contracts, a move that would pay off in unforeseen ways in later years.

Wipro, still riding high on its hard-earned credentials based on R&D work, joined the party when the pickings had already grown slim.

My first client, after eight months of relentless and random cold-calling, was Addison Wesley Longman, a publishing company that needed Y2K remediation,' says Gupta. 'It was one of the few [such projects] Wipro ever did. But that first win was such a relief!'

Gupta's experience was, painfully, replicated across the US and Europe, into the new millennium. A few lucky ones, such as Makarand Teje, landed in a new country, the US, and took over existing accounts in the Bay area. Most, like Rajan Kohli in the West Coast or Srini Pallia in Minneapolis or even Nagendra Bandaru in the UK, found themselves confronting months-long dry spells in alien cultures.

'And to think I chose the Midwest over Chicago or New York!' says Pallia. 'But I felt the challenge lay in opening up a market. Also, there were ten to

I was always impressed at how Wipro was learning the verticals and picking some, that they were just going to be super strong and deep in. The idea of taking human talent that was there in India and constantly retraining people on the latest stuff, working on a global basis, having to adapt ... There was this year 2000 thing which generated some business, but then there was this question of how do you grow from that point and, like Microsoft, Wipro has had to constantly learn new things. And when you actually do it with lots of people, that agility isn't easy to have. So, it's great that it has continued to this day.

Bill Gates,
Microsoft

fifteen Fortune 500 companies in the region. I thought if I could make a dent there, it'd make a difference both to myself and to Wipro. And within two years, we had at least five big brands as our clients, and I was the most valued person in sales two years running.'

Like Gupta, his boss Pallia managed to open his first account in Retail, a new domain for Wipro, only after eight to nine months. 'Failure was not an option,' he says. 'I'd landed in the US with my wife and my one-year-old daughter. For the first two weeks, I worked out of the public library, since I didn't have a laptop or mobile phone, or even a credit card to buy them with! Till such time I got an office on a low rent, I worked out of our tiny apartment. But mine is not the only such story. We didn't hire people to create the US market for us: passionate Wiproites parachuted into the US and worked to be successful and make Wipro successful. That is how Wipro Technologies was built.'

While there was no significant pressure from back home—business unit leaders in India knew there was nothing they could tell these men that they were not already beating themselves up about—for the most part, it was a long, lonely struggle for Wipro's tech pioneers. Perhaps it enhanced the triumph, when it finally came, of breaking into fresh sectors such as retail and financial services.

For all the exploration of foreign shores and future prospects, Wipro's software services continued to undersell when compared to its hardware and related services till 1999–2000. Among the several success stories Soota crafted over this period, perhaps the most startling was the Wipro Genius PC. Sidelined by a 1993 Wipro-Acer joint venture for computers, the homegrown PC was relaunched in 1998 as the SuperGenius, to coincide with the adoption of the Rainbow Flower logo. Despite a four-year absence from the market, it helped Wipro best rivals in computer system revenues for three consecutive years. The joint venture died in 1999.

❖❖❖

In the R&D section of the business, Mitta—having proved India could pull off high-caliber outsourcing—grew keen to develop Wipro's own intellectual properties. But Premji, unsure of their marketability, suggested an alternative: he would seed EnThink, a new company for Mitta, who would license the products developed at Global R&D.

Mitta was not the only one bitten by the entrepreneurial bug. The late 1990s saw a significant start-up wave in India, helmed by experienced professionals who wanted to try out their own ideas. Among them was Bagchi, who quit Wipro in 1998 to work with an MNC and, within months, began thinking of his own start-up. He found like-minded partners in N Krishna Kumar, then heading Infotech's e-commerce division, Kalyan Banerjee and NS Parthasarathy, both with Global R&D. But the cherry on their cake was Soota, who was also looking to do something on his own. Together with some others, they birthed a business-enabling solutions and technologies company called MindTree in 1999. A year later, they were joined by S Janakiraman, chief of Global R&D. And, separately, Mitta too brought down the curtains on his glorious twenty-year career at Wipro.

As the old millennium gave way to the new, Wipro faced a transformation of its own. Businesses were booming, and the future looked brighter than ever before. The leaders that Soota and Mitta had groomed were ready to take their place at the global table. And Wipro needed a commander at home in the changing world. Premji found him at GE, the company he had looked up to for so long.

Vivek Paul was India-born, US-educated, with stints at both Wipro-GE (president and CEO, 1993–95) and GE Medical Systems (GM of the global CT business, 1996–99). Aggressive, imposing and at ease in Wipro's two most important territories, he seemed just the person to shake up the technology business and drive it into the 2000s.

❖❖❖

Wipro's market cap peaked at Rs 695,280 million in January 2000, as the BSE hit its highest point till that date.[5] Media interest now spilled over into Premji's personal life. Reports speculated that if the owner of 75 per cent of Wipro sold his holdings, 'the money … could buy Reliance and Hindustan Lever, India's largest corporations, and Infosys'.[6] Premji, now crowned 'the richest Indian ever', dismissed the figures as 'notional'.

But the conversation on IT-generated wealth, which had been swirling around in the sector for a while, now came to a head. Within Wipro, there was some resentment over inequitable distribution, especially in contrast to other IT companies, which garnered many feel-good headlines around this time over employee stock options.

Then corporate treasurer, Shankar Jaganathan, however, points out that the comparison was unfair, especially because Wipro had introduced the Wipro Equity Reward Trust in 1984, followed by Wipro Employee Stock Option Plan in the late 1990s. 'Wipro was an established company that used

RIGHT
Azim Premji and his A-team (from left) Ram Agarwal, Suresh Senapaty, Arun Thiagarajan, MS Rao and Dileep Ranjekar on the cover of a newsmagazine, March 2000.

Wipro's market cap peaked at Rs 69,528 crore in January 2000, making Premji, as the largest shareholder, the richest Indian at the time. He dismissed the figures as 'notional'.

LEFT
A number of leaders left Wipro to form MindTree, a start-up in the tech space, in 1999. The founders (sitting, from left): Anjan Lahiri, Ashok Soota, Scott Staples, (standing, from left) Kalyan Banerjee, Rostow Ravanan, S Janakiraman, Subroto Bagchi, N Krishnakumar, Kamran Ozair, NS Parthasarathy.

stock options as a retention tool or as variable compensation for senior managers. It was never given in lieu of salary,' he says, whereas start-ups like Infosys typically offset lower compensations with stock options.

For Premji, a long-time believer in the social purpose of business, there was another conflict to resolve as well. 'From the late 1990s, [I began thinking about] the need for expanding the roles of private corporations in society,' he would later say in a speech at an event.[7] 'Do private corporations exist only to create value for their immediate shareholders? Or do they have another role to play?

'The more I thought about it, the more convinced I got that we needed to play a role beyond business. ... [We have] been fortunate enough to be successful. This success had given us a certain voice and influence in society. In my view, this voice and influence came with a responsibility to engage with society beyond issues of business.' Over the next few years, this thought process would lead to multiple small and big socially minded initiatives in healthcare, education, environment and sustainability, peaking with the establishment of the Azim Premji Foundation. But more on that later.

❖❖❖

In its 1994–95 annual report, when profit after taxes was Rs 321.9 million, Wipro set down goals for the new millennium: by 2000, it hoped to be among the top ten Indian corporations, and increase value and profitability for stakeholders, looking to take in Rs 3,000 million in profit after taxes. In the report for 1999–2000, Premji announced that they had exceeded their target by Rs 6 million. And lest one think their job was done, he followed it up by saying, 'With hindsight ... the goal should have been more ambitious.'

With Paul at the helm, Wipro was ramping up its ambition. At a landmark visioning exercise for 150-odd senior members of the Wipro leadership in 2000, Ghoshal led the ground-up formulation of the war-cry '4x4': a turnover of $4 billion by 2004. Paul declared, 'This is not empty vision. It is an opportunity that this country has not had in centuries. It is really up to us to seize the moment.'

Notwithstanding a few skeptics—led by seventeen-year veteran Sudip Banerjee who felt that the market wasn't big enough for this goal yet—4X4 was seared into every leader's consciousness the next day, when Premji, then fifty-five, appeared without his distinctive moustache: he claimed the target made him feel young and energized. He had come a full circle from his earliest days with the company, when, as a twenty-one-year-old, he had grown a moustache to add gravitas to his personality.

Few at Wipro remained unaffected by Paul. 'He injected a lot of hope, a lot of optimism, a great sense of freedom, the belief that we were on the cusp of big change,' recalls Pratik Kumar, whom Paul chose to lead his HR team.

The first US-based CEO of an Indian tech corporation, Paul introduced global internal practices to the growing company—the headcount was around 6,500 at the time—such as writing a weekly mailer and putting in place SAP processes, which touched every employee.

The early 2000s was a period of growth for the Indian IT industry. Paul focused strongly on enterprise services and on acquisitions as drivers for Wipro's growth. His strategy marked a departure. 'We had to understand the customers' businesses – that was good change for Wipro. It helped us understand individual vertical markets and we were a little ahead of the competition in thinking like this,' says Bhanumurthy Ballapuram, President and Chief Operating Officer at Wipro, in retrospect. He sums up Wipro's changing direction in terms of three outcomes: Acquisition of new customers, expanding into new territories and growing new capabilities like in applications or infrastructure.

In the first few years of the new millennium, US-based leaders, such as Gupta, Pallia, Kohli and Teje, opened one coveted logo account after another: Best Buy, Target, 3M, Hollywood Videos, British American Tobacco, Farmers Insurance, Putnam Investments, Capital One, Mastercard, JP Morgan, Hartford Insurance and Northwestern Insurance in BFSI. Across the pond, in the UK, the energy and utilities sector threw up Southern Water, Thames Water and Wales West Utilities.

While none of these wins was easy, the Western economy at the turn of the century formed a rising tide that lifted all Indian IT boats; thus Wipro was competing with many of its domestic rivals away from home. Nor was it all plain sailing. The dotcom crash of 2000 triggered a telecom bust that took down core Wipro customers such as AT&T and Nortel, then worth $30 million together to Wipro.

Around the same time, long-standing client initiated tough price negotiations. Things came to a head when GE wanted a stake in Wipro Technologies as well as proposing reduction in price. When Premji rejected the idea, GE walked out. 'These two crucial moments [the telecom bust and GE walking away]

Practicing values

to create value. It's about understanding and responding to the needs of our customers, employees, shareholders and the society at large. It's about being aware and responsible for the social and business environment. With actions based on a foundation of values. It's about creating an organisation that is ever changing, yet with a constant expression; of integrity, of trust, of continuity. And that is what we believe makes us who we are.

WIPRO
Applying Thought

Corporate Overview 2005

led us to pivot from a 63 per cent R&D business to a 63 per cent enterprise business in a span of five years,' explains Sangita Singh, vice president and chief marketing officer for Wipro Technologies between 2001 and 2005.

But these years also set a change in Wipro's culture. With multiple opportunities and global ambitions to pursue, each business division took complete responsibility for its own growth. With a CEO in Santa Clara, Wipro's strong entrepreneurial culture, and a 'my-business-first attitude', the strong operational glue between verticals and service lines began to weaken. In addition, the declining share and voice of the R&D services business, Wipro's strong suit for well over two decades, created a new set of challenges for Wipro (more on that later).

And then there was 9/11. Premji was actually in the New York area to meet clients when the planes flew into the twin towers at the World Trade Center on that morning of 2001. Four Wipro employees working with Kohli's client March & McLennan, housed on the ninety-seventh floor of Tower One, died in the terrorist attacks, while a fifth had a narrow escape. Wipro memorialized the deceased by naming conference rooms in its Sarjapur campus after them.

The 9/11 tragedy also exposed a fault line that Wipro failed to counter. The system redundancies developed for Y2K helped the telecom and transport services to recover right after the attacks. The financial markets, too, were able to open within five days, thanks to the back-up processes put in place for Y2K. The tech companies that had gained a toehold in that space thus acquired a competitive edge over Wipro, especially in the BFSI game.

However, business was so abundant that these setbacks hit Wipro only fleetingly. If one client pulled out, there were two others lining up to take its place. The only concern was juggling deployment and ensuring a pipeline of available engineers, so much so that the employee headcount grew to 40,000 by 2005, making Wipro the largest private sector employer in India.

As outlined in the 4x4 strategy document, Paul also spearheaded acquisitions in a bid to help Wipro evolve into an end-to-end solutions provider. With an aim of contributing $1.6 billion towards the $4 billion target, Wipro's buys began in 2002 with Spectramind, one of India's first business process outsourcing (BPO) outfits set up by entrepreneur Raman Roy, who had previously helped American Express and GE with their BPO operations in the country. The second bead in Wipro's 'string of pearls' acquisition strategy was NerveWire, a Massachusetts-based consulting firm in the financial services business: Wipro expected its ninety domain experts to add forty client relationships to their portfolio. In between, the company also picked up AMS's global energy business.

While Wipro did not realize the $4 billion target, Paul grew the IT business from $150 million to $1.4 billion by the time he put in his papers in 2005. More intangible, but perhaps as critical, was the image makeover Wipro underwent in these six frenetic years. From a competent but low-key Indian company, it came to be regarded globally as a powerhouse of tech talent. If the world took notice of the NYSE listing, where Premji and Paul stood as equals with Welch and Grasso, its solid record in execution and delivery lent depth to the newfound recognition.

❖❖❖

To say this decade and a half was transformative for Wipro would probably be an understatement. It was no longer a consumer products company first with solid capability in hardware. By 2005 Wipro was known the world over as an IT company first, with allied businesses in FMCG and hydraulics. The only part of the story that remained unchanged was Premji and the values that he imparted to his company from his earliest days.

The theme of the 2004–05 annual report summed it up well: Wipro believed it created value by practising values. In his letter to the stakeholders, Premji wrote, 'Our unyielding commitment to Wipro Values has been, I believe, the core reason of our success.' The report outlined how the company created value not only for shareholders but also for customers, through quality and innovation; for its employees, through building technology, and behavioral and leadership competencies; and for the larger community, by improving the quality of school education.

Wipro took ownership of the idea that economic progress and social progress went hand-in-hand. The next phase, the report signed off, would be 'Wipro's journey into the soul of its business'. ◆

wipro

2005–2020

It is more difficult to give money away intelligently than to earn it in the first place.

Andrew Carnegie

Chapter I **6** I 2005–2020

A Role Beyond Business

In the latest part of its story, Wipro has undergone several changes that have carved out a distinct position for it in the world.

Central to this was Azim Premji giving away most of his economic ownership of Wipro Ltd to the Azim Premji Foundation, thereby making it the single largest stakeholder of the company. Set up in 2001, to contribute to developing a 'just, equitable, humane and sustainable society', the Foundation started its work to help improve the Indian public education system. Over the years, Premji's philanthropy has made the Foundation's endowment one of the largest in the world, enabling it to scale-up and broaden its work significantly, a process that continues unabated. All this makes Wipro Ltd an unusual business enterprise, where most of the economic value it creates for its shareholders goes directly towards serving some of the most disadvantaged and vulnerable people of the world through the work of the Foundation.

Along with redirecting the value created by Wipro Ltd to philanthropic causes, Premji planned his succession too. One major step in this direction was the appointment of Rishad Premji as chief strategy officer for Wipro's IT business in 2010, three years after he joined the company. On 31 July 2019, Rishad succeeded the senior Premji as Chairman of Wipro Ltd. Right from the time of Rishad's induction into the information technology business in 2007, Premji had insisted that Rishad's appointment was not a step toward his taking take over as the chief executive officer. This instead represented

Premji described the 2008 financial crisis as a reset cycle rather than a recession cycle. While Wipro's target was to grow ahead of the competition in each business, the world of technology and its clients faced real disruption after 2008. The IT landscape was being restructured and reimagined.

ABOVE
Launched in 2006, the Electronic City campus became a showcase for Wipro's businesses focused on environmental sustainability. The campus includes a biodiversity zone and a butterfly park, and has its own paper pulping plant and micro windmill. It also harvests rainwater.

continuity of ownership in Wipro Ltd, a need made even more pertinent by the subsequent transfer of economic ownership of Premji's shares to the Foundation.

The third significant change in this period was the demerger of the three non-IT businesses from the IT business (Wipro Ltd) to form Wipro Enterprises Ltd (WEL) in 2013. On an exponential growth path ever since, WEL has explored new territories with a rare cultural sensitivity, seizing opportunities around the world and establishing its leadership position in the industries it operates in.

In comparison, this period was relatively turbulent for Wipro's technology business. The turmoil was brought on by the global recession triggered by the financial meltdown of 2008, which, coupled with some key technology changes, led to disruption in business models of several client industries. This was further exacerbated by some factors internal to the company.

Despite the recession, changes in the global IT delivery model and the consumerization of IT, Wipro's IT business held on to a steady growth, crossing $5 billion in revenue during 2008–09. This was accompanied by significant leadership changes, along with noticeable changes in some aspects of the culture—both of which would later have significant impact on Wipro Ltd.

❖❖❖

The early 2000s were boom years for the Indian IT industry. Thanks to its deep technological roots, investments in new capabilities and domains, expansion into new territories and aggressive acquisitions, Wipro was well positioned to make the most of it.

In 2004, Wipro Technologies (as the Global IT Business was called then) crossed $1 billion in turnover, on the base of growing business from many existing clients and propelled by expanding IT services opportunities in new industries such as energy, utilities and retail. For instance, in 2004, Wipro Technologies bagged a long-term $1.1 billion contract with Anglo-Dutch energy major Shell, covering IT applications, maintenance and infrastructure support. In early 2008, Wipro Infotech (the India and Middle East focused IT business) bagged a nine-year, $500 million contract with mobile network operator Aircel in India, followed by a $550 million deal with Uninor (now Telenor) the following year.

While Wipro's growth was coming from a diverse set of industry verticals, its closest rivals were riding high mostly on IT opportunities from the banking, financial services and insurance industries. The difference would become starker in the following years.

After Vivek Paul's departure in 2005, Premji had taken on direct responsibility for Wipro Technologies, with five executive presidents reporting to him. Among these, apart from PR Chandrasekhar, who joined the business in 2000, four—Girish Paranjpe, Suresh Vaswani, Sudip Banerjee and AL Rao—had had long careers in Wipro.

Part of the reason for creating such a structure was that Premji did not have a clear successor in mind after Paul left. At the same time, he did not want to go outside the company to hire a CEO. His plan was that this interim period, in which he was directly responsible for the IT business, would allow him to assess and decide on the next CEO for the IT business. In hindsight, it was not the most optimal organizational situation. The absence of a clear executive leader created an operational vacuum, as also a strain on the culture of the organization.

This situation was very different from how Premji had grown and run Wipro, but for the very initial part of his tenure. Ever since the late 1970s, when he had separated the businesses into independent units, Premji had assumed the role of the custodian of Wipro's values and set the overall direction and vision for Wipro, while the CEOs ran the business operationally and worked with him to translate those values across the organization. With Premji having to manage both these roles now, and given that Wipro had always been fiercely entrepreneurial, a structure like this seeded fragmentation of its operational culture, which, along with some other significant developments later, hobbled Wipro Ltd's growth in this period.

❖❖❖

Most observers inside Wipro and elsewhere, had believed Premji would choose one of his five presidents to be the next CEO. The announcement, when it came in 2008, surprised most people. Premji named not one but two CEOs: Girish Paranjpe (head of the BFSI business) and Suresh Vaswani (president of Wipro Infotech).

The two-CEO structure was unusual but not unknown—at least one other IT major had a similar structure. Premji believed their complementary strengths would benefit Wipro and allow it to integrate the global and India–Middle East IT businesses to leverage complex deals. 'Their leadership qualities were very different: Suresh was all about the numbers; Girish would come to them last. Suresh was rigorous and action-oriented; Girish was the strategic big-picture thinker. And both had a very, very strong employee connect. It isn't easy to create that kind

LEFT
In 2008, Wipro's IT business appointed two CEOs, Suresh Vaswani (left), then president of Wipro Infotech, and Girish Paranjpe, then president of the BFSI vertical.

Taking over from the joint CEOs, Kurien adopted a two-pronged approach. To defend the existing IT business, he sought to make Wipro's offerings more efficient. Alongside, he invested in new technologies, setting up a separate unit to focus on digital transformation.

LEFT
TK Kurien, president, Wipro Consulting, Telecoms and Strategic Initiatives, took over as CEO in 2011, when Wipro dismantled the two-CEO format.

of loyalty in a professional set-up. But both did,' says Jatin Dalal, then with Corporate Treasury. Dalal would go on to become chief financial officer of Wipro Ltd in 2015.

But 2008, the year the two CEOs entered office, was no ordinary year. Within six months of Paranjpe and Vaswani taking over, the simmering financial crisis in the US boiled over, scalding the world.

Wipro's IT business hadn't seen anything like this before. 'Every morning, we'd come in to work and see a BFSI account either shrink or evaporate [impacted by the financial meltdown]. Then came the telecom crisis, brought on by the arrival of cheaper Chinese makes. It really hit all the large European original equipment manufacturers (OEMs)—Motorola, Alcatel, Lucent, Nokia—and us, in turn, as they were all our clients,' remembers Dalal.

The two CEOs, recognizing that these were very stressful times, pulled out all the stops. 'They ran a very successful, very unique campaign,' remembers Dalal. 'It required teams to grow their margins by 10 per cent in four quarters. Though times were tough, the really hungry people—immediately marked as our next generation of leaders—managed to coax out positive growth. Unfortunately, it couldn't be sustained ... and, while our growth slipped, our competitors were performing better.'

For a brief while, it seemed Wipro would catch up. However, soon Wipro began to lag many of its peers in revenue and margin growth.

The financial crisis led to the worst recession the world had seen since the Great Depression of the 1930s. When the financial industry experienced a quick, sharp fall, governments around the world stepped in to stabilize the sector, leading it to recover sooner than expected. However, other industries took much longer to mend. This translated to a bigger blow to Wipro's business as compared to its peers, because Wipro had significant business in industries that took longer to rebound, and comparatively less significant business in the financial sector.

As often happens, tough external conditions magnify internal issues of organizations. The operational fragmentation seeded earlier combined with Wipro's deep entrepreneurial culture would have been inconsequential in a more benign environment, but this severe external turbulence fed those differences. The combined result of all these factors took a toll, and Wipro's IT business began to feel the strain. In 2008–9, IT business growth fell from 43 per cent the year before, to 18.5 per cent.

By the end of 2010, Premji sensed that a simpler organization structure with a new leader was likely to address many of the key issues being faced by the IT business. TK Kurien was appointed as the CEO in place of Vaswani and Paranjpe. The sudden departure of the joint CEOs, both with long Wipro tenures, rattled many within the company. In these circumstances, Kurien started with a calming hand—but he would soon shake things up himself, much of which was necessary.

❖❖❖

Wipro was facing internal challenges along those in the world it inhabited and the world of technology, and its clients were facing real disruption. The IT landscape was being restructured and reimagined. The emergence of free, open-source operating systems like Linux and the mainstreaming of internet-based platforms like Facebook, Apple, Amazon, Netflix and Google (FAANG) changed forever the way industries—right from banking to utilities to healthcare—thought about technology.

Businesses needed a swift transition to cloud and mobile technology, which in turn had to enable many more functions, be it marketing, finance or operations. Traditional consumers of IT renewed focus on cost and flexibility, demanding new usage models and changed financial contracts.

Wipro recognized that a rapid response was essential if its customers were to achieve all these goals. Kurien pursued a two-pronged approach: defending the existing IT business by making Wipro's offerings more efficient, while simultaneously investing in new technologies and setting up a separate unit, Wipro Digital, to focus on digital transformation. This was a bold call, made well before clients started investing significant money in a shift toward digital technologies.

A key part of this new technology strategy was Wipro Holmes, an automation platform, the name a cheeky riposte to IBM's Watson. For clients such as Citibank, looking to make their existing IT infrastructure more cost-effective and improve productivity by using technologies like automation, Wipro Holmes worked out brilliantly. 'Building straight-through processing, increasing automation, eliminating manual touch points—these were all high priorities for us,' says Jagdish Rao, Citi's global technology head. 'Wipro's investment in the Holmes platform was actually very encouraging for us. It's made a significant difference in automating many previous processes with manual handoffs,' he says.

❖❖❖

Designit®
a **wipro** company

The Designit expertise enhanced the perception of Wipro Ltd's customer-centricity. It told the world that Wipro Ltd was ready for a digital future.

ABOVE
A schematic depicting the Designit way of solving problems.

TOP
Rajan Kohli, global head of Wipro Digital and Consulting, at Designit's Copenhagen office.

OPPOSITE PAGE
A Wipro Digital team at work in London.

Wipro Digital was deliberately designed to be different from Wipro Ltd on many counts.

While most IT services companies focused on technology alone, Wipro Ltd offered an integrated approach of strategy, design and technology, all under one roof. This was unlike how things were done so far. Clients typically went to one set of firms to get strategy advice, another for design when required, and then to technology companies like Wipro Ltd to operationalize that strategy and design. Recognizing that technology and business were now two sides of the same coin, and that clients wanted complete ownership of outcomes from their service partners, Wipro Ltd decided to offer these capabilities under one roof.

Predicting that Digital would grow to be one of its strongest service lines, Wipro Ltd moved Rajan Kohli, then senior vice president and global head of BFSI, to lead Wipro Digital in 2015. But it was clear that building each capability ground-up was simply not feasible. The Wipro Ltd leadership zeroed in on Designit, one of the world's largest strategic design houses, which had made waves with its empathetic solutions addressing a cross-section of needs—from breast-cancer patients to millennial customers of banks. By this time, Wipro Ltd had enough experience in acquisitions across geographies and capabilities to be confident of making it work; it had also developed the ability to support a diversity of people, technologies, processes and practices.

Even so, Rishad, by then the chief strategy officer at Wipro Ltd, was thrown off by the first meeting with the Copenhagen-headquartered Designit in an arts bar in London. 'I remember thinking, "I don't think this is going to work. They're so different from us,"' says Rishad. 'But what we discovered at that meeting and over the next nine months is that our commonalities or the kinds of offerings or experiences of our companies mattered less than our value systems. The alignment of values and sensibilities was as important to them as to us.'

It was clear that the strategic acquisition would benefit both: Wipro Ltd in its move to scale up Wipro Digital and for Designit in its global ambitions. 'Wipro has been very entrepreneurial, which is who we are also as a company. So, that kind of spirit and that idea was very valuable and was very needed,' says Kjersti Lund, then global executive director of Designit.

Equally important, she says, was the respect with which Wipro Ltd approached Designit. By the time the $94 million deal was inked in July 2015, that sense of being a good fit had percolated through the organization. 'The teams across Europe actually celebrated the new collaboration by going out for Indian food,' Lund says. 'It was a very, very positive starting point.'

'Our engineers and designers had to work together—not an easy ask in a technology company,' says Kohli. 'Clients don't want thinking from one person and doing from somebody else. They don't have the time. That's why it was important to build the design–engineer–scale team end to end.'

❖❖❖

By most measures, it seemed that Wipro Ltd was doing all the right things to maximize the opportunities thrown up by a new world: energizing client-facing teams, identifying and investing in new technologies and building new partnership models. Yet something continued to be amiss as Wipro Ltd's growth lagged behind many of its competitors.

It was around this point that the Wipro Ltd leadership came around to recognizing aspects of its 'culture' as a factor in its dip in relative performance over the years, specifically in the way people and teams worked with each other.

It was an idea that needed more work, but Kurien had his hands full focusing on growth, clients and technology solutions. Also, he had (self-confessedly) an impatient, mercurial temperament, which sometimes intimidated his team and others around him. It was felt he needed a chief operating officer who could look inside Wipro Ltd, while the CEO

From a digital twin of an oil rig that allows for remote problem-solving to a virtual retail experience or an entirely automated vehicle, state-of-the-art technology at the innovation centers attests to Wipro's capability as an imaginative, creative thinker.

ABOVE
The Technovation Center in Bangalore mirrors the latest developments of the Silicon Valley Innovation Center, showcasing the best and latest of Wipro's technology innovations to the world.

TOP
Azim Premji at Wipro Ltd's Silicon Valley Innovation Center, Mountain View, California, 2018.

persisted with his vital front-facing role, as also as a likely successor to Kurien, who was nearing retirement. A long search led Premji to Abidali Neemuchwala, who had spent twenty-three years at TCS, most recently as the head of its BPO unit. Neemuchwala understood the value of culture and its invisible yet critical role in an organization, and was a good foil for Kurien.

Neemuchwala became CEO in 2016, upon Kurien's retirement from Wipro Ltd. He continued to build on Wipro's investment in technology and amped-up sales functions, while also improving client satisfaction and operational excellence.

The results could be seen best in accounts like the Lloyds Banking Group (LBG), which was undergoing a significant transition. In the aftermath of the financial crisis of 2008, LBG had to survive near bankruptcy and turn itself around on the back of a digital transformation of its business. Its new chief information officer, Morteza Mahjour, was on a mission to 'make revenue by doing digital and becoming customer-centric'. Wipro Ltd had long shared the LBG business pie with other Indian-origin service companies, and was up against stiff competition.

Mahjour met Kurien, Neemuchwala and Shaji Farooq, the president and chief executive for the BFSI business, having assessed that Wipro Ltd would not make the cut to be a digital transformation partner. The meeting was a turning point.'I got a sense of their commitment and transparency. They really took the strategy, understood it and came back with additional resources,' says Mahjour.

As LBG's digital transformation was underway, Wipro Ltd's rapid strides with Wipro Digital made all the difference, along with the added expertise of Designit. 'We took it as a demonstration of Wipro's customer-centricity, a sign that they were investing proactively in the account,' says Mahjour. He could see the company was transforming the organization for a more customer-centric, digital future. His feeling was vindicated again in 2020, two years after he left the company, when LBG renewed its digital deal with Wipro Ltd.

In these last few years, Wipro Ltd has driven ahead with its investment in technology and future-oriented businesses. This is often enabled by setting up localized teams in countries with those cutting-edge skills, along with significant investments and acquisitions that tap into the global technology innovation ecosystem.

Wipro Ltd is charging ahead to reclaim its roots as a company with technology leadership in its DNA. Today, it seems to be on its way. A glimpse of this is visible in the Technovation Centers in Mountain View, California, and in Bangalore.

Built to help clients engage first-hand with Wipro Ltd's technological and creative prowess, both innovation centers have immersive zones showcasing dramatic walk-through concepts, like a remote customer activity at a bank or a virtual reality (VR)-enhanced digitized experience of an oil rig that allows remote problem-solving, to a virtual retail encounter, and an entirely automated, state-of-the-art vehicle. A rapid prototype lab displays Wipro Ltd's investments in and optimization of robotics, drones, AI, machine vision, hyperspectral imaging, 3D printing and much more that back up Wipro Ltd's 750-odd patents.

❖❖❖

LEFT
Abidali Neemuchwala joined Wipro Ltd as its COO in 2015, and became the CEO following TK Kurien's retirement in 2016.

ABOVE
Amalner, Wipro's oldest outpost, continues to thrive, seventy-five years after it was set up. Today it is a factory manufacturing Santoor, the consumer business's leading domestic brand.

TOP
Vineet Agrawal, CEO of Wipro Consumer Care and Lighting, Bangalore, 2020.

In 2013, Wipro Enterprises Ltd demerged from Wipro Ltd as a private, non-listed company with revenues of nearly $2 billion. For the businesses grouped under WEL, this period has been one of realizing global ambitions.

WEL, WIN FOR THE WORLD

In the last fifteen years, Wipro Consumer Care & Lighting (WCCLG) and Wipro Infrastructure Engineering (WIN), which together now constitute Wipro Enterprises Limited (WEL), have scripted a story of dramatic success. In 2013, WEL demerged from Wipro Ltd, becoming a private, non-listed company, now with revenues of nearly $2 billion. WEL also has two joint ventures—Wipro-GE, set up in 1989, and Wipro Kawasaki, formed in 2011.

For these businesses, this period had been one of realizing global ambitions. It began on a high note with the acquisition of Unza in 2007. WCCLG was already on a spectacular growth trajectory with nine consecutive quarters of over 25 per cent organic growth (2006–08), making it the fastest-growing consumer business in India. But the acquisition of Unza, Southeast Asia's largest independent manufacturer and marketer of personal-care products, with operations in 40 countries and more than 4,000 employees at the time, would reshape even this trajectory.[1]

'Our intent was never to acquire such a big company,' says Vineet Agrawal. 'It fell into our laps and sort of spiraled. At $246 million, Unza was the biggest acquisition we were looking at across Wipro—its size was equal to our consumer business then.' But he had wide backing. Jagdish Sheth, one of the directors of the board then, recollects, 'I wanted us to buy Unza for two reasons: One, the Unza brands were very valuable. And two, WCCLG was still very domestic, but their competition would always be global.'

As they did their groundwork, Agrawal and his team became aware that Unza employees—who owned 30 per cent of the company—would prefer being bought over by a British or American business: cultural biases made them resistant to Indian ownership. The Wipro team worked around them to visit factories and study the numbers. But the 'drag-along' clause, which meant the buyer could buy 100 per cent of Unza even if the employees held out, helped WCCLG clinch the deal. Today, however, the erstwhile Unza employees are a full, enthusiastic and vibrant part of WCCLG.

The news of Wipro's acquisition of Unza shook the Asian FMCG world. Unza, which had a revenue of Rs 6,800 million for the year, took WCCLG revenue to more than Rs 15,000 million, and gave it a pan-Asia footprint overnight.

❖❖❖

Besides the mechanics of an overseas acquisition, the biggest takeaway for WCCLG in the Unza chapter lay in being culturally sensitive. Agrawal decided to move gently. 'There was some pressure to change the name immediately, but we stalled,' he remembers. 'Our first priority was to understand the business.'

But then it struck Agrawal that if they knew very little about the business they had acquired, the employees of that business knew even less about Wipro. Working with the Wipro tenet that people were the greatest asset, he drafted a plan to 'sell India and Wipro to Unza'.

In three batches, seventy-five Unza managers, mostly Malaysian Chinese, came to India, a country none of them had ever visited. 'We picked them up from the airport, made presentations about India, took them around the Electronic City campus to give them an idea of the size of Wipro, offered trips to Mysore or Agra,' remembers Agrawal. 'The climax of their visit was a group photo with AHP, whom they'd seen only on the "global rich" lists.'

When the apprehended personnel trouble erupted within two months of the takeover, the 20 per cent restricted stock units (RSUs) built into the buying price were rolled out immediately, which separated the stayers from the leavers. Those who signed up were overjoyed: RSUs had never been a practice at Unza. Wipro was as careful with HR policies, introducing no drastic changes but ensuring a balance between old practices and new.

On the business front, too, Wipro was deliberately slow and careful. They installed a single liaison person in each country to coordinate data, run internal audits and monitor compliance issues. Soon, they began quiet yet substantial value-adds to Unza's back-room processes, from manufacturing to loan restructuring to negotiating fragrance costs. The Unza team appreciated the inputs, more so when all savings accrued to the individual business units.

'We really pushed the manufacturing edge in terms of operating efficiency and shifted focus to more profitable categories of products. So, our margins got a double boost. The extra money went into advertising to build brands,' says Kumar Chander, who took over as managing director of

Wipro Unza Malaysia in 2009.

In many ways, Agrawal says, Unza helped them draft the WCCLG acquisition template: dealing with perceptions of the country and the company, understanding business practices, appreciating local nuances of commitment and delivery, and most importantly, building trust with a group of people whose very lives had been upturned by a change in ownership.

'Unza really helped Wipro and Vineet [Agrawal] understand a different customer psyche and gave them confidence for acquisitions,' says VS Kannan Sitaram, venture partner, Fireside Ventures, who observed WCCLG both as peer and competitor at Hindustan Lever and Dabur. 'Companies like Dabur and Marico followed the Indian diaspora, exporting their products first and then going onshore and moving on to acquisitions in those locations. Arguably, Santoor had no pull for the diaspora. So, they [WCCLG] went into different geographies [through acquisitions].'

Beginning 2009 (in that financial year, WCCLG crossed $500 million in revenue), the acquisition of the English brand Yardley took the company progressively deeper into the Middle East, and to Australia, north and west Africa and Europe, while the 2012 buyout of LD Waxson strengthened its presence in Hong Kong, Malaysia, Singapore, Taiwan and China. Following the demerger in 2013, WCCLG surged further into China by acquiring the family-run FMCG company Zhongshan Ma Er in 2016, and made inroads into the Philippines and South Africa, respectively, with personal-care companies Splash and Canway in 2019. Canway was the twelfth acquisition of WCCLG in sixteen years, capping a total spend of $950 million.

❖❖❖

If WCCLG asserted itself with the Unza acquisition, the engineering business symbolized its soaring ambition with a change in name in 2007. It dropped Wipro Fluid Power to call itself Wipro Infrastructure Engineering (WIN), indicating it would no longer limit itself to hydraulics.

The newfound drive could be traced to Anurag Behar. Charged in 2004 with determining the fate of the business, he assessed that its high-quality engineering capabilities and dominant market share in hydraulic cylinders in India (around 60 per cent then) made it an excellent launchpad for bigger ambitions. 'The hydraulic components we made were absolutely critical to our clients' products, and were difficult to engineer and manufacture. Which is why we would always be an integral part of our clients' long-term future product plans,' Behar says. 'This meant recurring business.'

By 2006–07, WIN's revenue was growing organically at 39 per cent over three consecutive years. With the fundamentals sound and with road-infrastructure projects, such as the Pradhan Mantri Gram Sadak Yojana, giving a fillip to key clients in the construction and earth-moving industries, Behar set about streamlining and scaling the existing business, diversifying into related segments and new geographies.

The first big step was the acquisition of the Sweden-based Hydrauto Group AB in 2006. 'It was the perfect fit,' says Sunil Rajagopalan of the $31 million Hydrauto deal, which included a 700-strong workforce, four plants in Sweden and one in Finland. 'Costs in Europe could be reduced by our India base, while we gained clients in Europe, and product lines,' he explains.

WIN, too, went about the integration of the acquired business methodically and with respect for the people of the acquired entity. It required the personal attention of the leadership team—for almost three years, Behar's life involved shuttling between India and Europe, three weeks here, then two weeks there. So was the case with the rest of WIN's leadership. This experience gave them the confidence and playbook for later acquisitions and expansion.

By the mid-2000s, Behar was convinced that climate change and environmental issues will be one of the defining forces for human society in the mid- and long-term. He remembers, 'I read journals like *Nature* every week and went for tutorials to scientists. Over a period of time I became absolutely clear that climate change will transform everything for society and so for business. We had to have a stand on it and then follow through with action,' Behar says. Pratik Kumar, Wipro's head of HR, and Lan, then head of treasury and investor relations, were his teammates in this process of discovery. True to his style, Premji debated and discussed this intensely, with Behar and others, with chats over lunch or walks, and also in quarter reviews and board meetings He picked the brains of global business leaders wherever he met them. 'One morning in 2006, AHP sent me a mail, "Ok, I am convinced, what should we do?"'says Behar.

Thus began Wipro's pioneering journey on environmental sustainability, complementing its already deep commitment to society. This manifested in Wipro pledging to becoming more sustainable (and continually achieving it)—on carbon footprint, water usage, waste, biodiversity and more. As also pursuing the development of businesses that leverage opportunities arising from the dynamics of climate change and the

WCCLG acquired Unza, Southeast Asia's largest independent personal-care company, in 2007. A few years later, Wipro strengthened its presence in the region by buying LD Waxson and then Zhongshan Ma Er. The 2009 acquisition of the English brand Yardley helped them make inroads into the Middle East, north and west Africa, Europe and Australia. In 2019, WCCLG acquired South African company Canway, its twelfth buy in sixteen years, capping a spend of $950 million.

efforts to contain it.

Consequently, Wipro founded two businesses in 2008 within WIN: Eco Energy and Wipro Water. Besides using learnings from Wipro's efforts toward reducing its own carbon footprint, Eco Energy tied up with fourteen global technology partners and solution providers to advise companies on reducing their carbon consumption. Wipro's new campus in Electronic City—the IT hub in Bangalore—became a showcase of sorts with a biodiversity zone, a butterfly park, rainwater harvesting, a paper pulping plant and a micro windmill.

The offering found takers among clients of Wipro's consumer and IT businesses: Among other projects, Eco Energy set up a geothermal data center for Aircel in Gurgaon; green lighting for Delhi Metro; a biogas plant for Taj Kovalam, Kerala; green lighting, cooling and recycling units at the Asian Paints greenfield plant in Rohtak, Haryana; and LED lights at the Indian Institute of Management Bangalore campus.

The water-treatment business—taking off from the expertise of its acquisition, Mumbai-based Aquatech Industries—adopted an engineering-procurement-construction format, building water-treatment plants for medium and large industrial clients.

Events moved rapidly in 2010, Behar moved to the Azim Premji Foundation and Pratik Kumar took charge as CEO of WIN. Kurien stepped in to lead Wipro EcoEnergy, which was separated from WIN. Soon after, Kurien took over as the CEO of the IT business, merging EcoEnergy in to the consulting part of the IT business. Wipro Water continues to grow within WIN.

❖❖❖

The demerger from the IT business, in 2013, was 'aimed at realizing the growth aspirations of all our businesses', as Premji puts it. 'It was just causing too much confusion with investors. The IT business was really the bigger part of the business. Plus, we wanted to take more risks in the consumer business with acquisitions,' explains Premji. 'This demerger [was to] enhance value for our stakeholders and provide momentum for growth by giving each of the businesses greater flexibility.'

It was a particularly eventful period for WCCLG. While the company was in the throes of the demerger, Agrawal was finalizing the acquisition of LD Waxson and was shedding its vanaspati brand, Sunflower, the very origins of the company.

'Sunflower had been at the core of the business for many of the early decades,' Agrawal explains why the rumor mills went into overdrive. 'People wondered what would follow. I worked really hard on the timing of all three things—the demerger, the Sunflower announcement and the LD Waxson acquisition—and they all came through in the same month. I think the LD Waxson buy-out took care of a lot of speculation.'

The growth path WCCLG chose for itself was propelled by its enhanced understanding of products, brands and markets. As Sitaram points out, 'Unilever proved that brands move easily across cultures. But products are not brands. [To make products work,] you need to understand the psyche of the local consumer. Once you build it, you leverage that.'

An increasingly confident Agrawal and his team have proved this maxim time and again. Enchanteur, the flagship offering from Wipro Unza, is WCCLG's second-largest brand at $150 million, while Safi, from the same house, is the biggest halal brand in the world. In 2018, WCCLG touched $1 billion in revenue. And in a sweet run-up to Wipro's seventy-fifth year in business, Santoor became the second-biggest soap brand in India in value at $300 million—overtaking HUL's Lux.[2] For a brand that few, including HUL, took seriously for years, the prize is vindication for an unorthodox marketing strategy, intuitive advertising and constant improvements in keeping with consumer desires.

❖❖❖

WIN now has a grip over an extended manufacturing space. While the hydraulics business generates the biggest revenues, it is among the top aerospace companies in India as well as a leading player in industrial automation.

ABOVE
Wipro Infrastructure Engineering's new manufacturing plant at the Aerospace Special Economic Zone in Devanahalli, Bangalore.

TOP
Pratik Kumar, CEO, Wipro Infrastructure Engineering. Bangalore, 2020.

LEFT

Wipro Infrastructure Engineering seeded its additive manufacturing printing business in 2013. In 2017, it went on to produce the first India-made 3D components for use in space by ISRO.

The infrastructure engineering business, though smaller in revenues, has been equally agile in pushing boundaries. WIN now has a presence across the globe, including in Israel, acquiring HR Givon Ltd in 2016 to gain a toehold as a manufacturer of parts in the aerospace industry. Today, the business focuses on industrial automation, 3D engineering (started in 2013), aerospace and water, apart from its mainstay, the legacy business of hydraulic components.

Kumar focused on industries that make heavy use of hydraulics, particularly the aerospace and defense segments. With their expertise in hydraulic actuators, WIN got a foothold in aerospace when Airbus put WIN in touch with its Spanish subsidiary Compañía Española de Sistemas Aeronáuticos S.A.U. (CESA).

CESA outsourced manufacturing of actuators and related precision-engineered components for Airbus to WIN. 'We subsequently entered into a technology-transfer agreement with CESA,' says Rajagopalan. 'As business expanded, we invested in a 75,000 square feet SEZ facility in Devanahalli, Bangalore, in 2013.'

WIN had caught the global tailwind. In a couple of years, the OEMs for Boeing and Airbus—together controlling 80 to 90 per cent of the global market—were registering record sales, driven by skyrocketing demand from emerging economies. With Airbus already an end-customer, WIN set its sights on Boeing.

A strategic acquisition, Kumar realized, could be a huge help. The Israel-headquartered Givon, manufacturers of structural parts for aircrafts, fitted the bill. 'Givon catered to Boeing and others in the US,' says Rajagopalan. 'By acquiring it in 2016, we made inroads into North America and other geographies, built a different product line with multiple factory locations and began servicing another Tier 1 aerospace company.'

❖❖❖

In 2013, WIN ventured into another new area: additive manufacturing. 'An economy cannot leapfrog by missing the manufacturing bus. [Additive manufacturing] is our opportunity to catch up, especially given our design skills,' Kumar said in an interview a year later.[3] In less than four years of investing $2 million in a 3D-printing plant, WIN made India's first fabricated 3D-printed antenna for ISRO's GSAT-19 satellite. It also ventured into 3D consulting for competency building, R&D services and turnkey solutions, and began work on its own industrial-grade 3D printer.

Next came industrial automation. 'We wanted to leverage our domain understanding of manufacturing, which was scalable on a global level. Automation ticked all the boxes,' says Kumar. 'In addition, it was not capex [capital expenditure] heavy and didn't stress the balance sheet too much.'

WIN found its first industrial automation client in JCB—leveraging a twenty-five-year-old client relationship from the hydraulics business—for whom it set up a conveyor line in their Jaipur factory. Within a year, it acquired Bangalore-based robotics company Incitecam to scale up capabilities.

WIN now has a grip over an extended manufacturing space. While the hydraulics business—its oldest and strongest, with more than a million cylinders sold—generates the biggest revenues, the global revenues of the aerospace venture make it one of the top aerospace companies from India. It is also among the leading industrial automation players in the country. ◆

Wipro Cares, set up in 2003 as a charitable trust, has scaled up operations over the years, enabling Wipro Ltd employees to contribute funds and volunteer time toward social causes.

ABOVE AND RIGHT
Wipro Cares is active in communities where Wipro is operational, spanning sectors such as education, health, environment and support for children with disabilities.

The idea of a 'good company' has sparked many kinds of debates—philosophical, political and in the vast literature surrounding sustainability. Somewhere in the mid-1990s, John Elkington introduced the notion of the triple bottom line—the need to examine a company's social, environmental and economic impact. It caught on but was much abused. Reduced to the snappy catchphrase of three Ps—people, planet and profit—it became a mere accounting tool where a narrow definition of profit shifts the needle. In 2018, Elkington asked for the recall of the triple bottom line, refusing to be made party to mere lip-service to progress. But the framework lives on. The world has moved to the idea of a quadruple bottom line where culture, purpose or even spirituality is the magic element missing so far.

It is interesting to note that whichever parameter or framework one may choose, Wipro stands the scrutiny. It is a company which understands that its purpose is to grow shareholder value, while equally contributing to a better world. Back in 2006, its 'Good Citizen Manifesto'—a statement of Wipro's responsibility to the larger community—had declared: 'Our belief is that since organizations have power, they have an obligation to do good.' And it did so much before it became mandatory by law for large corporates to set aside 2 per cent of their profits for corporate social responsibility in India.

On its journey to becoming a 'good citizen', Wipro has made several transformations, as also a host of small changes that matter as much cumulatively. From the mid-2000s, it became a leader in pioneering green initiatives across the board. It reduced its carbon footprint and water usage consistently, while improving multiple other environmental and social parameters, thus continually improving its 'sustainability', defined by any measure. All of this led to its being repeatedly cited as one of the world's most sustainable companies by the Dow Jones Sustainability Index or the Carbon Disclosure Project.

Its social initiatives started in a small way in 2001, and have expanded in scale and scope while remaining true to the basic principles: of focusing on a few chosen fields, deep engagement with partners as opposed to mere 'check-writing' and shunning the limelight.

Starting with training schoolteachers in India, to help them move away from rote learning and instead foster the ability for 'Applying Thought' (Wipro's motto then) in their students, today Wipro Ltd's efforts span a synergistic range: from helping develop a vibrant civil society and NGO ecosystem, to support improvements in the education system, to specific niche programs like Wipro Earthian, a program to sensitize schoolchildren and college students to issues of biodiversity, water, food and waste. While education remains the focus for Wipro Ltd across the world, it has also added significant work over the years on environment, in sync with its overall commitment to ecological sustainability.

In 2003, Wipro Cares was set up as a charitable trust to enable contribution of employees to social causes. 'All our social initiatives needed deep expertise and full involvement; while seeing the company do all this, employees also had the urge to contribute. So, Wipro Cares was set up. This enabled employees to contribute money as well as their time in the form of volunteering efforts. And Wipro would match every rupee they contributed,' explains PS Narayan, vice president and head, Sustainability, Wipro Ltd. The work of Wipro Cares focuses on the proximate communities of Wipro Ltd's operations, spanning education, health, environment and support for children with disabilities.

Driven by the principle of contributing to its social context and communities, it was inevitable that Wipro start something significant in the US. In 2012, it set up the Wipro Science Education Fellowship in the US in partnership with University of Massachusetts, Boston. A two-year professional development program for teacher leadership, it focuses on improving science education in school districts that predominantly serve disadvantaged communities. The program now spans multiple states, with seven university partners and hundreds of teacher leaders. 'We're trying to provide sustainable change in science education in underprivileged school districts,' says Arthur Eisenkraft, Distinguished Professor of Science Education at University of Massachusetts, Boston, and the director of the program.

Wipro Ltd continues to expand such initiatives, big and small, across the world. Another notable one is in the UK, where Wipro Ltd worked with King's College London to create the curriculum for a two-year master's program in science-technology-engineering-mathematics (STEM) education, and it partnered with the Sheffield Hallam University, South Yorkshire, for the Wipro Teacher Mentor and Wipro Science Fellowship programs.

But the most significant and definitive expression of being a company that has a purpose above and beyond what most businesses have, has been the transfer of 67 per cent of the economic ownership of the

On 31 July 2019, Premji retired as the Executive Chairman of Wipro Ltd. 'Leading Wipro from 1966 till now has been the greatest privilege of my life. It has been an extraordinary journey—growing from being a small vegetable oil company to the diverse global business that we are today. It is the deep commitment and hard work of Wiproites across generations that has helped shape the organization of today,' he wrote in his last letter.

ABOVE
Azim Premji, Founder Chairman, at Wipro Ltd's headquarters on Sarjapur Road, Bangalore.

company by Premji to the philanthropic organization he set up to serve the most disadvantaged people in India.

'Sustainable philanthropic activity requires a constant source of revenue,' points out KR Lakshminarayana, Wipro's erstwhile chief strategy officer and now the chief endowment officer for the Foundation. 'Traditionally, endowments are invested to generate that revenue. Here, there's an endowment that's invested and an operating company that produces profit. So, a big reason for Wipro Ltd's existence is that its profits go to help needy communities.'

❖❖❖

On 31 July 2019, Rishad took over as the Chairman of Wipro Ltd, as Premji retired. 'Leading Wipro from 1966 till now has been the greatest privilege of my life. It has been an extraordinary journey—growing from being a small vegetable oil company to the diverse global business that we are today. It is the deep commitment and hard work of Wiproites across generations that has helped shape the organization of today. Wipro is an exemplar of a successful, ethical and a socially responsible organization,' Premji wrote in his last letter as the Executive Chairman of Wipro Ltd.

In these early days of his role, Rishad's one key priority has been to fire up the 'growth mindset', similar to the early 2000s, which had so defined Wipro then. With many of its technology bets paying off and soaring customer satisfaction, Rishad feels that Wipro Ltd is ready to seize a new world of opportunity. Wipro Ltd's recent big deals in multiple industry verticals, along with a definite uptick in revenues from new areas such as cyber security, cloud, engineering services and digital, boosts this confidence.

He found a new partner in his journey in Thierry Delaporte, who took over as CEO in July 2020, six months after Neemuchwala stepped down. Delaporte is as drawn by the legacy of Wipro Ltd as the challenges it faces in a rapidly evolving world. 'It's the best brand in the industry,' says Delaporte. 'It's a company where everything is driven by the heart,' he continues. 'People are constructive, they're positive, they love their company. They want to do the right things,' he points out, adding, 'I'm the luckiest because I'm working with people who have placed the interests of Wipro Ltd before their own interests. These are incredible values.' Delaporte holds that change in the future will come from within Wipro Ltd, in the way people think.

❖❖❖

This is something that the new Chairman has been fostering throughout the organization, since assuming office in 2019. 'Our customer mix, our people, our capabilities—we are very good on every front,' says Rishad. 'But some of our ways of working are coming in our way. Our challenges are more internal than external.'

Some of it, arguably, has a long history. Rapid change in the IT industry is perhaps the most oft-cited cliché. But there was one structural change that happened comparatively slowly over a decade or so, with deep implications for Wipro Ltd. This was the relative slowdown in growth of the Technology and R&D solutions versus Enterprise services and solutions, the latter becoming bigger and bigger through the early 2000s. Wipro's traditional strength was in providing core technology and R&D solutions, and as its share grew smaller in the overall business of Wipro, it sparked internal friction on deciding what (and who) was more relevant for Wipro's future. It led to other issues too.

❖❖❖

'The organization growing so fast had its own problems. It wasn't a very rigid organization at the time. Role definitions were not clear then. There were good things and bad about this. The good part is that you had people who took full responsibility, who would take the ball from the center of the court to the goal. But at the same time, there were some things that are not easily measurable ... that could easily take a backseat—like setting up systems. One would do what was needed to deliver to the customer. But you wouldn't wait for some other function or team to do something for you ... that process was not so [clearly defined]. But when you scale, it's not easy to scale with such methods,' says Bhanumurthy BM, president and COO, Wipro Ltd.

All this left a telling effect. 'Somewhere along the way, as we sought to throw off straitjackets, become even more entrepreneurial, we let go of necessary control-and-coordination, we started becoming dysfunctional,' says chief human resources officer Saurabh Govil, who joined the human resources function from GE in 2009 amidst the unfolding financial crisis.

Rishad is asking fundamental questions and driving change in Wipro Ltd. 'Are we very siloed and think only about our own unit? Are we driving metrics that drive distorted behaviors? Are we very input-centric, instead of output-centric? Are we responsive enough? Are we collaborating enough? Are we communicating enough?' he asks. There is need for renewed synergies, he feels.

Rishad's focus has been on creating

CLOCKWISE FROM TOP, LEFT
Wiproites in Curitiba, Brazil, participate in the Spirit of Wipro Run, 2014.

Wipro Pride celebrations in London, 2018.

Wipro Ltd CHRO Saurabh Govil (standing, in black) at a meeting with his HR team in Houston, 2017.

While integrity and ethics have always been the touchstones for how people in Wipro made every decision—from the businesses it chose to enter to how it framed its HR policies—it is the narrative of finding its purpose and living by those principles that makes Wipro's story so relevant to our lives today.

habits that are rooted in Wipro's values, the Spirit of Wipro. These habits—Being Respectful, Being Responsive, Always Communicating, Demonstrating Stewardship and Building Trust—address business and also the role in society.

By bringing the focus on these behaviors, which he believes have come to be diffused by the passage of time and by the vastness of the operations of Wipro, Rishad intends all the committed values of Wipro to manifest in its culture, everywhere, every day and for everyone.

'Culture for me is the most important determinant of a company's success. And culture is shaped by the values of an organization. While values define the soul and norms of the organization, they manifest in the form of culture, by the repeated and observable behavior of the people of the organization—action that should be true to those values,' says Rishad.

Mindful that changing culture and habits takes time and a great deal of effort, he likens it to a marathon, one that he is committed to winning.

❖❖❖

'History may not repeat itself, but it often rhymes.' – Unknown

Much of what happened in Wipro's story in the early part of the twentieth century is history to us. Many of us were not born then, but if we look closely, we can trace a line through the history to our everyday lives today. Resilience is one such theme that remains consistent throughout Wipro's story and as the events of 2020 have demonstrated, it has an important role in our lives too.

Historians say that 2020 was the sixth worst year in human history. Hopefully, most of us will not witness such a year again in our lifetime. So many of us lost so much. Businesses around the world suffered massive losses, lives and relationships were upended, and for the more disadvantaged amongst us, livelihoods and loved ones were lost. Some of us may never go back to being the people we were before the events of 2020.

The one way in which we will change hopefully is that we will become more mindful of our place in the world, of our responsibility to our families and find a sense of purpose to the communities we live in. We will learn to value what is most dear to us and learn to make choices to live more responsibly.

And it is here that the story of Wipro can serve as a great inspiration. While integrity and ethics have always been the touchstones for how people in Wipro made every decision—from the businesses it chose to enter to how it framed its HR policies—it is in the narrative of finding its purpose and living by those principles that makes Wipro's story so relevant to our lives today.

While our lives can only be lived forward, we can only connect the dots by looking backwards. And it is in joining the dots of the Wipro story that we realize how, at every moment, life presents us with choices. How we respond to those choices shapes our lives. From the time a young twenty-one-year-old found himself at a crossroads, making the most difficult choice of his life—whether to continue pursuing his dreams or take over the responsibility of the family's business—every moment in Wipro's story resonates with such choices. What if that twenty-one-year-old had made a different choice for himself? Where would Wipro have been today? No one knows the answer.

But if we understand that our responses shape our future, if we have faith in ourselves to see our choices through, if we have enough courage to stay true to our values and if we believe that we are here for a larger purpose, our time on this Earth would have been well served.

That in a nutshell is the story of Wipro. ◆

LEFT
Rishad Premji, Chairman, Wipro Ltd. Bangalore, 2020.

The Foundation Story

ABOVE
Ganeshram has a student work out a math problem at the government primary school in Ruponi Bagdawon Ki Dhani, Rajasthan.

THE FOUNDATION STORY

Towards a just, equitable, humane society

'Master, thaaro jaat ke?' In a tiny desert town in Rajasthan, a schoolteacher tries his best to dodge an insistent six-year-old's question about his caste identity. The little girl is unwilling to settle for a discussion on gender identities or anything else. She wants specifics on caste. She is a part of the world she inhabits.

The teacher knows that he is the path for the girl to expand her horizons. To retain the rootedness in all that is good in that closely knit community, and yet demolish all the prejudices and chains. He is the path for her to be empowered, to grow, to fly.

He works with the child, pushing the question aside for the moment. But it festers inside. In a public school in north India, one that largely serves the underprivileged, could education change the world for a six-year-old girl?

The teacher believes—must believe—it will.

Across the country in rocky north Karnataka, in another public school, his colleague shares this belief. She laughs as she points to a hut on the outskirts of a village. A six-year-old used to throw pebbles at the teacher each time she went to cajole him into the classroom. The boy from a migrant community had little appreciation for the confines of a classroom and a language so alien. The teacher took a year to learn the boy's mother tongue, Lambani, and has now started teaching in the dialect to keep the student in the classroom. She believes the child can learn, that every child can learn, if she could learn how to teach them right.

Education in India is deeply shaped by sociopolitical, economic, cultural and physical contexts, all of which are bewilderingly and gloriously diverse. This poses challenges in each dimension, from access to education to the curriculum, teachers'

ABOVE

Dileep Ranjekar, or DKR as he is universally known, is one of two chief executives of the Azim Premji Foundation. He had a long stint as Wipro's Corporate HR chief and gave form to the vision and concept of the Foundation, which he joined in 2002 as its first CEO. At a government primary school in Champawat, Uttarakhand, 2020.

capacity and the resources that students can access at home.

Across India, teachers battle highly skewed teacher–student ratios in classrooms, the unique challenges of first-generation learners, the problems faced by underprivileged families, and the trials of a physical terrain that is a desert, a remote mountain or an arid tract of land, which makes migrants out of its populace.

Contrary to popular discourse and its reductive narrative of the public school teacher as the source of all malaise, the Azim Premji Foundation's work with teachers over the last twenty years has borne witness to the immense change brought about by them—teachers who are committed and have faith in, and an abiding love for, their students. The teacher who scales a rocky hill-face braving the monsoons in Uttarakhand to reach her school on time every day, the teacher who spends every evening after work and most weekends at the Foundation's Teacher Learning Centers to improve his classroom teaching, the headmaster and his team who run an informal hostel so that children of seasonal workers don't need to drop out of the school system when their parents leave their village in search of work, the science teacher who frustrated with the loss in translation, has taken to writing textbooks in Hindi, the teacher who battles caste in the village single-handedly along with his students—the list goes on.

Extending support to these individuals, who are an accurate representation of public school teachers, by and large, is the wide-reaching team of the Foundation, spread across the most disadvantaged of regions. They live in small towns and villages when they could be in bustling metros. They build bonds, make communities their own, put their lives' work in these remote, desolate areas, driven by their faith in the transformative power of education and their immense willpower.

The Foundation's fieldwork in education seeks to improve the equity and quality of the Indian public education system. Since the heart of it is the teacher, a significant part of this fieldwork is with them—hundreds of thousands across multiple states in India in over 400,000 schools. The Foundation also works on other aspects of education: curriculum, assessment, textbook and content development, policy and capacity development, education leaders and institutions. This work is spread across even more states. The Foundation played a key role in the development of the National Education Policy 2020, which India had undertaken again after thirty-four years.

All of this extensive work in the field happens through the Azim Premji Foundation District Institutes, realized in close collaboration with the state governments. The Foundation also runs eight 'demonstration schools' to help in the capacity development of public school teachers and education leaders. A significant part of the teachers' engagement with the Foundation's work is voluntary. They attend workshops and discussion sessions, or drop in at the Foundation's Teacher Learning Centers after school hours, on weekends or during school vacations. This is a testament to the teachers' commitment and the work that the Foundation's field team does.

There is a second, critical aspect of the Foundation's work in India. To help deal with the critical shortage of talent and research in the social sector, the Foundation set up the Azim Premji University in Bangalore in 2010. The University conducts research and runs teaching programs in a range of fields, from school education and public health to development and law. Its undergraduate program offers liberal education in its truest sense, with deep, multidisciplinary curriculum.

Housed in a 100-acre, 2.6-million-square-foot campus, the University is expanding. Half of its students are supported by scholarship. This is possible only because the long-term financial model of the University is to recover only 20 per cent of its overall expenses from student fees, while 80 per cent is supported by the Foundation. Thus, the campus and the student body fully reflect the socio-economic diversity of India. The Foundation is setting up a similar university in Bhopal in central India, and plans to set up a third university in the North-east. Both the fieldwork and the University operate and are energized by their own long-term strategy and goals.

In 2014, the Foundation built a third significant thrust to its work—the Philanthropy (in addition to the fieldwork and the University). Through the Philanthropy, it provides financial support through multi-year grants to other not-for-profit organizations (NPOs), such as to a night shelter in Bangalore where homeless laborers get a meal, a chance to bathe and sleep safely till they find their feet, standing between disaster and the possibility of building a better life. Or, a grant to help women marginal farmers in Rajasthan shift to sustainable agricultural practices, to help improve their family income and nutrition, and to prevent distress migration.

The Philanthropy also supports NPOs that work for the most disadvantaged and marginalized people—the homeless, persons

ABOVE

Anurag Behar (first from left), CEO of Azim Premji Foundation, too joined the Foundation after a long stint at Wipro. He started his career in Wipro–GE, later moving to the Wipro Corporate Office, and became CEO of WIN in 2004. He took up his current role in Foundation in 2010. At an outdoor class in Dhamtari, Chhattisgarh, 2020

OPPOSITE PAGE

Premji interacts with children at the inauguration of Shalegaagi Naavu-Neevu, a programme to improve the quality of school education in Karnataka, at Vidhana Soudha in Bangalore, 2009.

with disability, women survivors of violence, adolescent girls at risk, street children, elderly poor, manual scavengers, ragpickers, migrant workers, transgender people and other gender minorities, farmers with marginal landholding and vulnerable tribal groups. To these vulnerable groups, the grants offer immediate care, access to essential services and the possibility of a dignified future. In all this, the Philanthropy supports 'good people doing good work', unfettered by notions of 'whether it is eliminating root cause'. This is simply because it truly believes that such good people do change the world, one step at a time.

The Philanthropy also engages in systematic collaboration with state governments and NPOs to address large humanitarian and development challenges. This includes reducing child malnutrition, preventing human trafficking, offering legal access to undertrials, improving gram panchayats and welfare delivery, and shifting to agro-ecological farming practices.

All this comes together clearly and simply. The Foundation's quest is to contribute to developing a more just, equitable, humane and sustainable society in India, which the Constitution committed to in 1950.

While the Foundation's overall work is premised on a long-term approach, the global pandemic prompted an immediate response to an unfolding healthcare and humanitarian crisis. On 1 April 2020, the Foundation and Wipro's IT and non-IT businesses together committed about $150 million (Rs 11,250 million) to contribute towards the nationwide efforts to address the crisis.

In a lightning-quick operational response, the Foundation moved on a three-pronged approach. Teams on the ground were mobilized to provide immediate humanitarian assistance in the form of cooked meals, dry ration and relief to vulnerable communities—this was a team of over 65,000 people covering over 400 districts. This included the Foundation's own field team, public school teachers whom the Foundation works with in 'normal times', team members of partner NPOs supported financially by the Foundation, and the alumni of the University. Second, the Foundation built a comprehensive healthcare response in collaboration with the public health system, local administration and NPOs. Starting with mobilizing communities, monitoring and surveillance, and testing, this extended right to secondary and tertiary care. Third, the Foundation started systematic, deep, on-the-ground interventions to address the huge loss of livelihood caused by the pandemic.

This moment of crisis, however, makes clearer the shift in Wipro's history, of its will to work for the greater good. Set up in 2001, the Foundation has been seen as a testament to Premji's deep, abiding sense of responsibility towards society. In two decades, it has worked to improve the school education system, created institutions that can sustain long-term intervention, and addressed social and developmental challenges.

Over time, Premji has irrevocably donated most of his wealth to the Foundation, which now owns an economic interest in Wipro Ltd. Sixty-seven per cent of all value created by the company goes towards making a difference in the lives of some of India's most disadvantaged citizens. Similarly, the Foundation owns a substantial portion of Wipro Enterprises Ltd and of Premji Invest, besides a diversified portfolio of investments. The Foundation's endowment, contributed by Premji, is now valued at $ 24.5 billion (Rs 1.83 lakh crore).

Wipro's work finds a new significance: the Foundation enables it to change the lives of the most vulnerable and disenfranchised population in the world. The Foundation has become the beacon of the deep sense of purpose that drives Wipro forward. ◆

Field Institutions

ABOVE
Like many schools in Rajasthan, the Government Upper Primary School Dhokali Nadi, Baytu, in Barmer district, serves a cluster of habitations (dhanis) in the area, and children walk through the desert to reach the school.

TOP LEFT AND RIGHT
Ganpatlal uses flashcards to teach his second-grade students at the Government Primary School, Ruponi Bagdawon Ki Dhani. The school serves several dhanis near the town of Baytu, in Barmer.

LEFT
Haam Singh has the fifth-grade students engrossed with his theatrical teaching style during a Hindi lesson at Government Upper Primary School Fatdai Nadi, Siwana.

ಮಾನವನ ಹೃದಯ

TOP, LEFT AND MIDDLE
At a small government school in Anpura village, Yadgir, Karnataka, children walk in early before classes begin. They take turns to clean the premises before the morning assembly. Student ministers, elected annually by the children, assign teams to decorate the courtyard with a rice-flour kolam. Instead of traditional symbols, they draw a diagram from their textbooks each day.

LEFT
Social science teacher Jaipal Reddy has adopted a student-led interactive approach to teaching. 'I don't teach. They [students] design the discussion and I fill gaps,' he says. His confident, quick thinking students have responded well to this approach. They sit in circles, discuss the lessons among themselves and present to their classmates the talking points from the day's lesson, peppered liberally with pop-culture references.

ABOVE
The Foundation has been working with government schoolteachers in Yadgir, one of the most disadvantaged districts in Karnataka, since 2001. The terrain is rocky, there is shortage of drinking water, and it lags on most human development indices. Like in all the other places it works, the Foundation is deeply engaged with teachers across the district, inside and outside the school, to help enable the best educational outcomes for their students.

ABOVE
The students at Government Upper Primary School in Chintkunta love science and maths thanks to Naranappa, the science teacher. A regular at the Foundation's Teacher Learning Centers, he is part of a learning community of science teachers in the region. With the Foundation's help, he has put together material for a tiny laboratory his students simply love working in.

LEFT AND BELOW
A student uses his mobile phone's torch function to see a slide under the microscope, while another demonstrates a concept of physics to her classmates. Most students here are first-generation schoolgoers from a farming community, and they are excellent at sports, with several of them qualifying for Karnataka's state volleyball team.

ABOVE
Children from the Government Primary School, Pahi, Uttarakhand return home after school. This village is part of Bhatwari block in Uttarkashi that was severely damaged in a cloudburst in 2014.

RIGHT
Government Primary School, Siror, in Uttarkashi, on the banks of the Bhagirathi river. The road (leading to Gangotri) is on the left bank and children walk across a bridge to get to the school.

ABOVE
At Government Primary School, Pahi, the morning assembly is an important educational event. Children conduct the assembly independently, practice public speaking, discuss the news and put up short cultural performances. Among other things, this develops their confidence and fosters teamwork.

RIGHT
Children put on an enthusiastic performance as they sing during the morning assembly at Government Primary School, Dang, in Bhatwari block, Uttarakhand.

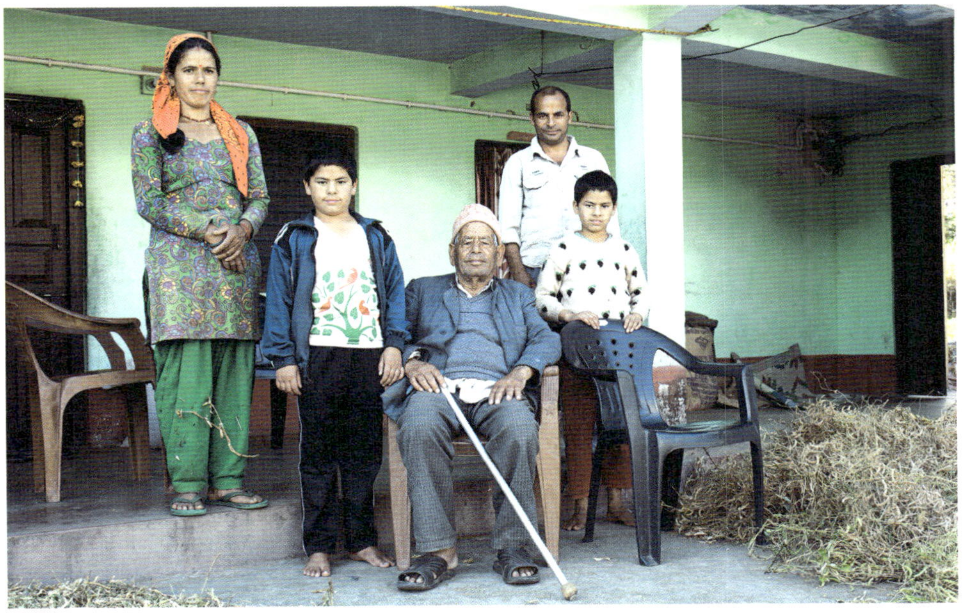

ABOVE
Children at Government Model Primary School, Maneri, take charge of their lunch every day, helping with all chores related to the mid-day meal that is cooked and served by school employees, designated the 'bhojanmata'.

LEFT
Like in most rural areas, students live in multi-generational families and help with household chores after school. These children's father also went to the same school, Government Primary School, Pahi. However, a few years ago enrollment dropped to single digits. Thanks to a new head teacher's efforts, villagers found renewed faith in the local school, sending most of their children there. It now has about forty students.

RIGHT
Rekha Chamoli has taught at the Primary School, Ganeshpur, Uttarkashi, since 2009. The school has forty-one children enrolled in five classes and two teachers. For long, parents were only too eager to enroll children in the private English-medium school nearby. Chamoli, feisty, self-assured and articulate, and her colleague Manju Rana, quiet, unassuming and equally committed, have turned things around. They have created an environment of hope, of change and one where children are confident, curious and eager to learn on their own. Chamoli's diary of her teaching life has been published as a book by the Foundation, which she credits with shaping how she reflects on education.

LEFT
Sunder Nautiyal is the assistant teacher at Government Inter College, Kotdwar Gamari in Uttarakhand. He teaches science to high school students and makes his own demonstration tools, like this wire-and-box toy to explain the difference between centripetal and centrifugal force. A huge challenge is developing a scientific temperament in students, given the deeply held superstitions children absorb from their socio-cultural milieu. Inspired by like-minded education professionals he met at the Foundation's workshops, Nautiyal started writing in the local language to explain different topics—a short drama on photosynthesis, for instance—to make science interesting for his students.

ABOVE
Haam Singh started teaching at the Government Upper Primary School Fatdai Nadi, Siwana some sixteen years ago. His first 'classroom' was under a tree in the school compound. Thanks to Haam Singh and his colleagues' hardwork and dedication, community support for the school and teachers has grown in these years, and new buildings and classrooms have come up. Singh still teaches some of his youngest students outside, under the shade of a tree in the school, for the fun of it .

RIGHT
Kashibai, the head teacher of the Government Primary School, Gaddada Narayana Tanda, is considered part of the community in her students' families. The settlement has many members of the Lambani tribe, known for their rich artisan skills. The men of the community often migrate in search of employment, and the children speak in a language quite distinct from Kannada, the medium of instruction in Karnataka. Kashibai taught herself the Lambani language to ensure her students learn well. She visits and learns at the Foundation's Teacher Learning Centers whenever she can get some time away from the eighty-eight students at the primary school.

ABOVE
Science teachers at a workshop organized by the Foundation at Viratra Mata, Chohtan, Barmer, in 2019. This large-scale 'camp-like' workshop was attended by teachers from across Rajasthan and was on the theme 'Let's Know Our Sky'. Here, teachers are measuring the angle and length of a shadow cast by a stick. They would later use this activity in their classrooms to teach students how to find out the latitude of a particular location.

TOP, LEFT
Foundation member Deepak Rawat (second from left) facilitates a summer science workshop at the Teacher Learning Center, Gopeshwar, Chamoli, in Uttarakhand. The teachers are working on an experiment that would help them teach the workings of the respiratory system of plants.

TOP, RIGHT
Teachers experiment with puppetry as a pedagogic tool at a Foundation workshop in Barmer, Rajasthan. The teachers learned to make puppets, which they took back to their classrooms to use while teaching primary grades.

ABOVE
Teachers from different districts in the Garhwal region at a summer science workshop in Chamoli. They use commonly available material, like a water bottle and string, to devise an experiment to help engage students in a lesson on force and motion.

ABOVE
The Azim Premji School in Yadgir was set up in 2014. Like the government schools, it is free for all students and provides mid-day meals, uniforms and textbooks. The school, an integral part of the Foundation's efforts to help improve the public education system, is a 'demonstration' school for pedagogical and school-management practices for government school teachers and officials.

LEFT AND MIDDLE
Children in grades one, two and three learn in small groups. Teachers use activities, exercises and locally sourced material as learning aids. A math class in progress has students using seeds and bundles of ice-cream stick to keep count.

BELOW
The entire school comes together at assembly in the morning, where children put up a play based on their learnings. To complement the vibrant learning environment at the school, the teachers are engaged with the community. They visit the students' homes frequently, ensure attendance, understand the context the children come from, and involve the community in the school.

ABOVE AND RIGHT

The Foundation's campus in Gulbarga sits amidst cotton fields. It also houses the Azim Premji School and the District Institute, along with a hostel for teachers who participate in the Foundation's workshops, which are often a week long. The campus is recently constructed. Children run in with great pleasure, queuing up for the assembly with evident anticipation. The national anthem is followed by a musical performance by a group of students. The community's deep faith in the school is a result of the Foundation's work in the district.

LEFT AND BELOW
The Azim Premji School in Dineshpur, in the Udham Singh Nagar district of Uttarakhand, came up in 2012. At present, it has 417 students. The school has its own building with spacious classrooms and other infrastructural facilities, including a library with a collection of close to 5,500 books. They also use a wide variety of textbooks and other teaching-learning materials, including found objects. The students (left) are working on an art composition with material collected from their surroundings, an exercise that helps develop awareness of their spaces as much as it builds appreciation and understanding for local materials.

Philanthropic Initiatives

RIGHT
A women's group with a community worker at the end of a meeting to discuss the effective disbursement of a grant received by the partner NPO to empower livelihood here. This community makes a living out of cattle herding and most of the grant's funds went toward buying goats.

RIGHT
An activity session at a day care center for the elderly from economically vulnerable households in the community. At this center, the men and women come in by 10.30 am. A small assembly starts the day off with activities followed by lunch and naptime, singing, dancing, exercise sessions in the afternoon and then coffee before they return home.

ABOVE

A pond to irrigate farming land nearby, designed and built as part of environmentally and economically sustainable agricultural practices. A mobile phone application shows watershed gradient, helping design efforts to prevent depletion of groundwater.

LEFT

Social workers work closely with the city police to ensure the homeless in the area can find refuge in this shelter. Many of the homeless have some means of livelihood, but are unable to find a home because they do not earn enough, are new migrants, or their places of work are too far for them to commute to.

RIGHT AND BELOW
Community workers from a partner NPO help women who face domestic violence with the written procedures involved in filing a police complaint.

BELOW

Child care shelters provide care and protection to children in need of such support. These are not only safe homes, but provide children with a full life experience including caring adult presence, as also exposure to art and crafts, music and good education.

ABOVE AND TOP

Small and marginal farmers, often with a focus on women and women's collectives, are a significant area of the Foundation's support work. From encouraging sustainable farming and pisciculture methods to enabling women to form self-help groups and much else, partner organizations work to reduce vulnerabilities on many fronts.

RIGHT
An awareness campaign in the Dharavi community in Mumbai, focusing on mental illness. The posters seek to educate community members about suicide and schizophrenia.

ABOVE
A group of village women attend a session on livestock management. The aim is to enhance household income, improve food security and strengthen community collectives.

ABOVE
Across the country, the Foundation supports several not-for-profit organizations that work with people with disabilities, with a particular focus on the rehabilitation of children with neuromuscular and developmental disabilities.

BELOW
Work with the farming community, especially the women, is wide-ranging and includes learning-exposure visits for self-help group members to experience best practices such as the rice-intensification methodology **(top, left)**, or the raising of awareness on optimal methods of pest management and seeding concepts in large groups at village organizations **(below)**.

Azim Premji University

ABOVE
The new Azim Premji University campus in Bangalore sprawls across 100 acres. The 2.6 million square feet of buildings are phase one, with room for expansion in the future. Founded in 2010, the University's teaching programs are focused on preparing the students to contribute to education, livelihoods, health, sustainability and other fields of human development. A second campus will come up in Bhopal, planned for 2023, and then a third in the North-east. The research at the University is also focused on issues of human development, equity and justice. The University, the Field Institutes and Philanthropic Initiatives work closely together to further the Foundation's vision.

ABOVE AND RIGHT
The University currently has 800 masters and 450 undergraduate students and 140 faculty members. This will go up to about 5,000 students and 400 faculty members by 2023–24. The graduate programs include Master of Arts in Education, Development, Public Policy and Governance, and a postgraduate law degree focused on Law and Development. The undergraduate programs offer majors in the entire range of disciplines, from Physics and Math to Economics and Philosophy, along with interdisciplinary studies such as Education, Development, Sustainability and Data Sciences.

LEFT
The four-year integrated teacher-education program is one of the most significant programs of the University, arising as it does from one the Foundation's most extensive efforts, to help improve the teacher-education system in India through its various interventions.

BELOW
Azim and Yasmeen Premji confer a master's degree upon V Anjali Naidu, a student of Development, at the Azim Premji University's convocation in 2018.

LEFT
To ensure that students from disadvantaged backgrounds find an equal opportunity at the University, it offers financial assistance to over half the students. The learning environment is enriched by the diversity of the students, who come from all states of India and from across the socio-economic spectrum. With the University's close alignment with the Field Institutes, students are immersed in fieldwork as part of their curriculum.

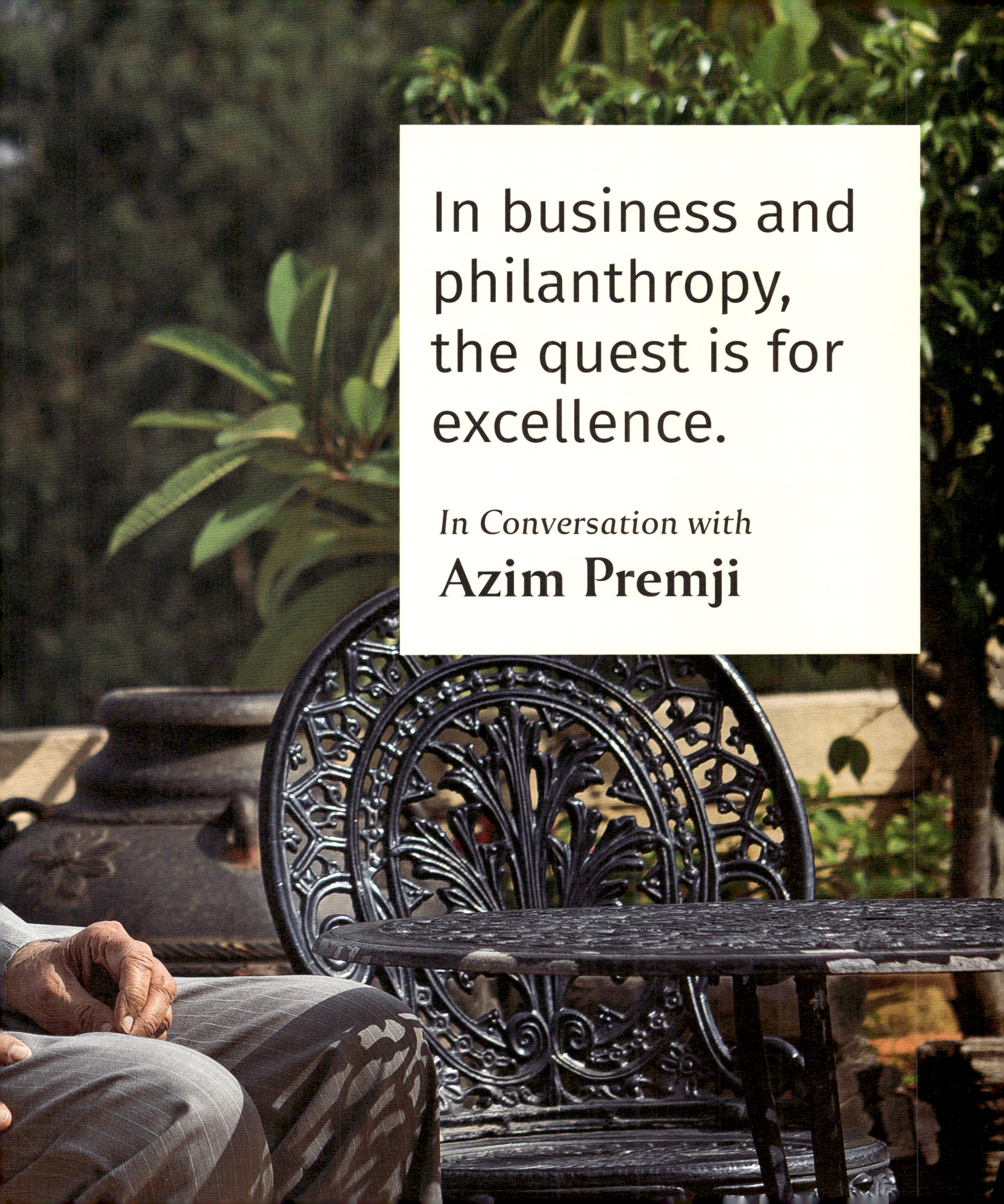

In business and philanthropy, the quest is for excellence.

In Conversation with

Azim Premji

LEFT
Azim Premji as a student at St. Mary's School, Bombay.

Why did your father start Western India Vegetable Products Ltd? What was the background to that?
I am not sure. Maybe he thought there was good money to be made. He wanted to become an industrialist versus being a trader. His family had a trading background. My grandfather started [his life earning] Rs 2 a week. And then he set up a rice business, which became a very profitable global business. We had large offices in the Middle East and Africa. My father took that over from him. And then the rice trade business got nationalized. So private traders couldn't work in that anymore.

My father saw an opportunity in oil milling. He set up the plant in Amalner because that area grew a lot of groundnut. But the business didn't do very well. In 1966, when I joined, the net worth of the company was just Rs 20–21 lakh. And it was not paying much dividend. I don't think my father professionalized the management enough. His key man, the general manager, was from the royal family of Sachin (in Gujarat), who really learned on the job. And in turn, he got his son in.

When did you decide that you were going to run the business and give up your studies?
There was no alternative but for me to come back. The business had to be run. There was not enough professional management to run it. ... The five years after my father's passing were very hard for us. We had to convince banks to give us a bridge loan, but we didn't have a balance sheet to be eligible for one. Which is why I couldn't go back. It was all firefighting.

Growing up, did you have any sense of the business?
No. My father was interested in many things. He was Chairman of the Electricity Board for the State of Bombay, covering Gujarat and Maharashtra. And he would work up to 12–12.30 every night because of that honorary responsibility. Then he became Chairman of the Federation of All India Food Grain Dealers' Association. That was the time they wanted to nationalize the [rice] trade. So he was constantly lobbying with the government. He was governor of Rotary Club—I don't think he missed a single meeting in his entire life!

So, he really got himself diverted, giving 40—or maybe 50—per cent of his time to all these activities. Which is why he could not concentrate enough on the business. And he didn't professionalize the business enough to be able to afford to do this. He worked extraordinary hours.

I used to visit the Amalner factory with my father; he was known as Sethji. He was a very empathetic person; people really loved him. When I came back, they started calling me Sethji. I got rid of that.

We had an office in Calcutta, a big commission-agency business in foodgrains. The son of a very old employee headed the show there, but he did not understand the business. It constantly ran into losses. I had to fire him when I came in, and replace him with a professional. So, there was a major effort to professionalize the organization, to get people who were qualified to do the jobs.

Was that daunting? You must have been so much younger than them in age.
Yes, but because it was a family concern, the family head was accepted. That was not the challenge. I worked hard. I worked intelligently, so I got acceptance very quickly. I never found that a challenge.

Is it true your father turned down an offer from MA Jinnah to join his ministry in Pakistan after Partition?
Yes. He was a prominent Muslim business leader at that point of time. And I think Jinnah was looking for talent. And he might have met my father and gotten impressed with him. He had the commercial background. I think he was offered the finance or the commerce ministry—I am not sure, but it was a very senior position. My father was clear that India was his homeland, his people, his country.

What was your childhood like?
I have some recollections. I started in a school run by this lady at Malabar Hill, I think. I forget the name of the school. I worked very hard even as a student. I fell in love with my French teacher (smiles). I played very hard as well. I used to play all kinds of things all the time; I remember playing with tops. We had a bungalow, about 1,200 square yards. It was green all around.

In the seventh grade, my mother admitted me to St Mary's School. The principal said he'd take me in a lower class because the exams were three months away. My mother insisted he take me in the current class, for which I didn't have the qualifications. The principal said, no way, he comes from an average school and he has lost a year. My mother was able to convince him, though—and I did well in the exams because she really helped me work very hard. And the principal, too, took a real liking to me because of this.

St Mary's had very high quality academics and a lot of sports, big grounds. We used to go skating every afternoon; we had cricket, quite a lot of it. I never enjoyed football.

I thought I'd get a job at the World Bank after Stanford. But I had to rush back because my father died very suddenly in August 1966. I got so involved in the business, I wasn't able to go back to school. Many years later, I suddenly got an urge for a degree. So I petitioned the University and asked them if I could secure my remaining credits. I had a decent academic ranking and I was able to convince them. So I did two courses by correspondence and they gave me a final degree in electrical engineering.

I enjoyed skating a lot and I enjoyed cricket. I was not a very good player. I was an all-rounder but average.

Were you athletic as a child?
Reasonably. My mother liked walking. Father never got time for all this. When we were kids, our family would rent a cottage in Mahabaleshwar and every day my mother would come for long walks with us. We would be there for a month, our immediate family as well as cousins, and we used to have a ball.

In my youth, I played a lot of cricket. There were lots of fields in Bandra. I played a fair amount of tennis, because we were members of the Willingdon Club, a twelve-to-fifteen-minute drive from home. We used to go for long walks on Juhu beach, we'd either drive or cycle there. The beach was pristine at that time.

Later, I would jog regularly. I gave that up when I turned fifty-six or fifty-seven, after a knee injury. We had big German Shepherds, one of them jumped on me and I fell. So, I had to stop.

We also heard that you used to walk up fourteen floors to the Bombay office!
It is a very good way to build stamina. I learned this at Stanford. I was in an experimental Harvard Step Test. There was a gym professor who was doing research on how football players got so much energy—he figured that running up and down the field helped them build their stamina. Walking up the staircase became the equivalent of a Harvard Step Test for me.

Growing up, you were obviously from a well-to-do family. Was it evident in your upbringing?
(Shakes head to indicate no.)

As a child, what was your ambition?
I wasn't forced to think of a career. We were given a lot of freedom at home. Our parents never forced us to study; they left it to us. But they took life seriously and encouraged us to do the same.

You were very close to your mother; you often talk about her as your inspiration. When she became the Chairman of Wipro, did she have any official duties or roles?
She was like an Emeritus Chairman. She had poise, intelligence, people respected her for the work she was doing at the Children's Orthopaedic Hospital. She had the experience of building and running a complex hospital. She ran the show [at Wipro] when I went back to Stanford for a few months for summer school in 1967.

Did you ever take her inputs or advice on running the business after you took over?
Yes. She didn't understand the business because my father never involved her. But her fundamentals were very clear. Her judgment of people was very sound. She had a certain ethos, which a twenty-year-old wouldn't have had.

What do you remember of your paternal grandfather, Khan Bahadur Hasham Premji?
I never met my paternal grandfather. But I've heard he was a very straightforward person. Once he was in his car, it passed over a puddle and splashed water on a pedestrian. He felt so bad [about the accident], he insisted on dropping the pedestrian home.

My maternal grandfather was a doctor. He was famous for visiting poor patients, not charging his fees and leaving money for their medicines under the pillow, but in a way that wouldn't make them feel cheap.

Do you have any family connection back to Kutch?
We were originally from Kutch, but I've never been there. I cannot speak Gujarati or Kutchhi, though I can understand some Gujarati.

Why did you choose to study engineering in Stanford? Was that your decision or your parents'?
I wanted to go abroad. I had a group of very close friends who were also going abroad. At that point of time, from what I recollect, [the government] only gave foreign exchange for engineering courses. Even though I wasn't really interested in engineering, it was the only way one could get the foreign exchange to go overseas. So [I went for engineering] not by choice but by regulation. Which is why I took so many non-engineering courses there.

If the foreign exchange constraint was not there, what would you have studied?
I'd have gone there and looked around before deciding on my specializations.

What were your goals when you set off for Stanford?
I was thinking of getting a job in the World Bank or [its] equivalent. But I had to rush back because my father died very suddenly [in August 1966]. I got so involved in the business,

ABOVE
At Stanford, where Azim Premji studied electrical engineering in 1963–66. Premji is seated fifth from left.

I wasn't able to go back to school for my degree.

Many years later, I suddenly got an urge for a degree. So I petitioned the engineering committee [at Stanford] and asked them if I could [secure my remaining credits] by correspondence. I had a decent academic ranking and I was able to convince them with the help of an executive sponsor from the engineering department. So, I did two courses by correspondence, and whatever else was required, and they gave me a final degree in electrical engineering. But they told me, 'Don't come for the graduation; we don't want to set a precedent.' So, they made an exception for me at that time. Now I think there have been more cases like that.

Did you like engineering?

Engineering helped me to think in a more disciplined way. So, it was a major asset. The technicalities of it may not have been useful but the discipline of it was.

What was Stanford like for you?

It was good, if intense. I had done two years of college in India (I studied science in St Xavier's) before going to Stanford and was able to get a lot of credits for that—I could do a five-year course in three or three-and-a-half years. In retrospect, I think I made a misjudgment: the courses in India were not of a mark to give me the credits, so I had a lot of catch-up to do in Stanford to be at the top of the class. It had me working harder than I should have—I should have had a little more space and time there.

Stanford had a very strong engineering department, especially electrical engineering, which ranked number one. The faculty had some real stalwarts, including two or three Nobel Prize winners. It was very competitive; at the same time, people had the opportunity to cater to different interests, like sports and community activities.

I was a member of an eating club, which was less formal than a fraternity [was]. We didn't live under the same roof, but we did eat all three meals together. A group of us contributed every month towards hiring a cook and the cost of the food. There were people of different levels—graduates, undergraduates, people who were doing their PhDs. And that was an interesting experience because one made close friends. And you got the best of both worlds. I was living in campus housing, so I had two roommates.

Did you also work on campus?

Yes, I worked as a night-shift telephone operator and in the cafeteria cleaning dustbins and plates. Because one required a supplementation of the exchange my father was able to send me. It was an interesting experience because it gave me, for the first time, the dignity of labor. I had never worked before. And that also added pressure because you had to work, you had to study and, at the same time, you had taken credits to cut down your five-year course into three-and-a-half.

What was the night telephone operator's job?

It wasn't too intense—the phone would barely ring ten to twelve times a night since only urgent or emergency calls could go through. So, if you had girlfriends calling up, you had to monitor those calls and cut them. The load was not heavy and the salary was very little too. But you could study during that time. It was a luxury to be able to catch up with work.

How often could you visit home?

I didn't visit at all.

Because of the expenses or because of the course load?

Expenses.

And your family? Did they visit you while you were there?

My mother visited me once soon after I landed in the US. Nobody else—we were not an international company at that point of time. I think my mother stayed for a month. I was not used to the food; she would cook for me. I built up a rash because I got so nervous there.

In your first year?

First three months. One had had a very protected life. That was quite a hit.

And her coming helped?

Yes.

STARTING OUT

When you first took over the business in 1966, were you just doing things intuitively?

[I was working] intuitively. I had zero experience in business. I was trained as an engineer, and I took a lot of courses in Western civilization and English as my electives. I did not take any business courses. So, what I studied was hardcore engineering and a lot of humanities and social sciences. So, I did things intuitively.

For example, productivity (of people) would fall every summer in Amalner; the excuse was that the temperatures

WIVP personnel in front of the company guest house in Amalner in 1977. Consumer products would remain Premji's largest business till 1994, when it was overtaken by IT.

went up to over 105 degree Fahrenheit. I ended that myth by spending an entire summer there. It established that if you get used to it, you can do solid work even during the worst of the heat. We couldn't afford air-conditioners and there were power cuts all the time.

Also, when I came on the scene, we were pricing on a full-cost basis, not on variable cost. So, we did a complete re-engineering of our cost-accounting system. I spent not less than six months and a huge amount of time each day working with the team and completely overhauled the costing system. And, broadly, that cost system is valid even today.

Why was it important to take up that as your first project?

We used to shut down the plant often during periods when we couldn't cover all costs. The overhaul fundamentally changed that. We continued production as we were able to recover the variable costs and make a positive contribution towards overheads. So, we no longer needed to shut down the plant. Seems very natural today, but it was quite revolutionary then, particularly for us, having run with that older system for twenty-five years before.

How did you learn all this?

One learned from books and from the people one worked with by asking the right questions. We bypassed, for instance, the chief accountant, who did not get these concepts, and worked with a cost accountant, a younger fellow.

The other system we changed was procurement. We used to buy wet groundnuts. The water content affected the yields. We went to a laboratory to get a read on the water content and then priced it accordingly—because the water didn't give any yields, dry groundnuts did. So that changed the way we procured, and made it more scientific.

We set up an equivalent of the Marwari pratha system, the daily accounting of profit and loss, which Marwari companies use even today. They know the production, sale and margin on a daily basis. That was never heard of in the vanaspati industry.

We started weekly calls with every region in which we sold vanaspati to get an idea of the sales we'd made and the average price of the sales, which helped us determine the margins. Such weekly calls were unheard of then. And we set up a competition among different regions to optimize the sales realizations. We were monitoring online our profitability for the week and the month and we were able to base our decisions for buying and selling on that. This supplemented the variable cost system very well.

Was there anything in your Stanford years that prepared you for it? We are just trying to understand how a twenty-one-year-old grasped these concepts.
I read. I went to professors at the [Jamnalal] Bajaj Institute of Management [Studies] and told them, 'I cannot enroll full time here, but can you recommend me your course books?' I read a great deal to understand various business subjects. I also did a few short courses at IIM Ahmedabad. One was forced into it because of the quality of people we had at that time. Most of them were very loyal, very committed, but many were completely ineffective in their jobs. We benchmarked very heavily with Hindustan Lever. One saw the contrast in the way they ran their business versus the way we ran ours. So, one got triggered by the comparisons, the benchmarks we did with other successful companies.

A few years in, you started recruiting young professionals. How did the company's old guard react to it?
We recruited very high-quality people and put them in specific roles. They were able to get reasonably good acceptance because they were placed in jobs where they ran the show and reported to me directly. The organization was very flat then. They were quite humble and didn't rub people the wrong way in terms of demonstrating their superiority.

You spent hours and days recruiting each of these early professionals. What were you looking for?
High commitment, the capability to work hard—because we had a hard-working culture—and an ability to get to the root of the problem. We gave a lot of importance to their extracurricular activities [in school and college]; we looked for people who had leadership positions in sports or in debates or if they participated in theatre, to gauge their [mental] breadth. If studies were his only focus, we would weigh it less. We didn't go for the toppers in the class—I don't think we'd even get applications from the toppers, they were in so much demand; we went for the solid middle line, the 80–70–60th percentile. It was difficult to look for track record because at that time business schools were taking in freshers [with no work experience].

Were you consciously hiring fresh graduates?
Yes, it was easier to pick people from campus than pinch the best talent from competition. We didn't have the reputation to do that.

Did you already have the idea of diversifying from vanaspati? Were you hiring talent in anticipation of that?
We were diversifying from selling commodity vanaspati to branded vanaspati through retail distribution. When I entered the business, 99 per cent of our vanaspati was sold in bulk packs to the wholesale trade. The retailer would unseal the 16.5 kg tin and dispense it by weight. As a result, our brand, Sunflower, got little play—and it even got abused. Sunflower was a premium brand, even in the wholesale market, and people would put other brands into our tin of vanaspati and dispense it. So, we started emphasizing consumer packs.

We pioneered the flexi pack in 1981 in quarter kg, half kg and one kg. At that time, HLL was experimenting with flexi packs (but they were hesitating because of negative market feedback). We hit the market first and then they followed. It was a major innovation at that time.

Alongside, we started investing in advertising. We signed up HTA. We took a strong brand positioning of '*shuddh ghee ke baad pehli pasand*' (the first choice after pure ghee). I personally worked very closely in advertising, branding and packaging.

We started weekly retail distribution for both the bulk packs and the small packs. We captured the data from the salesman to understand stocking levels, etc.

I spent twelve to fifteen days a month in the field, overseeing the distribution system when we were trying to get it off the ground, gauging how the brand was perceived, building relationships with retailers and distributors.

So, you took a combination of best practices from the Marwaris to the MNCs. What was your guiding principle for all this?
Very simple, running a profitable, successful business. We really took up our profitability. We were the envy of the vanaspati industry. We were the most profitable vanaspati company in the country—among twenty to thirty such companies.

We've heard that you would go into HLL offices, you had good relations with the leaders there. Why were they helping you?
I was very young at that time, people felt sorry for me and shared a lot of information with me (laughs).

I went to professors at the Bajaj Institute of Management [Studies] and told them, 'I cannot enroll full time here, but can you recommend me your course books?' I read a great deal to understand various business subjects. I also did a few short courses at IIM Ahmedabad.

ABOVE
From left: PS Pai and Azim Premji with Dr Gulbanoo Premji in Amalner.

What was your modus operandi? What did you tell people?
[I'd] just be straightforward. [I'd say:] I want to learn from you. Can you please help me? I want to run a successful business like you are running. What should I be doing? How do you do it? Can you share some information with me? If you are humble, people share a lot. They may not share the core secrets, but they will share a lot. I was the youngest member in every association. I became active in the toiletry association, the vanaspati association, the solvent extraction association; so, one kept meeting colleagues who were much more senior to me. And I built a rapport with them.

You weren't shy of approaching them?
No, [I thought] at the most they will say 'no, I cannot share this with you'.

We heard you'd use the bathroom to jot down notes from these meetings. And the next day, you'd share the notes with your team.
One was able to remember a lot of the conversations, so one just noted points. I dictated quickly, you know, before wastage takes place in your memory.

Where was this coming from? Was it because you'd seen tough times when you came into the business?
No. You set standards for yourself and try to beat those standards. It is an ongoing process. Set high standards. Be self-motivated to achieve those.

You were trying to outdo yourself? Wasn't wealth the end goal?
No. It took a huge effort on my part [decades later] to buy a second-hand Mercedes. And soon I got so embarrassed by it, I switched over to a hybrid Camry.

When you were renaming Western India Vegetable Products, how did you pick Wipro?
[It is a] very generic name. Very western sounding, which is an asset in our country. Simple, easy to read.

MOVING INTO INFOTECH

In a previous interview, you were asked, 'How did a vanaspati company get into IT?' You said, 'Diversification was fashionable those days.' What did you mean?
It was also strategic. We went into a business which was hi-tech, had huge opportunities, gave us differentiation by technology as well as after-sales recurring revenue. It was a major market opportunity because IBM had exited [in 1977].

When did you know the IT services business was going to be the mainstay?
The early 1990s. Business really took off then.

In 2010, I decided to give away most of my wealth to the Foundation. My family got behind it fully. We have never been a greedy family.

ABOVE
Yasmeen and Azim Premji with sons Tariq (left) and Rishad (right) at the Azim Premji Foundation, Bangalore, 2020.

What made you get into the software products business (Wipro Systems) in 1983?
We wanted to be in product software but, unfortunately, we went into consumer products software. Strategically, we should have gone into product software for specific industries. We did build a telecom package, but we were not very successful [with it]. I don't think we invested enough in it; we missed that bus. We had a small company (in Wipro Systems), which we could have used as a nucleus ... it was a major strategic blunder.

How did you decide to move to Bangalore? What was that related to?
Cost of living. We couldn't afford Bombay anymore. Bombay real estate was expensive in those days also. Bangalore was relatively so much cheaper. Less cost, more quality, more engineering talent concentration here.

When you look at entering a sector, how much weight do you put on integrity, on how clean the business is?
Absolutely fundamental. It's one reason we didn't look at real estate—we didn't want to use agents, because agents are a backdoor way of giving kickbacks, aren't they? We were very selective in the government business we took. IT is a reasonably clean business, it's export-oriented. Toiletries [consumer care] is also a clean business. Even hydraulics is a very clean business because you deal with large companies, it's a technology business.

For the first thirty years, Wipro was a manufacturing company. Then it pivoted into a services company in the 1990s. Was it very difficult to shift the mindset from a manufacturing to a services company?
We got the right management. So, I didn't personally run it. It was run by professionals. I think we were good in picking those professionals.

GLOBALIZATION

Wipro was an inward-looking domestic company. Around 1991, the time of globalization, we find you saying, 'Let's become customer-focused, outward-looking.' What was on your mind?
We were building a global presence, so we had to be a global company. We couldn't just be a domestic, inward-looking company. Competition was getting global within the domestic market. Competition was opening up in terms of IT services, products, even in toilet soap. And opportunities were opening up globally.

In 1993, Wipro did a visioning exercise with management guru Sumantra Ghoshal on how to think about the future. Was it a reaction to global competition arriving at Indian shores or was it driven by something else?
It was mostly driven by the fact that we were going global. We had to be looking out and, also, looking in with a different lens because of the intensity of competition being built up by global companies entering India. Such was not the case prior to the 1990s, when everything was licensed, and India didn't have the image to attract global investments. There were Unilever and Johnson & Johnson, but they were few and far between. Proctor & Gamble wasn't a strong presence and Colgate was there, but not in competing products.

Was it difficult to shift the mindset from being a domestic company to a global company?
While it happened very gradually, I don't think it was terribly difficult, no.

PARTNERING WITH GE

The 1990s was mostly about joint ventures. You made a very significant decision to tie up with GE.
In healthcare systems. We were also discussing a joint venture with HP in IT that never came about. HP was a great name. The company was at its peak at that time. They had very solid values, similar to ours.

What were you looking for in joint ventures? Were you feeling that being on your own was not going to be enough? Was this a confidence issue or was it ambition?
[These explorations were led by] ambition, it was not a confidence issue. In global IT services, you didn't require a global partner. In the domestic market for hardware, we thought a global partner would help bring the latest technology and help us address the high end of the market.

How did the tie-up with GE happen?
Healthcare systems was quite like the IT business, selling to large customers. We brought all these competencies [to the table]. GE was looking for a partner and we pitched and, finally, we won. They had selected another Indian company to be their partner; we got Jack Welch to reverse that

GE was looking for a partner for a joint venture. We pitched and, finally, we won. They had selected another Indian company to be their partner. We got Jack Welch to reverse that decision. I wrote him a personal one-page letter. I think I spent two days drafting it.

ABOVE
Azim Premji and Jack Welch, CEO of GE, during the latter's visit to Wipro GE in Bangalore. The joint venture for the manufacture, sale and service of diagnostic and imaging products was incorporated in 1990 and continues to go strong.

decision—something that had never happened before.

Word is you made a personal pitch to Welch.
Yeah, I wrote a personal one-page letter. I think I spent two days drafting it. We didn't like [the idea of] losing.

Was it a business decision? You felt this was going to be a huge opportunity and you didn't want to miss it—or was it more personal?
It's a combination of both, I think. GE was a good, strong name and we were hoping to get a lot of management-expertise learning and transfer from them (which happened, but not as intensely as we thought it would). The joint venture has gone through its ups and downs, but it's a very successful business today.

Were you very closely involved with it?
A lot initially, including interviewing from A–Z to get the right teams in place and transferring key people from Wipro into that joint venture. I worked very closely with [GE's Asia-Pacific head] Chuck Pieper. I studied GE deeply—it was at its pinnacle during those times. Like IBM, they were studied and covered very extensively. Absolute benchmark companies.

Joint ventures are tricky; most don't work out. What makes this one work even so many years later?
I think an ability to have employees—starting with the CEO—think in terms of the joint venture, not in terms of either partner. That was a very important criterion, [they had to internalize the fact that] they work for the joint venture. Their interests had to be the interests of the joint venture. Don't pander to either party; do what is right.

I think that's a very successful approach—and it works even today though GE is a very dominant force. The Wipro influence has got diluted, but they still have a lot of respect for us. It's a 50–50 venture in spirit even though they have 51 per cent shareholding.

Do you like a good fight? What do you fight for?
Not for the sake of a fight. I fight for our rights. Whether in a joint venture or in a business deal or anything else in life. But I equally fight for the rights (internally) of our partners, clients, etc. We must be fair—to everyone.

Our work in the Foundation is also a fight—a fight for justice, equality, humaneness ... a better world.

What did you get out of it other than a financially successful venture?
We got reasonable transfer of management technology and expertise, their training initiatives, their appraisal initiatives, the way they planned their future. GE had very strong leaders across the board, very high-quality people and, despite their aggression, their people are fair. They may have politics within their organization and with partners they're dominating—but [they're] very fair.

Some of GE's leaders became larger than life. How are things different at Wipro?
The chairmen in GE become demigods, I don't think the chairman here [at Wipro] is a demigod. That's the major difference.

You seem very aware of it. Is [the low-key approach] your personal style or something you worked on because you felt it was not good for the business?
Personality.

Is that just in Wipro, or are you like that in other parts of your life as well?
You'd better ask my wife that—have you met her?

I have.
I hope she said nice things about me (smiles).

She said you've been very intense and very driven for as long as she has known you. And your mother told her you were always like that. But your colleagues say they liked working here because you allowed people to challenge you.
You get the best from people when you let them speak out. They shouldn't fear speaking out. That's how you create a very open environment and that's how you get rid of politics. Our major strength is that there's little politics in the organization, whereas large companies [generally] have a lot of politics.

DIVERSIFICATIONS

Other than IT, there was a series of other businesses that Wipro got into through the 1970s and '80s and '90s: Fluid Power, Peripherals, Lighting, Finance, to name just a few. How did you look at new opportunities?
One was looking at the excitement of doing something new, more than anything else. It was fashionable to look at

completely unrelated diversifications in those days. ... The Indian market was so raw (for instance, the waiting time for scooters was three years!) that you could diversify and still get into leadership positions because competition was only just growing. It's far more mature now. Diversifications are no longer easy.

Wipro Beckman was a forerunner to Wipro GE. Not a very successful business. We went on a major trip at that time to do joint ventures. We were negotiating very actively for a joint venture with GE in lighting and it didn't go through. We had really learned the business in the process of [working towards] the joint venture, so we decided to do it on our own. It's an average business, reasonably successful, but nowhere close to our toiletries business.

How did Wipro Finance happen?

That was a major disaster; it could have destroyed the whole company. We went into it because it was a booming business at that point of time. We didn't realize its complexity; we didn't realize the complexity of collecting money. We underestimated the number of crooks in the business. We didn't have strong credit controls nor was the leadership focused adequately on risk. It was a mess. We wrote off a lot of money—and it was a hell of a lot of money at that point of time—but we paid back every single paisa to people. It was a separate company. We could have declared it insolvent and not have had to pay any of the debts, but we didn't declare ourselves insolvent.

Why didn't you do that?

Personal reputation, personal obligation to people. Honor.

You shut it down within a few years. Did you lose sleep over it before shutting it down?

Of course. The write-off was something like 30 per cent of Wipro's net worth. You have a lot at stake in a new business. There's an emotional connect with a new business. It's not easy to sever it.

Wipro Finance seems so out of character with everything else you have done. Most of the businesses have manufacturing, R&D, technology ... this is pure play services.

Finance is very hi-tech, don't underestimate it.

You do due diligence before you start businesses. So, how did you not see the risks in this business?

We didn't do due diligence; we messed it up. We didn't take care of our accounts receivables. It's as simple as that. We didn't do due diligence of the parties we lent to, and later found that the same party had borrowed from four people against the same assets. It was very bad risk management. Risk management is critical to the finance business. If you don't do risk management well, you're executing badly.

Wipro Finance taught us hard lessons. Don't be stupid. Don't underestimate competition. If you want to build scale in a business, you need to be dominant, you can't do a fringe business. If you try to do a fringe business, exploit a short-term opportunity. You have to get the right management in place ... which, through hard experience in the industry, you learn.

[In hindsight] I think we should have focused on building our existing businesses better. In the last twenty years, there has been more consolidation.

Is there anything you regret not doing from a business opportunity perspective? Areas left unexplored or you didn't try hard enough in?

Maybe foods. It's a booming market. Look at ITC. Their atta, spaghetti are brilliant, and they're making good money.

Have you ever felt scared or nervous about taking these decisions to diversify?

Of course, you feel nervous about doing something new ... but you do it because you think you can make a success of it. Finance was probably when I felt most nervous.

Is there any business that you wanted to shut down in hindsight?

We stayed with the hydraulics business unduly long. It was bleeding. But once it turned around, we decided not to divest it. We could've considered divesting it much earlier, which we didn't do.

IT LEADERSHIP

Let's talk about the listing on the New York Stock Exchange. What was that day like for you?

We did a very small listing, fortunately [for us]. I think NYSE handled it well, we got Jack Welch down for it—he was at his peak in those days, and for him to invest the time and come down from Fairfield to NYC sent a strong message. We were the first real big technology cache on NYSE and they went overboard on us because they wanted more technology companies, everyone was going to NASDAQ. We got a king's treatment, it felt good.

Why did you choose NYSE over NASDAQ?
There were some technical reasons. It was more prestigious, positioned us differently, away from the pack. Also, because we were a more diversified business, NYSE made more sense [over NASDAQ, for tech stocks]. It was an important day for Wipro. The listing helped with customers.

In the early years, you had stable leadership in every business; CEOs had long runs. But after 2000, in the IT business, the CEO tenure became shorter and shorter. What do you attribute that to?
Vivek Paul left because he wanted to join a private equity company. After Vivek, I took over the business. Then Girish [Paranjpe] and Suresh [Vaswani] came. Which did not work out too well. Then TK [Kurien] took over. He took early retirement and now works with Premji Invest.

Any business goes through a lot of transformations all the time. In Wipro Ltd you have to reinvent yourself all the time, tech moves so fast. The customer demands are escalating so high. That's a very complex business—very, very complex.
(Editor's note: These interviews were recorded in January and February 2020, and do not reflect the latest leadership changes at Wipro Ltd.)

When Paul left in 2005, why did you decide to run the IT business by yourself?
I wanted to prove to myself that I could run it—do as good or bad a job as my predecessors and successors (laughs). I ran it, na! [We didn't want to take a risk and bring in an external leader and] no other leader was ready at that time. I think I ran the business for three years before the joint CEOs took over.

We could have gone to the market (to recruit), but we underestimated our draw, which we realize now. The fact that nearly 70 per cent of the company is owned by a philanthropic foundation, the fact that the company has a solid reputation, that the Chairman doesn't interfere with the CEO beyond a certain point, gives it a very strong professional reputation.

You've been very effective as a Chairman. What did you learn when running the business directly?
I've always been very hands-on. In that period, I ran the business with two or three people in almost CEO-like roles. I elevated some people, consolidated [others] under them. I thought I managed the transition [from Vivek leaving to taking over] very well. We didn't lose any key people, including people who got pushed down to reporting a level lower [than they did under Vivek] because of the consolidation.

So why did you give up in three years?
The Consumer business was growing. The Foundation needed my attention. I was putting in eighty-five-to-ninety-hour weeks, fifty-two weeks a year. It was strenuous.

What did you set out to do in those three years?
I think I got the team more charged ... It was fun! I liked that rhythm. It boosted my self-confidence, taking on that job and doing justice to it. Not adequate justice, but justice. It was fun working with twelve to fifteen direct reports, very good human beings, very motivated. They gave their life for the company, in a very real sense. Like most of our top management today. And having direct experience of that ... was fun.

We've heard that you give your leaders their responsibilities, then you refrain from micro-managing. Has that been true with all the CEO changes?
A little less so with Suresh [and] Girish. In their case, first, there was the coordination with two CEOs running the show. It meant that I was the only point of integration for some things. I think they worked beautifully as a team, but even then, an operation becomes difficult with two co-CEOs. So, I became a little more active as Executive Chairman.

In retrospect, the joint CEO plan was doomed to failure. Why did you do it?
No, I don't think it was doomed to failure. Basically, I thought that I didn't have one person ready enough [to be CEO]. So, we split the job into two. It's just that it did not work out to expectation. They worked wonderfully well as a team. It wasn't a failure of the model.

But so many people were skeptical even then [of the model working].
I credit their work as a team, [there was] zero politics. It is just that results fell short of expectations, as compared to competition.

Was the whole episode difficult?
Yes. And I don't think it was handled as well as it could've been, as I should have [handled it].

Would you have done it differently if you had the choice again? The two-CEO structure, the way it was handled, the separations?

Yes, I would've gone to the market and hired a good person. We didn't think a person located overseas would agree to join [us], with our center of gravity in India. I think that was a block with us then. One wasn't confident enough of working [in that particular role] with someone entirely alien to this culture. Maybe that was another [factor].

With each leadership change over the last two decades, a lot of people left the company.

We lost talent in high-quality middle management. We lost some people who could have been very competent senior management.

Why did they leave?

They saw opportunities outside. Or didn't have enough respect for their leaders. Or didn't think we took care of them adequately.

Is this during the time Wipro's growth began slowing down?

I suppose so. But I don't think that was the chief motivator, I think it was because we didn't look after these people well enough—in a few ways, not merely compensation.

How is that being corrected now?

We have really strengthened the quality of people we hire from campuses and laterally also. We have worked on their roles, the responsibilities, the compensation, many dimensions. For a period, on campus, we didn't differentiate adequately on compensation. We've changed that now over the past couple of years. Earlier, we weren't giving all this enough attention. Everyone was clubbed as equal. Now, we have differentiated very significantly. We're looking for talent. The idea is to groom them and give them very early responsibility. This is true across levels.

Why haven't there been many senior women leaders in Wipro? You're diverse in other ways.

We haven't recruited aggressively enough capable women leaders at the middle-management level to go into senior management. And what we tried to grow from within has not worked adequately. It has been complicated. For example, in spite of the fact that women in India often have house help, most of the house load falls on them ... too many of them would move with their husbands and we weren't multi-locational earlier. We lost a lot of good women to this. We also lost them once they had a child. We weren't able to backfill this loss of excellent women leaders adequately. I think we have just not been proactive enough on this. I think it's one of our major failures.

Also, I think as men we were most comfortable working with men. We must change it, but it has been a reality, particularly with Indian men. [We] must face reality if we have to change it.

DEMERGING WEL

Let's turn to WEL. Everything about it is different, the rhythm is different, the scale is different—you were managing 200,000 people in IT!

Everything was different. That's why we spun off our Consumer and Infrastructure Engineering business separately—it was confusing the investors. We wanted a more dedicated focus.

You'd always said no to demerging, so how did you finally convince yourself to go ahead with it?

It was just causing too much confusion with investors—are you an IT company? Or a consumer care company? It's the best decision we made. IT was really the bigger part of the business. Plus, we wanted to take more risks in those businesses through acquisitions—though it was taking risks at that time also [before the demerger]. That made the demerger more logical and understandable. After that demerger, we weren't undergoing the scrutiny (of short-term investors) of every acquisition, and we've done well there. That business would have had a Rs 50,000-crore market cap today.

Didn't you think of listing the two companies separately? Why did you take the Consumer, Infrastructure Engineering and Healthcare business private?

Listed companies are a headache in a way; it's so much more fun being a private company. And despite being private we have all the governance systems of a listed company, from quarterly reviews and quarterly board meetings to annual general meetings. It'd be a very easy switchover for us to list it, if we wanted to. It would not put any new pressure on management either. [But] I don't want a headache. We don't need the money, we are generating enough cash flows, we don't pay dividends.

Why doesn't that business pay dividends?
Why should it pay dividends? We generate a lot of cash flow for acquisitions. We invest in brands; we plough back money into advertising. Our advertising budget is Rs 400 crore, so we're happy with our present operating margin. Unilever runs it at 17 per cent, but we put the money back to grow. That's why we're growing at two to three times their rate. Two times their rate at least. [We give] full support to brands. We'd be tempted to try to show higher margins if we were a listed company, but we would have to take the trade-off on lower growth. Some of the acquisitions we've made, our margins get diluted, but we don't care about that since we maintain a fairly consistent 12 per cent margin.

Was the timing of it significant? It was done in 2013. Did something shift in you, or did something else happen?
No, it was just pressure for clarity from investors on the one hand. And the other, that business was getting large enough to be spun off. Then there's the significant slowdown of the IT sector over the past five–six years. It was anticipated because of the size of the IT businesses. And I've desired to grow Consumer Care and Infrastructure Engineering significantly through acquisitions, which we did. We're no longer answerable to external shareholders on a quarter-to-quarter basis on each such long-term decision, though we still maintain the discipline.

So Santoor is now the third-largest brand in the country?
Second; it's overtaken Lux.

Did you ever think in the mid-1980s, when you were much smaller than Levers, that one day you'd have a brand competing with theirs?
No. Santoor has been quite a spectacular brand, strong brand. It's a brand we have taken care of very well. We're very careful that what we do does not dilute the brand. Every brand extension is very deeply researched because we just cannot afford to send the wrong signals to the consumer.

Is it a kick, knowing that Santoor has displaced one of their brands?
You know, I think that [the consumer products] industry has very honorable competition. That's what I like about that industry. The standards were set by the multinationals earlier, not by Indian companies—not that Indian companies are any less successful now—and the toiletry industry, the personal care industry, has had very high standards.

What about infrastructure engineering? That's your second-oldest business after vanaspati. How do you look back on that?
It's a very cyclical business. We've tried to change; we've diversified the portfolio to different sub-segments of the business, which are relative. It's a business in which we have dominance globally now. In hydraulics, cylinders, various heavy off-the-road equipment, we probably have the second-largest market share. But it's not a tremendously profitable business because the original buyers keep squeezing you for margins all the time. We have to do cost takeouts all the time. But we are very strong on engineering and our global footprint.

WIPRO NOW

How do you look back on the last decade of Wipro Ltd?
We lost our leadership position, very clearly. But I think the structure is good, the people are good. I think we were the first movers—after Accenture—on digitization. We managed the transformation to be a strong quality organization in Wipro Ltd. Quality levels have improved, customer satisfaction levels have improved significantly. Size is a disadvantage, but not a critical one. We're large enough to swing the game.

Would you have liked to turn the ship around?
Yes. There'd have been more self-satisfaction. But I think it requires a fresh approach.

Was it distressful for you to leave Wipro?
No. It wasn't hard to let go. [My retirement was] decided in 2017. It made sense. Rishad was ready. I'd touch seventy-four. How long do you continue? Plus I wanted to devote much more time to the Foundation. Then there is Premji Invest, which is very large now. And WEL, which I get involved with once a quarter, again for a full day for each of them.

The Foundation and the Wipro Board meetings are fairly intense. And I over-prepare for them because that's my involvement in the whole situation. I'm not involved in the operations, but I read the papers carefully, also the second-level papers, and that takes time. So each Board meeting requires six–seven days of intense preparation once a quarter, a little more than that, in fact.

My work week is much more relaxed now; I work much more from home; I may not be in the office more than two days a week.

LEFT
Rishad Premji with school children at the Earthian awards 2019 at Wipro's Sarjapur campus. Launched in 2011, Wipro Earthian is one of India's largest sustainability education programs, aimed at fostering sustainable thinking and action among the youth.

BUILDING SUCCESSION

You took over Wipro quite suddenly [because of the untimely death of your father]. Were you conscious that your son Rishad be given the time to transition?
Well, he's been there for twelve years, on the Board for four. He has been decently groomed. It's not completely unfamiliar to him [as the business was to me, when I took over]. I think I should have gone two years earlier. But I was very determined to see if I could turn the company [around]—which I was unsuccessful at. So, I delayed it by two years. And then I thought it's getting too much.

[If we've had one major focus] from 2008, it's been building succession. And it's been successful. The acceptability of Rishad within the organization and without has been extraordinary. It's all part of a plan, it couldn't happen automatically.

When you started out, you said there would never be another family member in Wipro, which upset your mother so much, she didn't talk to you for a year. In that context, how easy was it for you to initiate the process of bringing Rishad into the company?
Not easy.

What were you grappling with?
One, that I'd made a statement. Two, I was not sure. But I had made up my mind to donate most of my wealth to the Foundation, and there had to be continuity in the ownership. So, we inducted him and he shaped up well, shaped up very well.

Were you worried about the signal it would send your professional managers?
I think it has been a brilliant induction. Absolutely brilliant. We did it very differently from how other companies have [inducted family members]. It made life easier for us, made life easier for him.

But it was clear that he would not be inducted as CEO or that the business wouldn't be handed over to him to run.
At that stage, yes.

PHILANTHROPY

Most people would be happy to have built one institution in their lifetimes. You have built two—Wipro and the Foundation.
Well, Wipro is not only IT. There is also the consumer,

engineering and healthcare businesses. Worth about $2 billion, a fourth the size of Wipro Ltd, and growing fast.

You are a businessman as much as you are a philanthropist. What is the knowledge you took from one life to the other?
Build scale—that's most important. Scale with quality. And pick the right leadership. Motivate that leadership. And that leadership should be able to pick strong people under them, people with a commitment to purpose. [This applies to] both Wipro and the Foundation. [Both are also] very culture-based—[like the Spirit of Wipro,] we have a Spirit of the Foundation also. It has permeated the culture, as it permeated the culture at Wipro. That culture is there in the fieldwork, at the University, in the Philanthropic Initiatives. And now we're trying to bring more seamlessness among the three.

At what point did you decide to give away most of your wealth to the Foundation?
Ten years ago [in 2010].

Was this a long time coming? Or was there a definite moment when you made up your mind?
[It was a] creeping thought. Well, I don't know how, I just decided.

You've said that your family completely resonates with this idea [of giving away most of your wealth to philanthropy]. When you first floated the idea, what was their response?
They got behind it fully, perhaps gradually, but totally. We've never been a greedy family.

You have three different areas of work under the Azim Premji Foundation. There's direct operations—the fieldwork. Then there's the Philanthropic Initiatives, where you work with partners and the University. In your mind, how does it all come together?
The fieldwork and the university are very well tied together. The core is education. At the University, we basically look for people (as students) with a social mission. They spend a two-to-four-year period [getting their degrees], a lot of it in the field. Ninety per cent of the [University] graduates go on to work in social causes. So, evidently, the model works. We also use the university to train a lot of the NGOs we work with. So that's quite closely tied together.

So far as Philanthropic Initiatives is concerned, it is an arm through which we support our partners because we want reach in areas other than education. That works well. We have strategic areas—areas where we want to scale in, and we also have areas where we just support good people doing good work for vulnerable groups, and we are not bothered about scale there.

But, overall, they come together because we want to make a difference to our country. All our efforts are working together in a complementary way to have more justice, equity and humaneness in our society. It's a commitment to contribute to making the promises and values of our constitution real for every citizen.

You may not even see the Foundation's work fructify in your lifetime, at least not all of it. Are you satisfied with how things have gone?
Oh yes, without a question. For example, I spend time with the NGOs we support through our Philanthropic Initiatives. It's remarkable, the kind of work and dedication some of these people have. In Delhi, we're associated with an NGO that works with eight-to-twenty-year-olds with a history of drug abuse. Half of them are HIV-positive. They were spending Rs 3,000 a day on drugs, which they made picking pockets, stealing cellphones. Then there is a smaller group of girls between the ages of ten and twenty. The girls were selling themselves, or their boyfriends were selling them. It was such a sad sight. But what this NGO does for them is remarkable. They are undernourished when they come to the shelter. The NGO looks after their food, education—and now they look cheerful. Similarly, the government schoolteachers that we work with, and we work with literally thousands of teachers and schools, their dedication is remarkable. They are making a difference to the lives of the most disadvantaged and building our nation.

How much time do you spend on the Foundation?
Fifteen to twenty per cent of my time. I like making field visits to the extent my back can take it.

What makes you hopeful when you see all this?
The change you can make in lives. Complete change. About 80 per cent of the girls will move on to other livelihoods. Ninety per cent of the boys will have normal lives. And that makes a huge difference. Children are learning better in schools—not only subjects but values.

Is there a role model for your philanthropic work?
Not really. We have built it with our purpose in mind. And

The fieldwork and the university are very well tied together. We look for students with a social mission, from non-metro areas. They spend a two- to four-year period getting their degrees, a lot of that time is spent in the field. Ninety per cent of the University's graduates go on to work in social causes. We also use the University to train many of the NGOs we work with.

LEFT
Children, photographed in 2019, crossing a bridge to get to school in Uttarkashi, a town in Uttarakhand, India.

OPPOSITE PAGE
A classroom, photographed in 2019, in a school in Gulbarga, a city in the state of Karnataka, India.

with the core idea that we have to build institutions that outlast all of us, are unwaveringly committed to the purpose, have strong values and have deep expertise.

For example, for the University, we wanted a very high standard of teachers. We got more than what we expected—because of many reasons, including [Wipro's] reputation and our philanthropic reputation. We're very selective about our students as well. We do reference checks to see the scholarships we give are merited—50 per cent of our students are on scholarships, part or full—and for some we even reimburse expenses because, otherwise, their families will have great difficulty. We try to assess students for their social purpose, who come from communities they'll go back to in the smaller towns or villages.

Twenty-thirty per cent of the people running the Foundation come from corporate [jobs to work] in the social sector, at one-third their previous salaries. It's a major sacrifice to make for a choice in life. The attitude of the people is different.

What would you credit that to?

Our leadership, the work we do, the values, the fact that we don't want credit for the work we do. That's how we're successful. When you start taking credit, you become overbearing and a threat to the unions, the politicians, the bureaucracy and others. We work with them; we give them all the credit; and much of it is really due to them. You are on their side all the time.

You're working very closely with the government, which you didn't do much of as a businessman. How has that been?

It's been good. The teachers are very good—it's complete abuse and absurd when people say government teachers are incompetent or truant. Maybe some are, but then so are some people in our company! Eighty per cent [of government schoolteachers] are committed, 20 per cent are outstanding, 60 per cent will act on the basis of the environment provided to them. It was a surprise to us earlier that they get so charged to do their job. For example, the field organization conducts intense monthly and fortnightly meetings of the teachers by providing the resources and the facilitators, and the teachers come on their own [initiative] on weekends. You can't get any Wipro people to come for training on weekends! There's a different level of dedication, expectation, sense of mission here.

From left :
Dileep Ranjekar,
Anurag Behar,
Azim Premji,
Rishad Premji and
Yasmeen Premji at
the Azim Premji
University convocation,
Bangalore, in 2019.

EPILOGUE

Have you had fun in these fifty years at Wipro?
Without question. The Consumer business was the most fun. You can touch and feel it. I spent a lot of time in the market initially. We built it from scratch, running with stockists, filling their forms ... and they really opened up, if I can be modest. Building the Santoor brand. The Sunflower brand. Yardley was an acquisition, but building that too. And making a success of the international acquisitions. We've really taken it places, we have some very powerful brands today.

We got an offer for Santoor from Unilever, which we had turned down. When our market cap peaked (in 2000), I went back to Keki Dadiseth and said I want to buy Unilever (laughs). And we were something like 70 per cent of the value of Unilever globally—$65 billion here, and Unilever market cap was $70 billion or $80 billion.

Of all the hats you wear, what has been your learning from each of them?
You have to have a quest for excellence, for leadership in whatever you do. Otherwise it's a mishmash. In WCC, we're right at the top, winning against Unilever, which is a very strong business, and against all global competition. We're number one, two or three in Asia-Pacific countries against global competition. It's very impressive. And in India, we're growing in the top two consistently.

In Aerospace, we're growing well. We did a good acquisition in Israel. In Automation, we've got off to a good start, with one small acquisition. That will put us in a different sphere. It's a very small market but it's really booming.

What's the mantra for success in WCC and WIN?
At WCC, get people who are strong marketers. At WIN, for new areas, you have to understand the technology. You have to make the right technological bets.

Which are the time periods you've liked the most?
I think I was at my best between twenty-seven and forty years of age. I was at my most creative. Then I started deteriorating. I over-professionalized, was perhaps too fast. You can get too guided by professionals; you lose the gut of entrepreneurship. Look at the pioneering things we did in the early days—our appraisal system, our stock option system, our pratha system—it was remarkable in those days. You had to talk on a 'lightning phone call' that cost a bomb because, half the time, calls wouldn't go through. Still, every week, we had that call for two hours. But it generated such tight accountability.

> Twenty to thirty per cent of the people running the Foundation come from corporate [jobs to work] in the social sector, at one-third their previous salaries. [I give the credit to] our leadership, the work we do, the values, the fact that we don't want credit for the work we do. That's how we're successful.

That's what you mean by creativity. You were able to create all these systems and processes for Wipro?
Yeah. Like the costing system we set up. Earlier, we used to close down the plant when we didn't achieve total cost, which meant the entire amount of overheads, we threw it down the drain. With the new costing system, we changed that; it was a fundamental change in approach.

Do you feel you lost creativity when you stepped back from running the business and you became Chairman?
Maybe, I don't know.

Did the fun go away when you stepped away from running a business?
There is fun in running a business, but also in overseeing a business.

Where have you been more successful between these two models?
I've been equally successful and equally unsuccessful. ◆

Interviewed by Mitu Jayashankar, 2020

E

CAST OF CHARACTERS

A LAKSHMAN RAO (AL RAO)
One of the first recruits at Wipro Infotech in 1980, Rao, a software professional, was fundamental to the growth of Wipro's R&D division. He moved to Vs in 1992 as vice president, Technical. As CTO, he played a critical role in establishing Quality systems. Ahead of his retirement in 2009, Rao was the COO for Wipro Technologies.

A SADASHIVAM
One of the first batch of recruits at Wipro Infotech, he was the company's lead man in the establishment of the hardware factory at Mysore. He was with Wipro till 1999.

AV SRIDHAR
After working in sales and marketing functions in 1981–87, Sridhar headed the Sun division at Wipro Infotech and went on to lead the Peripherals, Personal Computers and CAD CAM divisions. In 1995, he founded the E-commerce division and worked there before leaving in 1997.

ABDULTYEB E MASKATI
A member of the WIVPL Board in the 1940s, Maskati came from a family involved in a textile business that stretched from Siam to Japan.

ABID ALI NEEMUCHWALA
He joined Wipro in 2015 as COO and transitioned into the role of CEO in 2016. Under his leadership, Wipro focused on AI, automation, big data and cloud. He also led Wipro's efforts to localize its workforces across the world. He left Wipro in early 2020.

AMBI PARAMESWARAN
As part of FCB Ulka, he led the recasting of the advertising for Wipro's Santoor soap, honoring the time-tested 'mummy' theme but updating it for the mid-1990s. The ads were a resounding success for Wipro Consumer Products.

ANAND TALWAI
After joining Wipro in 1981, Talwai went on to lead Wipro's Communications Division; he also headed its Customer Satisfaction and Quality functions. Later, he was chief executive of two joint ventures, Wipro-BT and Wipro Net. He was with Wipro till 2000.

ANDY GROVE
The longtime chief executive and chairman of Intel, his path crossed with Wipro's when the then little-known Indian company used the 80386 microprocessor in the Series 386, a first in the world, in 1987. Grove wrote Wipro a personal note in recognition of the achievement.

ANURAG BEHAR
After a long stint at Wipro GE, Behar moved in 2002, to become the corporate vice president of brand, innovation and quality, of Wipro. In 2004, he took charge of Wipro's engineering business, led it to a high growth trajectory, and founded two new businesses, Eco Energy and Wipro Water. He is currently CEO of Azim Premji Foundation and also oversees sustainability and CSR for Wipro.

ARDESHIR DALAL
Dalal was an administrator and businessman associated with the Tata Group. He served as collector in various parts of India before becoming the first Indian to be municipal commissioner of Bombay in 1928.

ARDESHIR DARABSHAW SHROFF
An eminent industrialist, banker and economist who lived in the first half of the twentieth century, he was a vocal proponent of free enterprise.

ARTHUR EISENKRAFT
Eisenkraft is Distinguished Professor of Science Education, professor of physics, and director of the Center of Science and Math in Context at the University of Massachusetts, Boston. He is involved with Wipro Science Education Fellowship, USA.

ASHOK NARASIMHAN
He joined Wipro as general manager, Finance, in 1978 and in 1979, spearheaded Wipro's diversification into computer hardware by setting up Wipro Infotech. In 1983, he led the company into the software products business with Wipro Systems before moving out in 1988.

ASHOK SOOTA
With a background in manufacturing and operations, Soota joined Wipro in 1984 as the head of the Infotech business and helmed both the hardware and software arms till 1999. He helped Wipro expand into allied territories in hardware and become a hugely profitable business. In the process, he emerged as the popular face of Wipro in the IT industry and media.

AZIM PREMJI
Premji inherited a small vanaspati company in 1966 and grew it into a global IT giant over fifty-three years. He set up the Azim Premji Foundation in 2001, which works to help improve India's public education system, supports other not-for-profits to help people with deep vulnerabilities and runs a University.
His PE Fund, Premji Invest, set up in 2006, invests in medium and early-stage companies.
In 2019, he retired as chairman of Wipro Ltd and is now a non-executive, non-independent director. He continues to be chairman of the privately held Wipro Enterprises Ltd, the consumer, engineering and healthcare wings of the conglomerate. He is ranked among the top five philanthropists in India.

BEHRAM N KARANJIA
A member of the first board of WIVPL, constituted in 1945, he also served as mayor of Bombay in 1939–40.

BHANUMURTHY BM
He joined Wipro Systems in 1992 as a program manager and transitioned into several roles, including leading the retail and consumer goods vertical and building the business application service line. He has also led global delivery

operations, people supply chain, quality and information services. He is currently president and chief operating officer of Wipro Ltd.

BILL GATES
The co-founder of Microsoft Corp, Gates is a technologist, business leader and philanthropist. The Wipro–Microsoft relationship dates back to 2001.

BV VENKATESH
The first head of marketing and sales at Wipro Infotech who joined in 1980, he pulled off the first ever sale of Wipro's computer hardware system.

CHARLES PAUL (CHUCK) PIEPER
Handpicked by Jack Welch to lead GE's foray into Asia, Pieper shortlisted and then backed Wipro as a partner for its joint venture in healthcare technology in 1989. He was a member of the board of Wipro GE from 1989 to 1992.

CK PRAHALAD
An academic, author and corporate strategist, Prahalad came to be associated with Wipro from 1995, leading visioning exercises and advising on talent management, global market share and finding its identity as a technology company. He was a Distinguished University Professor at the University of Michigan.

DA PRASANNA
After joining in 1978 in charge of human resources, Prasanna laid down processes to attract talent and headhunted senior leadership for Wipro's various divisions. Later, he switched to a business role, heading Wipro's venture in medical devices through partnerships with Beckman Instruments and GE. He was CEO of Wipro GE Medical Systems till 2001 and left in 2003.

DEVJI TOKARSEE MULJEE
He was part of the first board of directors of Western India Vegetable Products Limited, constituted in 1945. He passed away in 1951.

DIJU RAHA
Vice president of International R&D at Bell Northern Research (later Nortel Networks), Raha came from Canada to India looking for software talent that would give them a cost advantage in the early 1990s. BNR gave Wipro Systems one of its first R&D-focused contracts.

DILEEP RANJEKAR
After joining WVIP in 1976 as personnel manager at the Amalner factory, he went on to head HR for the Consumer Products Division and then took over the HR function for all of Wipro. One of Premji's closest confidants, he played a significant role in building and nourishing Wipro's leadership bench. In 2002, he joined the Azim Premji Foundation and is currently its co-CEO.

DR (MRS) GULBANOO PREMJI
A medical doctor and founder of the Society for the Rehabilitation of Crippled Children, Dr (Mrs) Premji ran the Children's Orthopaedic Hospital in Bombay. Wife of Mohamedhusain Hasham Premji and mother of Azim Premji, she was chairman of Western India Vegetable Products Limited between 1966 and 1983.

FATIMA ISMAIL
One of the founders of the Society for the Rehabilitation of Crippled Children, she was a close associate of Dr (Mrs) Premji.

FEROZE S WADIA
An early shareholder of Western India Vegetable Products, Wadia was known for his disruptive questioning during shareholder meetings.

GANGARAM VALLABHJI
He was part of the first board of directors of WVIP, which was constituted in 1945. He resigned in 1961.

GARY COLE
A product manager, Cole pushed Wipro Systems to develop Instaplan, a project management system, for clients in the US in 1987.

GHANSHYAM DAS BIRLA
The founder of the Birla industrial empire and a close associate of MK Gandhi, GD Birla inherited the family trade in cotton and diversified into multiple other areas, such as aluminum, cement and chemicals.

GIRISH ELCHURI
One of the first campus recruits at Wipro Systems, Elchuri was program manager from 1983 to 1992. He was one of the first band of Wiproites tobe based in the US to develop products for the American market.

GIRISH PARANJPE
He joined Wipro in 1990 and went on to serve in several leadership positions— most notably as head of the BFSI vertical—before being appointed joint CEO of Wipro's IT business in 2008. A collaborative, thoughtful, big-picture leader, he and Wipro parted ways in 2011.

HASHAM PREMJI
He arrived in Bombay from Kutch in the late nineteenth century and joined the rice trade, growing his enterprise into a global business, with offices in then-Burma, the Middle East and Africa, and earning the sobriquet 'Rice King'. He is the father of Mohamedhusain Hasham Premji and grandfather of Azim Premji.

JACK WELCH
A legendary business leader of his time, Welch was chief executive of GE when they tied up with Wipro for a joint venture and a champion of Wipro's software services in the US. Welch and Premji shared a close personal relationship.

JAGDISH RAO
As global technology head of Citibank, Rao led the 2008 sale of a Citi captive to Wipro, a high point of a long relationship between the two entities. He is now Citigroup chief information security officer; Citibank Technology head;Citigroup Enterprise Infrastructure head and MD.

JAGDISH SHETH
A consultant with Wipro Consumer Products since 1985, the internationally renowned marketing guru also served Wipro as Board Member and Independent Director.

JAMSHEDJI RATANJI DADABHOY TATA
JRD Tata was an iconic Indian businessman and aviation pioneer who founded India's first airline, Air India, in 1932 and oversaw the dramatic expansion of the Tata Group, India's largest industrial empire.

JATIN DALAL
He joined Wipro in 2002 and helped set up Wipro's internal Shared Services division, functioning as its finance head till 2004. Subsequently, he worked in the Corporate Treasury, and then relocated to the UK as the Head of Finance for Europe region and the Global Finance Head for three BUs. Between 2011–15, he was CFO for Wipro's global IT business. Currently, he is senior vice president and chief financial officer at Wipro Ltd.

JAWAHARLAL NEHRU
India's first prime minister (1947–64), he came under some fire from free enterprise advocates for his socialist economic policies.

JOHN ELKINGTON
An author, entrepreneur and advocate of corporate responsibility and sustainable capitalism, he is also the co-founder of Volans Ventures, a company that works with issues of sustainability. He introduced the concept of a 'triple bottom line', referring to a company's social, environmental and economic impact.

JOHN MATTHAI
An economist who served as India's first railway minister (1947–48) and subsequently as India's finance minister, Matthai was a pathbreaking intellectual associated with the foundation of multiple national bodies.

KALYAN BANERJEE
Banerjee joined Wipro's R&D division in 1986 and spent thirteen years working there, until 1999.

KAMALJIT BAWA
Bawa is a Distinguished Professor of Biology at the University of Massachusetts Boston, and founder-president of the Ashoka Trust for Research in Ecology and the Environment, one of India's top-ranked environmental think tanks.

KANNAN JAGAN
Jagan joined Wipro Systems in 1988 and, in the two years he spent here, gave it a significant push towards software services.

KASTURBHAI LALBHAI
An industrialist and philanthropist, he co-founded Arvind Mills in 1931. He also set up several educational institutes.

KISHORE VANSIA
The son of Natwarlal Vansia, he worked as sales manager for WIVP in Bombay and later moved to the Amalner factory in the 1960s and '70s.

KJERSTI LUND
Lund was the global executive director of Copenhagen-based strategic design company Designit when it was acquired by Wipro in 2015. Currently, she is the European managing director of Designit and in charge of its global strategy.

KN BASRUR
A lawyer by training, he handled commodities trading for 25 years, before moving to Amalner as deputy general manager in 1970.

KR LAKSHMINARAYANA
Popularly known as Lan, he joined Wipro Finance in 1995 and went on to handle Internal Audit, Investor Relations and the Corporate Treasury for Wipro. He was CFO of Wipro Technologies in 2005-07 before moving on to become chief strategy officer with charge of M&A in 2008–11. Since 2011, Lan has been with the Azim Premji Foundation and is currently its chief endowment officer.

KUMAR CHANDER
After joining Wipro Consumer Care in 1992 in the sales function, he became the head of Marketing in 1999 and took on the responsibility for Lighting in 2002. Chander is currently the president of South East Asia and MENA Region and the Yardley India Business.

KUMAR MANGALAM BIRLA
He is chairman of the diversified Aditya Birla Group, with a net revenue of $4.83 billion in 2020.

LAxMAN BADIGA
Badiga joined Wipro R&D in 1981 and moved to Wipro Systems in 1983 to develop software products. After fulfilling multiple roles in the US and Europe, he returned to India to the Banking/Finance domain and went on to lead and grow various other verticals. He was named corporate vice president and CIO in 2005 and left Wipro in 2011.

LALA SHRI RAM
An industrialist and philanthropist, he joined Delhi Cloth & General Mills in 1909 at the age of twenty-five and used it as a base to build a manufacturing empire making a vast variety of goods.

MS RAO
Rao joined Wipro in 1975 to set up the diversification into hydraulics. Based out of Bangalore, he established in-house R&D and foreign partnerships for the business and led it for close to thirty years before retiring in 2004.

MAHATMA GANDHI
Mohandas Karamchand Gandhi is unarguably India's best-known figure in the resistance to colonial rule. A lawyer by training, he galvanized the business community in the struggle for independence from British rule.

MAHOMMED HUSAIN R CHINOY
The son of Rahimtoola Chinoy, a member of the original WIVPL Board, he succeeded his father to his seat.

MAKARAND TEJE
Teje joined Wipro in a sales role in 1992 and struck multiple important deals for Wipro

Infotech, including as product manager for Sun Microsystems. In 1996, he moved to the US, working banking and financial accounts for Wipro. In 2007, when he left Wipro, he was vice president, leading the global insurance industry business.

MANI SUBRAMANIAN
On joining Wipro Systems in 1990, he tried to gear the business towards mainframe services. That proved to be short-lived, but Wipro Systems snagged several large software-development projects during his three-year stint.

MANMOHAN SINGH
Economist and politician, Singh was the finance minister in PV Narasimha Rao's government and shaped the economic liberalization policies of 1991. He was India's prime minister from 2004 to 2014.

MOHAMEDHUSAIN HASHAM PREMJI
The founder of Western India Vegetable Products Limited, which grew into the Wipro conglomerate, he served in many key positions including president of the Indian Merchants' Chamber (1945), chairman of Electricity Board for State of Bombay (1954), chairman of the Calcutta Stock Exchange (1958) and member of the Central Board of State Bank of India (1958). Married to Dr (Mrs) Gulbanoo Premji, he is the father of Azim Premji.

MORTEZA MAHJOUR
Mahjour took charge as CIO at Lloyds Banking Group in 2008. He played an important part in partnering with Wipro Ltd to overhaul the internal IT systems of the group and pave the way for its digital transformation. He was with LBG as group chief information officer till 2018.

MS SEKHAR
He joined Wipro in 1972 as finance manager and became company secretary. A chartered accountant with an MBA, he was the company's first finance professional. He was with Wipro for six years.

N KRISHNA KUMAR (KRISHNAKUMAR NATARAJAN)
NKK joined Wipro Infotech in 1982 as regional manager, and went on to play multiple roles, including as vice president of Human Resources and chief executive of the Commerce and Financial Solutions at Wipro Ltd. He left Wipro in 1999.

NR NARAYANA MURTHY
He is a co-founder and retired chairman of Infosys, the IT consulting company with a revenue of $13 billion in 2020.

NAGJIBHAI M SHAH
After a five-year stint with the commodities business, Shah became WIVP's procurement manager in 1975, overseeing millions of rupees' worth of inventory. He retired in 1998.

NALIN THAKOR
A consultant to Wipro in the early 1970s, Thakor structured the Human Resources Department and laid down the fundamentals of Wipro Values. He also instituted the Wipro Employees Reward Trust, India's first stock-option plan for employees.

NATWARLAL VANSIA
A trusted deputy of Mohamedhusain Hasham Premji, Vansia was an integral part of the rice business in Burma. When WIVP came up, he switched from trade to manufacturing, and was in charge of the vanaspati factory in Amalner till 1975.

NAVAL H TATA
Adopted son of Sir Ratanji Jamsetji Tata, Naval Hormusji is father to Ratan Tata, Jimmy Tata and Noel Tata. Born in Surat in 1904, Naval was adopted by Navajbai, wife of Ratanji Tata, when he was thirteen. After joining Tata Sons in 1930 as a despatch clerk-cum-assistant secretary, he rose to become managing director of Tata Mills in 1947. He held multiple offices in advocacy and trade organizations, including the Indian Merchants' Chamber.

NR PARIKH
Parikh joined the company in 1969 as purchase manager in Bombay and also acted as interim deputy factory manager in Amalner for a while till 1979. He left Wipro Consumer Products in 1980 but came back in charge of projects and materials in 1984 and continued till retirement in 2000.

NS PARTHASARATHY
Parthasarathy joined Wipro R&D in 1985. He was the general manager at Wipro Infotech's solutions division, where he led Wipro's development center for some of its large clients. He left in 1999.

PETER HAMBLING
The chief information officer at Lloyd's Bank Group, he retired from LBG after a ten-year stint in 2017.

PS PAI
Pai joined Wipro Products in 1979 as the factory general manager at Amalner and quickly became known for his efficiency and economy. Besides making vanaspati an extremely profitable enterprise, he directed the move into bath soaps and, later, was also in charge of Wipro's lighting business. He headed the Consumer Care and Lighting business for over two decades, before retiring from Wipro in 2002.

PR BHAGWAT
One of Premji's first professional hires in 1969, Bhagwat had a degree and work experience from the UK. As a consultant, he oversaw expansion and engineering needs at Amalner.

PR CHANDRASEKHAR
Chandrasekhar joined Wipro in 2000 from GE India and went on to lead Wipro's European operations. In 2005, he was appointed president of the Americas and Europe for Wipro Technologies, before leaving in 2008.

PRADEEP DESAI
Desai joined WIVP as its first export manager in 1970. The first IIM-A graduate in the company, he contributed significantly to instituting professional ways of working. He went on to become factory manager at Amalner before leaving Wipro in 1976.

PRAKASH MUTALIK
Mutalik joined Wipro Infotech in 1980 as R&D manager and moved to Wipro Systems in 1984 as engineering controller, going on to be part of the Instaplan team. He left Wipro in 1988.

PRANLAL DEVKARAN NANJEE
Banker, businessman and philanthropist, Nanjee was the founder of Dena Bank and former president of Indian Merchants' Chamber. As one of WIVP's founder-directors, he hosted its first meeting.

PRATIK KUMAR
He joined Wipro Systems as an assistant manager in the HR function in 1991 and rose right to the top before moving to head Wipro Infrastructure Engineering, first as president and then as CEO, in 2010. Kumar is also a member of the board of Wipro Enterprises Ltd and a member of Wipro's Corporate Executive Council.

PS NARAYAN
Narayan joined Wipro Infotech in 1988 as a field engineer and quit in 1990. He returned in 1995 and held several roles—including area manager, head of Business Architecture, SAP Practice and Business Transformation—till 2007. In 2008 he created Wipro's sustainability charter as head of Sustainability and Social Initiatives, a position he continues to hold. He is also managing trustee and head at Wipro Foundation and visiting faculty at the Azim Premji University.

PURSHOTTAMDAS THAKURDAS
A cotton trader, businessman and industrialist from Mumbai, he was one of the founders of the Federation of Indian Chambers of Commerce & Industry in 1927.

PV NARASIMHA RAO
The prime minister of India from 1991 to 1996, he oversaw the economic liberalization of India, dismantling the License Raj and bringing the country back from an economic precipice.

R RAMAMOORTHY
Joining as an eighteen-year-old typist and filing clerk in 1974, R Ramamoorthy rose through the ranks to become an area sales officer for the Consumer business in 1981 and then sales and distribution manager for bulk vanaspati in 1987. He left the business in 1992.

RAHIMTOOLA M CHINOY
Scion of a leading Bombay business family, Chinoy was president of the Federation of Indian Chambers of Commerce and Industry in the 1930s and an associate of Mohamedhusain Hasham Premji. He served on the WIVPL Board.

RAJAN KOHLI
Kohli joined Wipro in 1995 in the Financial Services Division in India and moved to the US in 2000. He was chief marketing officer in 2010–12, before heading the Banking and Financial Services (BFSI) vertical at Wipro. He is currently the president of Wipro Digital.

RAJEEV BATRA
The Sebastian S Krege Professor of Marketing at Ross School of Business at the University of Michigan, Batra worked with Wipro Consumer Products as a consultant in the 1990s.

RAJENDRA KUMAR SHREEMAL
He joined Wipro in 1996 as financial controller and later transitioned into roles as business finance head, Americas Geo, CFO, Enterprise Solutions SBU. He was senior vice president, Treasury & Investor Relations, when he left Wipro Ltd in 2012.

RAJIV GANDHI
The youngest prime minister of India between 1984 and 1989, he made it a priority to promote technology through telecommunications, computerization and software exports.

RAM AGARWAL
After joining the vanaspati business as area sales manager in 1977, Agarwal later worked in multiple Finance roles before switching to Wipro Infotech, where he led exports and the Wipro-Acer joint venture. He went on to lead Wipro Peripherals, which he eventually bought out in 2001.

RAMAN ROY
Roy was the CEO of Spectramind, which was acquired by Wipro in 2002. He stayed on as chairman and managing director of the BPO unit before leaving in 2005.

RAMESH EMANI
After joining Wipro Infotech as senior software engineer in 1983, he switched to Wipro Systems after spotting the potential of software services. He went on to lead Telecom Solutions and then became chief technology officer and chief executive of e-Enabling Solutions. He served Wipro for 24 years and was the president, Telecom and Product Engineering Solutions, when he left in 2008.

RAMU IYER
A professor of computer science at IIM Calcutta, in the late 1970s, he introduced Premji to his former student Ashok Narasimhan, who went on to establish Wipro Infotech.

RATANSEY KARSONDAS VISSANJI
Son of an old Bombay trading family, Vissanji was the longest-serving member of the original board of WIVPL. He resigned in 1984, after thirty-eight years at the table.

RATILAL GANDHI
A leading trader of foodgrains and oilseeds, he served on WIVP's board till 1975.

RAVI LAJMI
One of the first three campus recruits from IIM-A and the company's first marketing professional when he joined in 1973, he worked on WIVP's branding and subsequent transition to brand Wipro. He was with Wipro till 1984.

RICHARD GRASSO
The chairman and ehief executive of New York Stock Exchange from 1995–2003, he was in charge when Wipro listed on the NYSE for American Depository Receipt in 2000.

RISHAD PREMJI
Rishad Premji joined Wipro in 2007 in the Banking, Financial Services and Insurance vertical and moved to become chief strategy officer with responsibility for M&As in 2010. He also conceptualized and set up Wipro Ventures, a fund for early-and mid-stage start-ups. In 2019, Rishad Premji succeeded Azim Premji as chairman of Wipro. He is Azim Premji's older son.

S JANAKIRAMAN

Janakiraman joined Wipro as an engineer in R&D in 1980 and went on to head the Systems Integration Group from 1983–85 and then the PC business. He was the chief executive at Global R&D before leaving in 1999.

SANGITA SINGH

Singh joined Wipro in 1992 in the Software Products Division. She also became the head of marketing for Cross Industries Solutions and SVP, Head, Enterprise Application Services. In 2015, she quit Wipro as chief executive, Healthcare and Life Sciences Business Unit.

SANJAY GUPTA

After joining in 1988, Gupta was in charge of sales in North India for Wipro Infotech for close to a decade before moving to the US in 1997. Later, he became senior VP, Telecom Vertical Markets, senior VP and business division head as well as senior VP, Office of the CEO. Gupta left Wipro in 2013.

SATH SATYANARAYAN

He led outsourcing efforts for Tandem Computers, then a $2-billion company, in the early 1990s and zeroed in on Global R&D for a fruitful partnership. The Tandem–Wipro relationship would last for nearly a decade.

SAURABH GOVIL

Since joining Wipro in 2009, Govil has shaped the company's people, processes and organizational structure. Currently, he is president and chief human resource officer.

SCOTT MCNEALY

The co-founder of Sun Microsystems, he was CEO from 1984–2006. The Wipro–Sun relationship began in 1987, when Wipro Infotech started assembling Sun workstations for sale in India, and received a fillip in the 1990s, when Global R&D set up Orbit 1, a support center for Sun.

SHAJI FAROOQ

Since joining Wipro in 2012, Farooq has headed Global Alliances, Strategic Marketing and Sales Enablement functions, besides leading the Advanced Technologies service line, which evolved into Wipro Digital. He stepped down in 2019.

SHANKAR JAGANATHAN

He joined Wipro's financial operations in 1985 and went on to work in investor relations, treasury operations and external financial reportingfunctions as corporate treasurer at Wipro Ltd till 2003. Between 2003 and 2006, he worked at Azim Premji Foundation as head, Technology Initiatives & Academics and Pedagogy.

SHOMBIT SENGUPTA

A brand consultant and artist, Sengupta overhauled the Wipro brand identity by designing the rainbow flower logo with the 'Applying Thought' tagline in 1998. Alongside, he recast the Wipro Values, reflecting a customer orientation for the first time.

SHUNU SEN

A marketing guru with a long career at Hindustan Lever, Sen is credited with the creation of household brands such as Lux, Lifebuoy and Surf. He passed away in 2003.

SOM MITTAL

Mittal joined Wipro Peripherals in 1989 and then became the head of the division in 1990. In 1993, he became the chief executive of Server, PC and Services Division. He left Wipro in 1994.

SOUMITRO GHOSH

Ghosh joined Wipro Infotech in 1988 and played leadership roles in E-commerce and the Sun alliance. In 2000, he founded the BFSI vertical as senior vice president and chief executive, going on to win customers worldwide. In 2013, he became president and chief executive for Wipro's India and Middle East markets, before moving on in 2017.

SP GODREJ

Son of Pirojsha Burjorji Godrej, co-founder of the Godrej Group, he was appointed chairman of the Godrej group of companies in 1972. He held many positions of eminence in trade and industry groups.

SR GOPALAN

Gopalan joined Wipro in the Finance department in 1984. He later became vice president, Finance, at Wipro Infotech and then the CEO of Wipro Finance, before moving on in 1999.

SRIDHAR MITTA

An MTech from IIT Kharagpur and a doctorate from Oklahoma State University, he was the technological backbone of Wipro's IT business from 1980 till 2000. He set up the R&D division for Wipro Infotech and pioneered the 'Lab on Hire' concept. He was chief technology officer and president of the technology division, before setting up EnThink, a company to develop his own IPs, seeded by Premji.

SRIDHAR RAMASUBBU

He joined Wipro Infotech in 1989 as commercial manager and, over his twenty-five-year career at the company, was CFO, International, and CFO, America and Europe. He helped set up the first-ever overseas development center for Tandem. He was VP, Investor Relations, when he left Wipro in 2014.

SRINI PALLIA

After joining Wipro Systems in 1992 as a product manager for Compact, Pallia has held various positions across different units at Wipro, including vice president and head, Enterprise Business Unit, Americas, senior vice president and global head of Business Application Services and chief executive of RCTG Business Unit. He is currently the president and global head of Wipro's Consumer Business Unit.

SRIRAM SRINIVASAN

He joined Wipro Technologies in 2005 asvice president and was global head of banking customers for Wipro in 2009. He worked closely with Rishad Premji when the latter joined Wipro in 2007. Srinivasan left Wipro in 2012.

SUBHAS GHOSHAL

National head of HTA, the advertising agency, Ghoshal worked closely with Premji to roll out the first Sunflower consumer advertisements in 1977.

SUBROTO BAGCHI

Bagchi joined Wipro in 1988 as manager, Customer

Relations and Sales Support. He later became the first chief executive of Wipro's GR&D and then corporate vice president for Mission Quality. He left Wipro in 1998.

SUDIP BANERJEE
Banerjee joined Wipro Infotech in 1983 as a sales executive and went on to become GM, Software Products Division of Wipro Systems in 1993–96. He also did a three-year stint in HR and was president, Enterprises Solutions, at Wipro Technologies, when he left in 2008.

SUMANTRA GHOSHAL
A management guru and business consultant, Ghoshal was with the INSEAD Business School in France in 1992, when he started working with Wipro Consumer Products to help it refocus and sharpen its business strategies.

SUNIL RAJAGOPALAN
He joined Wipro Fluid Power (now WIN) in 1985. He headed the Aerospace and Defense business in 2009 and became chief strategy officer in 2017. He left Wipro in 2018.

SURESH SENAPATY
Senapaty joined Wipro Corporate in 1980 as Audit& Systems Coordinator and quickly became the finance head for Amalner. He was, successively, CFO of Wipro Consumer Care, CFO of Wipro Infotech and the executive director and CFO of Wipro Corporation. He helped architect the demerger of the IT and non-IT businesses in 2013 before retiring in 2015.

SURESH VASWANI
After joining Wipro in 1985, Vaswani worked his way up into leadership positions in Wipro Acer and 01 Markets, among others. He was also executive assistant to Premji before going on to head the IT services and products business for India. In 2008, he was named joint CEO for Wipro's IT business. A dynamic, rigorous, popular leader, Wipro and he parted ways in 2011.

TS KRISHNAMURTHI
The founding partner of data analysis firm Alpha Systems, he was Wipro Infotech's first ever customer in June 1981.

TADASHI SATAKE
A hydraulics expert from Japan, he worked at Wipro Fluid Power (now Wipro Infrastructure Engineering) under the Japanese Experts Services Abroad (JESA) program in 1996–99, augmenting understanding of both market and technology.

TARIQ PREMJI
Vice president of Azim Premji Endowment Fund, he also serves as a board member of the Azim Premji Foundation. He is Azim Premji's younger son.

THIERRY DELAPORTE
Delaporte is the chief executive officer and managing director of Wipro Ltd, appointed in 2020.

TK KURIEN
Kurien began his career at Wipro with Wipro-BT before taking over the Telecom business at the turn of the millennium. He also headed Wipro BPO, the Eco Energy business and Wipro Consulting Services. A strong operations person with a customer focus, he ran a tight ship after taking over Wipro Technologies as CEO in 2011. He left in 2016 to become chief investment officer at Premji Invest.

V CHANDRASEKARAN
Chandrasekaran joined Wipro in 1989 as CEO of Wipro Beckman and soon moved to Wipro Infotech, revolutionizing customer support operations. In 1992, he took over Wipro Systems as its chief executive and laid down fundamental processes and operating procedures. He left Wipro in 1999.

V SAMPATH
A management graduate, he worked with MS Rao in planning Wintrol, the hydraulics venture, in the mid-1970s.

VARUN NIJHAWAN
Nijhawan joined Wipro Corporate HR in 1991 and moved to a business role as the head of Wipro Lighting in 1992. His untimely death in 1996 led to the collapsing of the Lighting business with Wipro Consumer Care.

VENKAT MOHAN
Hired for Wipro Systems in 1988, the engineer with a consulting background helped re-orient the floundering company towards exports. He moved on in 1990.

VICTOR JAYAKARAN
The first campus recruit for Wipro Infotech, Jayakaran joined the fledgling company as assistant engineer, R&D, and went on to become project manager and technical manager, based in the US. He left Wipro in 1998.

VIJAY MALLYA
Son of Vittal Mallya and chairman of the United Breweries Group, he pushed his father to consider computerization of their business empire in the early 1980s. It led to Wipro Infotech's first major hardware deal in 1982.

VINEET AGRAWAL
Agrawal joined Wipro Consumer Products in 1985 in Sales and Marketing and was part of the first Santoor launch in 1986. Besides rolling out various other products from the stable, he led the Wipro rebranding effort in 1998. After a short stint as chief executive of Wipro Peripherals, Agrawal led the Corporate portfolio for Quality, Brand and Innovation. In 2002, he was appointed CEO of Wipro Consumer Care and Lighting, a position he continues to hold.

VITTAL MALLYA
A leading entrepreneur of his time and the first Indian director of the Scottish-origin founded United Breweries Group, in the 1980s, Mallya controlled an empire that included 10 breweries and fourteen distilleries. He is businessman Vijay Mallya's father.

VIVEK PAUL
A GE alumnus, Paul was president and CEO at Wipro GE in 1993-95 before joining Wipro as vice chairman and CEO of Wipro Technologies. Wipro hit several milestones under his leadership,

including listing on the New York Stock Exchange and formulating the 'string of pearls' acquisition philosophy, before he left in 2005.

VS KANNAN SITARAM

Sitaram, a veteran of the FMCG industry with long stints at Hindustan Lever and Dabur, is currently venture partner and CXO mentor at Fireside Investment.

YASMEEN PREMJI NÉE CHINOY

A master's in psychology from Smith College, Massachusetts, she worked as a magazine editor and is the author of the novel *Days of Gold and Sepia*. She is a director at Azim Premji Foundation and on the Board of Governors at Azim Premji University. She is married to Azim Premji and mother to Rishad and Tariq.

ABOUT THE WIPRO STORY PROJECT

What tells the story of an archive best? The 140 interviews, 1,100 photographs, 2,600 documents and 1,100 films we collected and perused in three years? Or the hundreds of plates of cheese Maggi and thousands of cups of ginger tea we downed while getting there? What describes our research best? The method or the madness?

Wipro's story is older than independent India. In 2016, when we started the Wipro Story Project, we wanted to reconstruct the whole of it. As we mapped the arc, we had to unearth incidents, decisions and the rationale behind these. To do this, we turned to people associated with Wipro—employees (former and present), board members, clients, peers and analysts.

The research team traveled to Amalner, Mumbai, Kolkata, Bangalore, Dallas, Atlanta, New Jersey, New York and beyond in search of the pieces of this incredible story. Each person we spoke to put us in touch with many more, each tried to help us unearth secondary material, many turned over their personal memorabilia, including photographs and Wipro mementos, to us.

We also realized that material—documents, photographs, memorabilia—relevant to the company's history must be collected, stored and preserved. We found a space in the Sarjapur campus in Bangalore. But we wanted more than a physical repository of material that would speak of Wipro's heritage. Hence came the Wipro Archives, established in October 2017. But we had to first understand how corporate archives worked, and how we could create a living, breathing space that would add value to Wipro's people. We visited archival spaces in leading corporate business houses of India, such as Godrej, Tata and Cipla.

We went on a hunt for primary material at older Wipro offices and buildings. Amalner, where the company's first factory was set up in 1945, is an important location in the Wipro story. A warehouse in the factory, unopened for over a decade, yielded rich finds. Our archiving consultants, Eka, helped us clean, organize and make a detailed inventory of all the material found—including one of the most popular Wipro machines dating back to 1987, which used the Intel 80386 chip in a minicomputer for the first time and attracted global attention.

Transporting the machine from Amalner to the Archive in Bangalore was not an easy job. It was taken to the Wipro Consumer Care warehouse in Bannerghatta Road first and cleaned several times. Once it was delivered at the Archive, five people had to help carry it inside. When the team of engineers (now long retired) behind Series 386 visited the Archive, they could still locate the chip in the computer.

At Amalner, we found several business documents, too, the oldest being a file from 1949, with details of the inventory logged in Marathi. We found a Sunflower Vanaspati tin from the 1980s. We found a letter Azim Premji wrote to Grindlays Bank asking for a loan in 1974 before setting up the hydraulics business, which was Wipro's first diversification.

Simultaneously, we were trying to put on paper Wipro's history. We went back time and again to Wiproites, past and present, with our questions. The most astonishing and humbling part of working on this project was the alumni's warmth and willingness in sharing their stories. It did not matter if they had left the company twenty years ago: they opened doors and hearts and spent hours recounting their time at Wipro. It was like they were sharing the best part of themselves, where they self-actualized professionally and personally, without perhaps even recognizing it as such at the time.

For many, it was their first job or the longest job, and to be able to get into their heads, relive those days with them and partake in their stories was a privilege. Although many moved on to other jobs, they remained grateful that Wipro taught them to honor and respect one's own moral core. That they embodied this was clear when we met and spent time with them. Whatever emotion Wipro evokes in its people—and there are unpleasant or ambivalent ones as well—it is genuine.

With each story, our narrative became richer. The arcs we developed and scrapped, the drafts we wrote and deleted, the noisy, emotional brainstorming sessions fuelled by copious

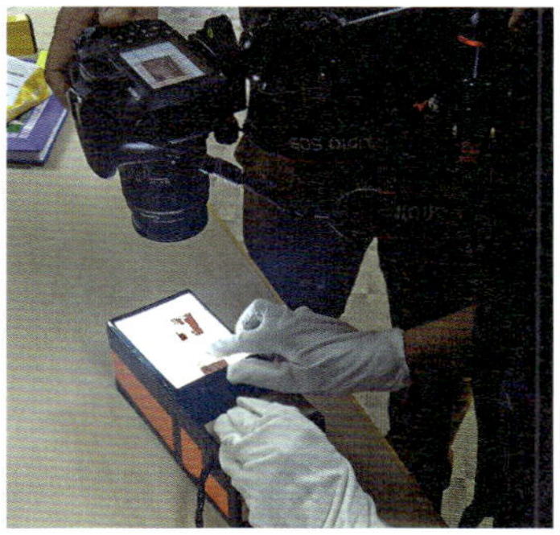

amounts of caffeine and carbohydrates, it all led us to realize how little we knew and how much more we needed to learn.

An important port of call was the National Archives of India, Delhi. Our most significant findings there were the licenses granted to Wipro for their various businesses. Crucial among these was the first license granted to the company—for the manufacture of microprocessors in 1979. This shed light on how Wipro's first computer was put together and the role that the Indian Institute of Science played in incubating the project. The licenses told us how many minicomputers were manufactured in the first five years, the kind of growth the company had in the initial years, and so on.

At the Consumer Care headquarters at the Sarjapur campus in Bangalore, we unearthed documents, product samples and artwork related to the business. We found vanaspati labels from 1972 and the first-ever launch poster of Santoor from 1986. We found correspondence between the people who ran the business, which helped us understand their strategies, and the reading material the company used, which shed light on the market context they were operating in.

By now, we were beginning to join the dots. The research for this volume, *The Story of Wipro*, started with primary material in the Archive, including the annual reports (dating back to 1946–47), strategy documents, business plans and correspondence between the senior leadership. With time, the Archive also built up a repository of the media reports of Wipro from the 1980s onwards. This deepened our understanding of the company's growth trajectory in the larger Indian and global context. We also took our search to external institutions, archives and libraries around the world, like the British Library in London, Duke University in North Carolina, the Intel Archive in California, the Indian Institute of Science in Bangalore, and the Nehru Memorial Museum and Library in Delhi.

Trying to record an interview in a noisy coffee shop in Atlanta, walking through pitch darkness into a dusty storage in Amalner, stuck in the Mumbai floods on the way to collect material, holding on to exhibition panels in the back of an open truck in Bangalore traffic, getting a sudden glimpse of a leopard atop a rock face in Yadgir—we have had stories to tell. Each episode made our discoveries all the more precious. We had to fight the urge to hoard the information, material and stories we collected. At several points in this project, we became petulant children reluctant to share all these, at times even with our sponsors. But the warmth with which our findings were received made us more and more excited about sharing 'our' story of Wipro with the world. For there is no one, definitive story of Wipro.

We must name a few individuals without whom we couldn't have come this far. Chitra Mohan at the Azim Premji Foundation removed every obstacle with a smile—working on everything from logistics and coordination to finding us resource people from across the country. Narasimha Murthy from the Corporate Communication team at Wipro Limited has been a pillar of support, unearthing photographs and nudging us in the right direction as we built up the Archive. Radha Radhakrishnan from Wipro Enterprises Ltd helped us with a larger context in which to frame our questions, streamlining our approach, and gave us primary material for the Archive.

The Story of Wipro is the first of many attempts to preserve Wipro's heritage. Mitu Jayashankar started the project in 2016. The initial team under her comprised Sumana Mukherjee and archivist Vinitha MV. The writing team expanded in 2019 to include Anindita Mitra and Ipsita Basu. At the Archive, Ajith KN joined Vinitha. The research team for this volume comprised Nilofer R D'Souza, Anusha Rajan, Boddapati Shivanand and Vasundhara Krishnan. Dileep Prakash, our visual editor, worked with the Archive team and the design partner, Wari Watai, to bring this edition to life.

But our work is far from done; we will continue to build the collection and hope for more contributions in the coming days. Our vision is for the Wipro Archives to be a space where various aspects of Wipro's, and by extension India's, business history are stored and accessed. We want this to be a space that helps understand and communicate to the world at large Wipro's legacy of values, its resilience and its rich history. In Wipro's seventy-fifth year, we hope to create a space that will further this project for decades to come. ◆

BIBLIOGRAPHY

CHAPTER 1

In a series of interviews by Mitu Jayashankar, taken in Bangalore, between January 2019 and November 2020.

CHAPTER 2

1. Roy, 'Trading firms in Colonial India'.
2. Pandit (ed.) 'Indian Merchants' Chamber'; IMC, 'Our Leaders'
3. *Historical Currency Converter.*
4. Siegel, *Hungry Nation*, p. 149.
5. The Times of India, 'Speech of the Acting Chairman Mr M.H. Hasham'. Mar 2, 1961, page 4.
6. Western India Vegetable Products Ltd (WIVP), Annual Report for 1965–66.
7. The Society for the Rehabilitation of Crippled Children (SRCC), 'About Us'.
8. John and Vashishtha, 'Eradicating Poliomyelitis: India's Journey from Hyperendemic to Polio-free Status', pp. 881–94.
9. Kini and Premji, 'Neurotripsy and Rehabilitation in Poliomyletis'.
10. James, 'Whispering Hope'.

CHAPTER 3

1. Premji, 'TIE Inaugural Address'.
2. Chaudhuri and Barman, 'Personnel Management Practices in Indian Family Business: A Case Study'.
3. The definition of professionalization can be traced to Dr Henrik Nilsson, who works on design, semantics and implementation of programming languages at the University of Nottingham.
4. Wilkins and Dyer, 'Toward Culturally Sensitive Theories of Culture Change', pp. 522–33.
5. Hindustan Unilever Limited, 'Doing Well by Doing Good', p. 16.
6. Premji, 'Letter to the Manager, Grindlays'.

CHAPTER 4

Seshadri "Progress in Megabytes." Ibid., p. 22.

CHAPTER 5

1. Premji, 'Speech to Wipro Employees on NYSE Listing'
2. Rediff Money Bureau, 'Wipro Debuts on NYSE'.
3. Ghosh, 'India's $30 Million Man'.
4. Rai, 'Wipro Power to Manufacture Sun Hydraulics Products'.
5. DQI Bureau, 'Shifting Gears Makes All the Difference'.
6. David and Saran, 'Wipro Becomes Most Valuable Indian Company'.
7. Premji, 'TIE Inaugural Address'.

CHAPTER 6

1. Actis, 'Acquisition of Unza by Wipro'.
2. Singh, 'Santoor'.
3. Mishra, 'Wipro Steps into $6 bn World of 3D Printing'.

IN CONVERSATION WITH AZIM PREMJI

In a series of interviews by Mitu Jayashankar, taken in Bangalore, between January 2018 and November 2020.

WORKS CITED

- Actis, 'Actis and Standard Chartered Private Equity Have Realised Their Investment in Unza Following the Acquisition of Unza by Wipro for US$246m', Actis, 9 August 2007, **https://www.act.is/media-centre/press-releases/actis-and-standard-chartered-private-equity-have-realised-their-investment-in-unza-following-the-acquisition-of-unza-by-wipro-for-us-246m/** (accessed 11 November 2020).
- Chaudhuri, K.K., and T.K. Barman. 'Personnel Management Practices in Indian Family Business: A Case Study.' *Economic and Political Weekly*, Vol. 16, No. 35, 1981, pp. M117–M120. **www.jstor.org/stable/4370166.** (accessed 17 October, 2020).
- David, Stephen and Rohit Saran. 'Wipro Becomes Most Valuable Indian Company, Azim Premji The Richest Indian Ever.' *India Today*, 6 March 2000. **https://www.indiatoday.in/magazine/cover-story/story/20000306-wipro-becomes-most-valuable-indian-company-azim-premji-the-richest-indian-ever-777179-2000-03-06.** (accessed 18 October, 2020).
- DQI Bureau. 'Shifting Gears Makes All The Difference'. *Dataquest*, February 15, 2000. **https://www.dqindia.com/wipro-shifting-gears-makes-all-the-difference/.** (accessed 18 October, 2020).
- Ghosh, Chandrani. 'India's $30 Million Man.' *Forbes*, 20 March, 2000. **https://www.forbes.com/forbes/2000/0320/6507144a.html#2c8fd2f7b96b.** (accessed 18 October, 2020).
- Hindustan Unilever Limited./ 'Doing Well by Doing Good', 2008, **hul.co.in/Images/hul_75years_special_issue__tcm1255-447470_en.pdf** (accessed 18 October, 2020).
- *Historical Currency Converter.* **www.historicalstatistics.org/Currencyconverter.html.** (accessed 16 October, 2020).
- IMC Chamber of Commerce and Industry. 'Our Leaders'. **https://www.imcnet.org/our-leaders.** (accessed 30 December, 2020).
- James, Teresa Viju. 'Whispering Hope', *The Times of India*, November 3, 1990. Accessed through ProQuest Historical Newspaper: *The Times of India*, p. A1.
- John, T. J., and V.M. Vashishtha. 'Eradicating Poliomyelitis: India's Journey from Hyperendemic to Polio-free Status', *The Indian Journal of Medical Research*, Vol. 137, No. 5, 2013, pp. 881–894. **https://www.ncbi.nlm.nih.gov/pmc/articles/PMC3734678/**
- Kini, M.G., and Gulbanoo Premji. 'Neurotripsy and Rehabilitation in Poliomyletis', *The Indian Journal of Surgery*, Vol. 12, No. 1, March 1950, pp. 53–57.
- Mishra, Pankaj, and ET Bureau. 'Wipro Takes Baby Steps into $6 bn World of 3D Printing with Lone Printer', *The Economic Times*,

14 October, 2014 **https://economictimes.indiatimes.com/tech/ites/wipro-takes-baby-steps-into-6-bn-world-of-3d-printing-with-lone-printer/articleshow/44807418.cms?from=mdr.** (accessed 12 November, 2020).

- Nilsson, Henrik. 'Professionalism, Lecture 5, What is a Profession?' University of Nottingham. Accessed at **https://en.wikipedia.org/wiki/Professionalization.**
- Pandit, Ramu (ed.). 'Indian Merchants' Chamber', *Platinum Jubilee Commemoration Volume 1982* Indian Merchants' Chamber, 1983.
- Premji, Azim Hasham, 'Letter to the Manager, Grindlays', sent on 29 May 1974, courtesy Wipro Archives.
- Speech to Wipro Employees on the Occasion of NYSE Listing', New York/Bangalore, 19 October 2000.
- 'Inaugural Address', 16th Annual TIE Event, 'History of Business Career, Opportunities and Challenges', 16 December 2008, Grand Ashok, Bangalore.
- Rai, Asha, 'Wipro Power to Manufacture Sun Hydraulics Products', Economic Times, 12 February 1997.
- Rediff Money Bureau, 'Wipro Debuts on NYSE at a Discount to Domestic Stock', *Rediff.com*, 19 October 2000, **https://www.rediff.com/money/2000/oct/19wipro.htm** (accessed 18 October 2020).
- Roy, Tirthankar, 'Trading firms in Colonial India', Business History Review, Vol. 88, No. 1, 2014, pp. 9–42, doi:10.1017/S0007680513001402.
- Seshadri, Malini. "Progress in Megabytes." Span, August 1990, pp. 20–23.
- Siegel, Benjamin R., Hungry Nation: Food, Famine and the Making of Modern India, Cambridge University Press, 2018.
- Singh, Rajiv, 'Santoor: Stay Regional and Gun for No. 1', Forbes India, 1 August 2019, **https://www.forbesindia.com/article/work-in-progress/santoor-stay-regional-and-gun-for-no1/54619/1** (accessed 12 November 2020).
- The Society for the Rehabilitation of Crippled Children (SRCC), 'About Us', **http://www.srcc.org.in/our-background/** (accessed 16 October 2020).
- *The Times of India*, 'The Vanaspati Manufacturers' Association of India: Speech of the Acting Chairman Mr M.H. Hasham', *The Times of India*, 2 March 1961, p. 4.
- Western India Vegetable Products Ltd (WIVP), *Annual Report for 1965–66*, courtesy Wipro Archives.
- Wilkins, Alan L. and W. Gibb Dyer, 'Toward Culturally Sensitive Theories of Culture Change', *The Academy of Management Review*, Vol. 13, No. 4, 1988, pp. 522–33, **www.jstor.org/stable/258372** (accessed 16 October 2020).

PHOTO CREDITS

Cover

ARTWORK Wari Watai

BACK COVER Brad Trent

Contents

PAGE 1 Wipro Archives

Chapter 1

PAGE 10 Illustration by Wari Watai

PAGE 13 Wipro Archives

PAGE 14 Anay Mann

PAGE 16 Harvard Business School

PAGE 18 Hemant Mishra / *Hindustan Times*

PAGE 20 Anay Mann

PAGE 21 Wipro Archives

PAGE 22 Wipro Ltd

PAGE 24 Anay Mann

PAGE 26 Wipro Ltd / Manoj Masand Photographs

PAGE 28 (Clockwise from top left)
Ajay Panwar, Project Manager, SBMA;
Ansu Abraham, Senior Grants Officer—
Corporate Relations, CBM; SwaTaleem Foundation;
Kottapuram Integrated Development Society;
Wipro Cares Initiative Picture Archive

PAGE 30 Anay Mann

PAGE 31 Wipro Ltd

Chapter 2

PAGE 34 (Background)
Dinodia Photos/Alamy

PAGE 34 (Left)
Yasmeen Premji Personal Collection

PAGES 35–37 Yasmeen Premji Personal Collection

PAGE 38 (Above)
Wipro Archives

PAGE 38 (Below, Left)
Yasmeen Premji Personal Collection

PAGE 38 (Below, Right)
Wipro Archives

PAGE 39 (Above)
Wipro Archives

PAGE 40 (Above)
IMC Chamber of Commerce and Industry, Mumbai

PAGE 41 (Top Left)
Yasmeen Premji Personal Collection

PAGE 41 (Top Right)
Wipro Archives

PAGE 41 (Above)
Yasmeen Premji Personal Collection

PAGE 42 (Box)
Wipro Archives

PAGE 42 (Bottom Right)
Wipro Ltd

PAGE 42 (Bottom Left)
Vanaspati Manufactures Association of India (VMAI)

PAGES 43–44 Yasmeen Premji Personal Collection

PAGE 44 (Below)
Society for the Rehabilitation of Crippled Children (SRCC)

PAGE 45 Society for the Rehabilitation of Crippled Children (SRCC)

PAGE 46 (Top)
Society for the Rehabilitation of Crippled Children (SRCC)

PAGE 46 (Above)
Yasmeen Premji Personal Collection

PAGE 47 (From Left)
Yasmeen Premji Personal Collection
Founder Chairman's office

Chapter 3

PAGE 50 Founder Chairman's office

PAGES 52–53 Wipro Archives

PAGE 54 Cemal Emden

PAGE 56 (Clockwise from top left)
Personal Collections of Dileep Ranjekar, Nagji M Shah
Pradip Desai, MS Sekhar; Founder Chairman's Office;
Wipro Archives; Dileep Ranjekar Personal Collection;
Ram Agarwal Personal Collection

PAGE 58 (Below Left)
IISc Archives, Bangalore

PAGE 58 (Below Right)
Wipro Infrastructure Engineering (WIN),

PAGE 60 Wipro Archives

PAGE 62 (Above)
Hans Winter/ Getty Images

PAGE 62 (Left)
Ninad Warekar Collection,
Bhaktawar Building Management

PAGE 64 (Above)
Dileep Ranjekar Personal Collection

PAGE 64 (Left)
Wipro Archives

Chapter 4

PAGE 68 Illustrations by Dhwani H. Trivedi,
Mansi Thakkar, Vivek V Ram

PAGE 70 Wipro Archives

PAGE 71 Ganesh Chikate Personal Collection

PAGE 72 Wipro Archives

PAGE 74 (Top)
Chris Stowers Photography

PAGE 74 (Above)
MN Suresh Personal Collection

PAGE 76 (Top)
M Divakaran

PAGE 76 (Above)
Sentinel Computer Corporation.
Computerworld, October 15, 1979, p.72

PAGE 77 J Naphade Personal Collection

PAGE 78 (Left)
Dr. Sridhar Mitta Personal Collection

PAGE 78 (Right)
Dr. Sridhar Mitta Personal Collection

PAGE 78 (Left)
JWT Archives, Duke University

PAGE 80 (Top Left)
Wipro Archives

PAGE 80 (Above)
M Divakaran

PAGE 80 (Left)
Wipro Archives

PAGE 82 Mark Richards/Zuma Press

PAGE 82 (From Left)
CPU of the Wipro S-386, Dataquest, April 1987, p.68
Konstantin Lanzet/Creative Commons

PAGE 83 M Divakaran

PAGE 84 (Left)
Dr. Sridhar Mitta Personal Collection

PAGE 84 (Above)
Girish Elchuri Personal Collection

PAGE 85 (Right)
Stewart Cheifet/ Archive.org

PAGE 85 (Far Right)
Dr. Sridhar Mitta

PAGE 86 (Right)
Wipro Infrastructure Engineering (WIN)

PAGE 86 (Below)
Wipro Archives

PAGE 86 (Above)
Wipro Infrastructure Engineering (WIN)

PAGE 88 Mahesh Bhat

PAGE 88 (Far Left)
Dr. Sridhar Mitta Personal Collection

PAGE 88 (Left)
Wipro Archives/India Today

PAGE 89 (Left)
Dr. Sridhar Mitta Personal Collection

Chapter 5

PAGE 92 Photographer Unknown / Artwork-Studio Snow Show

PAGE 94 Image is the property of NYSE Group, Inc. or its affiliates
and is protected by U.S. and international copyright and
trademark laws. © 2000 NYSE Group, Inc. All rights reserved.

PAGES 96–98 Wipro Archives

PAGES 99–100 Wipro Infrastructure Engineering (WIN)

PAGE 102 (Top)
Norm Betts/Getty Images

PAGE 102 (Left)
Dr. Sridhar Mitta Personal Collection

PAGE 103 Chris Stowers Photography

PAGE 104 Wipro Archives

PAGE 105 (Clockwise from above)
Wipro Archives, Ramesh Emani,
DA Prasanna Personal Collection

PAGE 106 (From Top)
Cyrus McCrimmon/Getty Images, Dr. Sridhar Mitta

PAGE 108 (Above)
Chris Stowers Photography

PAGE 108 (Left)

PHOTO CREDITS

	Mark Henley/Panos Pictures
PAGE 109	Wipro Archives
PAGE 110	Founder Chairman's Office
PAGE 112	Pallon Daruwala Photography/ Mistry Architects
PAGE 114	Wipro Archives/*Business India*
PAGE 116	Bill Gates' Office
PAGE 118	(Right)
	Wipro Archives/*India Today*
PAGE 118	(Left)
	N Krishnakumar
PAGE 120	Wipro Ltd

Chapter 6

PAGE 124	Wipro Ltd
PAGES 126–128	(Left)
	Rudra Sen/Wipro Ltd
PAGE 128	(Below)
	Namas Bhojani
PAGE 130	(Top)
	Wipro Ltd
PAGE 130	(Above)
	Designit
PAGES 131–133	Wipro Ltd
PAGE 134	(Above)
	Anay Mann
PAGE 134	(Below)
	Varchasva Dhunta
PAGE 138	(Above)
	Anay Mann
PAGE 138	(Below)
	Poornima Marh
PAGE 139	Wipro 3D/Wipro Infrastructure Engineering
PAGE 140	(Clockwise from top left)
	A. Joseph Rexon, Managing Trustee,
	Rehoboth Sustainable Development Foundation;
	A.Joseph Rexon, Managing Trustee,
	Rehoboth Sustainable Development Foundation;
	Deepak Acharya, General Counsel & SVP;
	Shahnawaz Shahid,
	Director-Programs, Sukarya;
	Kishan Nandlal Changlani,
	Sr. Account Manager, Digital, Wipro Ltd
PAGE 142	Rudra Sen/Wipro Ltd
PAGE 144	Wipro Ltd
PAGE 145	Anay Mann

The Foundation Story

PAGES 146–147	Purusottam Thakur, Azim Premji Foundation
PAGES 148–150	Dileep Prakash
PAGE 152	Purusottam Thakur, Azim Premji Foundation
PAGE 153	V. Sreenivasa Murthy/*The Hindu*
PAGES 154–165	Dileep Prakash
PAGE 166	Prema Ram, Azim Premji Foundation
PAGE 167	(Top Left)
	Mahesh Pokhariya
PAGE 167	(Top Right)
	Prema Ram, Azim Premji Foundation
PAGE 167	(Above)
	Mahesh Pokhariya
PAGES 168–173	Dileep Prakash
PAGES 174–177	Partner Organizations of Azim Premji Foundation
	(Philanthropic Initiatives)
PAGES 178	Sharmadip Basu
PAGES 179–181	Azim Premji University Community

In Conversation with Azim Premji

PAGE 182–183	Deepak G Pawar
PAGE 184	Yasmeen Premji Personal Collection
PAGE 188	Wipro Ltd
PAGE 190	Dileep Ranjekar Personal Collection
PAGE 193	Ganesh Chikate Personal Collection
PAGE 194	Anay Mann
PAGE 196	Founder Chairman's Office
PAGE 202	Ajay Menon Aj PhotoArtist
PAGE 204–205	Dileep Prakash
PAGE 206	Azim Premji University
PAGE 208–209	Pallon Daruwala Photography/ Mistry Architect

About the Wipro Story Project

PAGE 218–219	Wipro Archives

ACKNOWLEDGMENTS

We are thankful to all those who gave us their valuable time, spoke to us and donated material for this book. There is little doubt that this project would not have been possible without the support and goodwill of so many. The following is a list of people whose contributions have helped us complete this book successfully.

A
AP Ravish
Abhigna Kashyap
Abid Ali Neemuchwala
Adhitya Bhatia
Adira Thekkuveettil
Ajay Bhaskar
Ajay Parikh
Aji George
A Lakshman Rao
Alexander Kalinovsky
Alexander Beal
Alex Kendrick
Alex Manappurathu
Amardeep Santhoor
Amar Naga
Ambi Parameswaran
Amy Brown
Anand Padmanabhan
Anand Mirji
Anand Talwai
Angan Guha
Anil Chugh
Anil Jain
Anil Raibagi
Anil S Angadiki
Anil Sethi
Anindya Roy Choudhury
Anita Ganti
Anita Garware
Ankita Chugh
Ankur Khurana
Anurag Behar
Anurag Shinde
AR Ganj
Arghya Mukherjee
Arthur Eisenkraft
Arumugham Mahendran
Arun Singh
Arvind Shah
A Sadashivam
Ashis Kumar
Ashish K Ghoshal
Ashish Saxena
Ashok Ganguly
Ashok Narasimhan
Ashok Soota
Ashutosh Chaturvedi
Ashwatha Amarnath
AV Sridhar
Avinash Kumar
Ayan Mukerji
Azim Hasham Premji
Azra Naaz

B
Bhagwan Sharma
Bhanumurthy Ballapuram Bhavana
Bhalekar
Bianca Ghose
Bill Gates
Binoy Wilson
Biplab Adhya
Bitan Basu
BV Venkatesh
BV Vijayakumar

C
Chinmay Mohapatra
Chinmay Tumbe
Chirag Sutar
Chitra Krishna Mohan
Chuck Pieper
Clinton Bonner
Colin Rozario
CV Kamath

D
DA Prasanna
D Ramesh
David Dion
Debashish Roy
Deepak Gujarati
Deepak Jain
Deepak Panda
Deepika Sharma
Deepika Sorabjee
Dhriti Pant
Diju Raha
Dileep Basole
Dileep K Ranjekar
Dnyanesh Patkar
Donna Allen

E
Eashwari Deshpande
Elvis Rodrigues
Emma Ladurantie
Eravi Gopan

G
G Annapa
G Satyamurthy
G Sundararaman
Ganesh Chikate
Ganeshwara Rao
Girish Chandra Elchuri
GK Iyer
Guru Sankayya Moger
Gurunath Goudar
Gyanendra Shukla
(Cherry Hill)

H
H Balakrishna
Harish Shah

I
Indu Venkatesh
Issac V George

J
JN Naphade
J Venkatesh
Jack Welch
Jagdish Sheth
Jagdish Rao
Jasdeep Bhatia
Jatin Dalal
Jayashree Mishra
Jonas Allen
Jon (Eric) Olson
Joshua Thoppil
Joyce Vijay
JP Shivakumar
JP Shivaswamy
Justin James
Justin Wieland
Jyoti Doshi
Jyotirmay Datta
Jyoti Rane

K
K Gurujrao
KR Sanjiv
Kalyan Banerjee
Kamakshi Rao
Kamalesh Mishra
Kannan Jagan
Kannan Sitaram
Kavita Khetarpal
KB Ravi Menon
Keka Banerjee
Keki Bugwadia
Kjersti Lund
KN Padmanabhan
KN Prabhu
Kothandaraman Gopalan
KR Lakshminarayana
Krishna Nacha
Krishnakumar Natarajan
Kumar Chander

L
Laxman N Chaudhari
Lee Cole
Liril Gupta
Lukose Sruthi

M
M Divakaran
M N Suresh
M Seethapathy Rao
MS Sekhar
Madhu Mohan
Mahendra Ayyalasomayajula
Mahesh Bhatt
Mahindra Patil
Mahrooh Basar
Makarand Teje
Mahadevappa SM
Mahesh S Kobalkar
Mahesh Chandrasekar
Malcolm Alvarez
Malini Narasimha
Manish Rathore
Manoj Prakash
Md Iqbal Shaikh
Mir Mohammed Ali
MN Suresh
Morteza Mahjour
Mukta Pant
Mythily Ramesh

N
N Balasubramanian
N Komala
NJ Rao
N Mohan
Nagamani Murthy
Nagarjuna Sadineni
Nagender Arya
Nagendra Bhandaru
Nagesh Rao Yadav
Nagji M Shah
Nakshatra Tyagi
Namas Bhojani
Namdeo T Chaudhari Nandakumar
Narayanan Vaghul
Naveen Rajdev
Nikki Glee
Ninad Warekar
Nischala P Murthy
Nitin Goyal
Nitin Parab
NS Parthasarathy
NS Ramnath
Nuruddin Salati

P
Pallon Daruwala
P Murali Shankar
Pankaj Mridul
Patrick Dupuis
Pawan Kumar
Poornima Marh
Pradeep Desai
Pradeep Gupta
Pradeep Kumar Sharma
Praful Karania
Prakash Mallya
Prakash Mutalik
Pratik Kumar
Prem Koshy
Prema Ram
PS Narayan
Puk Sjeldan
Putul Mathur

R
Rachel B Gross
Radha Radhakrishnan
Raghavendra Kanekanti
Rahmath Cazi
Raja Veluswamy
Rajan Kohli
Rajsekhar Basu
Rajesh Stephan
Rajesh Itagi
Rajiv Pathak

ACKNOWLEDGMENTS

Ram Agarwal
Ramesh Emani
Ravi Lajmi
Ravindra Kumar
Ravindra Mudgal
Revathi Kasturi
Rishad Premji
Rohini Haskar
Roshan Dias Victor
Roy George
R Ramamoorthy
R Sivakumar
R Vasudevan
RV Jagirdar

S

S Janakiraman
S Rudresh
Sakti Chatterjee
Sambuddha Deb
Samir Kumar
Sandeep Devaji Gayakawad
Sangita Singh
Sanjay Anandram
Sanjay Gupta
Sanjay S Chowdhury
Sanjay Semwal
Sanjay Teni
Sanjeev Kumar
Sanjib Kumar Maiti
Santosh Karagada
Sath Sathyanarayan
Satish Khanderia
Saugata Gupta
Saurabh Govil
Saveeta Mohanty
Scott McNealy
S Giridhar
Shankar Jaganathan
Shashidhar Sabnavis
Sheik Mohamed Ishaq
Shivananda Salgame
Shipra Poddar
Shombit Sengupta
Shweta Adlakha
Shyam Sundar Laxminarayana
Siva Sagar
Som Mittal
Somasundar
Sonia Arora
S Prasanna Rai
Sridhar Mitta
Sridhar Ramasubbu
Srini Pallia
Srinivas Chamarthi
Srinivas Devareddy
Sripathy Kaur
Stephen C Snyder
Subhash Bhamara
Subhash Khare
Subroto Bagchi
Sudhir Sethi
Sudip Banerjee
Sudip Nandy
Sue Yanovitch
Sumathi Srinath
Sunil Maheshwari
Sunil Rajagopalan
Sunita Cherian
Surendra Dixit
Suresh Senapaty
Sushma Amin
Swapna Sathe

T

Tapan Dutta
Tarun Rai
Thiagrajan Nagarajan
Thierry Delaporte
TK Jithendran
TK Kurien
Tom Derrick
Tripta Sharma
TV Sethumadhava Rao

U

Umashankar Periodi
Umesh Nanda
Usha Dantu
Usha Iyer
Usha Sathyanarayana

V

Varchasva Dhunta
V Chandrasekaran
VN Mujawar
V Rama Kumar
Vallabh Kulkarni
Venkat Srinivasan
Venkateswara Rao Renati
Venu Pemmaraju
Victor Jayakaran
Vijaya Verma
Vijish Thankachan
Vinay Rawat
Vineet Agrawal
Vineet Tripathi
Vinod Kadavil
Vinod Rajan
Vishnu Vardhan
VR Venkatesh
Vrundha Patare

Y

Yasmeen Premji
Yazad Balaporia
YK Maheshwari
Yoga Narasimha

We also extend our gratitude to the various libraries, archives and institutions around the world for letting us use the materials and resources at their disposal

Archive.org
Advertising Agencies Association of India
Asiatic Society
British Library
Bunge
Cargill
Cherry Hill
Cipla
Computer Society of India
Confederation of Indian Industry
Deen Dayal Family
Department of Information and Publicity, Bangalore
Dignity Foundation
Eka Cultural Resources and Research
Exxon Mobil Corporation
FCB Ulka
FE Dinshaw Commercial and Financial Reference Library
Film Heritage Foundation of India
Fluid Power Society of India
Forbes Gujarati Sabha
GK Vale
Hamilton Studios
Higginbotham Bookstore
HM Passport Office
HTA
IDG
Indian Institute of Science
IMC Chamber of Commerce and Industry
INTACH Bangalore
Intel Archives
Itihaasa.com
JN Petit Institute
J Walter Thompson Company Collections
Duke University
Karnataka Small Scale Industries Limited
M Moser Associates
Maharashtra State Archives
Mistry Architects
More Megastore, Mahadevapura
National Archives of India
National Archives of the United Kingdom
Nehru Memorial Museum and Library
Nehru Centre
Netaji Research Bureau
New York Stock Exchange
Public Broadcasting Service
Rupam Studio, Amalner
Span Magazine
Sparsha Trust
State Bank of India Archives
Survey of India, Dehradun
The Foundation of Ecological Security
The Society for the Rehabilitation of Crippled Children
Vidhan Soudha State Archives
Yardley London

We thank the following members of the Azim Premji Foundation who helped us write this book

Yadgir field team
Barmer field team
Davanagere field team
Gulbarga field team
Uttarkashi field team

We are also deeply indebted to the following teams in Wipro for their unwavering support and cooperation in helping us gather material for this book

Corporate Communications
Facilities Management Group
Finance
Founder Chairman's Office
IT Management Group
Wipro Consumer Care and Lighting
Wipro Foundation
Wipro HR
Wipro Infrastructure Engineering

We also thank the following newspaper/journal archives for allowing us to use their material

Cybermedia
Deccan Herald
Hindustan Times
The Indian Express
The Times of India
The Hindu

INDEX

INDEX

INDEX